ASHEVILLE
A View From The Top

Sponsored by the Asheville Area Chamber of Commerce

ASHEVILLE
A View From The Top

Written by **Lisa Bell**

Corporate profiles by **Lynda McDaniel**

Featuring the photography of **Tim Barnwell**

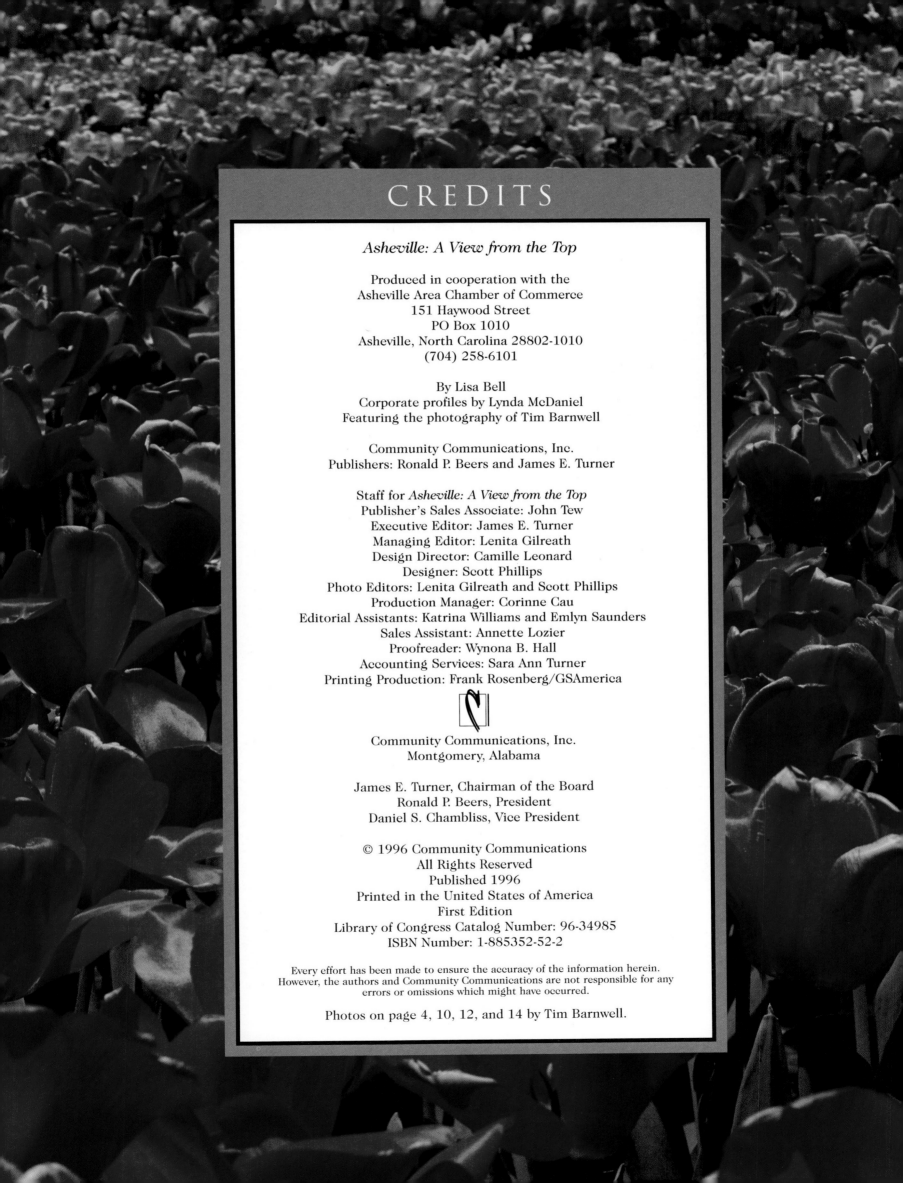

CREDITS

Asheville: A View from the Top

Produced in cooperation with the
Asheville Area Chamber of Commerce
151 Haywood Street
PO Box 1010
Asheville, North Carolina 28802-1010
(704) 258-6101

By Lisa Bell
Corporate profiles by Lynda McDaniel
Featuring the photography of Tim Barnwell

Community Communications, Inc.
Publishers: Ronald P. Beers and James E. Turner

Staff for *Asheville: A View from the Top*
Publisher's Sales Associate: John Tew
Executive Editor: James E. Turner
Managing Editor: Lenita Gilreath
Design Director: Camille Leonard
Designer: Scott Phillips
Photo Editors: Lenita Gilreath and Scott Phillips
Production Manager: Corinne Cau
Editorial Assistants: Katrina Williams and Emlyn Saunders
Sales Assistant: Annette Lozier
Proofreader: Wynona B. Hall
Accounting Services: Sara Ann Turner
Printing Production: Frank Rosenberg/GSAmerica

Community Communications, Inc.
Montgomery, Alabama

James E. Turner, Chairman of the Board
Ronald P. Beers, President
Daniel S. Chambliss, Vice President

Published 1996
Printed in the United States of America
First Edition
Library of Congress Catalog Number: 96-34985
ISBN Number: 1-885352-52-2

Photos on page 4, 10, 12, and 14 by Tim Barnwell.

PART ONE

CONTENTS

Foreword 10
Preface 12
Part I 14

18

CHAPTER ONE
Looking Back: A Historical Perspective
Asheville and Buncombe County have a rich and colorful past with a cast of many characters—Thomas Wolfe, George Vanderbilt, and E. W. Grove to name a few. These and other pioneers, including our Cherokee neighbors, helped to mine and polish our mountain home into the gem it is today.

CHAPTER TWO
Downtown: Down-home Hospitality in the Heart of the City
Take a stroll down Wall Street...sip a cappuccino at a trendy sidewalk cafe...enjoy a free concert in the park. Is this Asheville or the Big Apple? We may have a smaller downtown, but you'd be hard pressed to find a more interesting one.

34

50

CHAPTER THREE
Mountain Magic: Your Spirits will Soar
Our mountains attract about 2 million visitors a year, some seeking a quiet getaway; others in search of the Appalachian folk art and culture we're famous for. Quilts, handmade pottery, and crafts are found throughout the area. Cruise along the scenic Blue Ridge Parkway and you'll find mountain magic as close as the next exit—at one of our many festivals and roadside craft stands.

CHAPTER FOUR
Attractions: So Much to See–So Much to Do
We like to think our "Great Outdoors" is greater than most. After all, with miles of mountains, scores of streams, and acres of protected forest land, the Asheville area offers abundant hiking, biking, fishing, and canoeing. Feeling like a spectator instead of a sports participant? Take in a Tourists baseball game, or visit America's largest private residence, the Biltmore House. And shop 'til you drop—into one of our many fine restaurants.

76

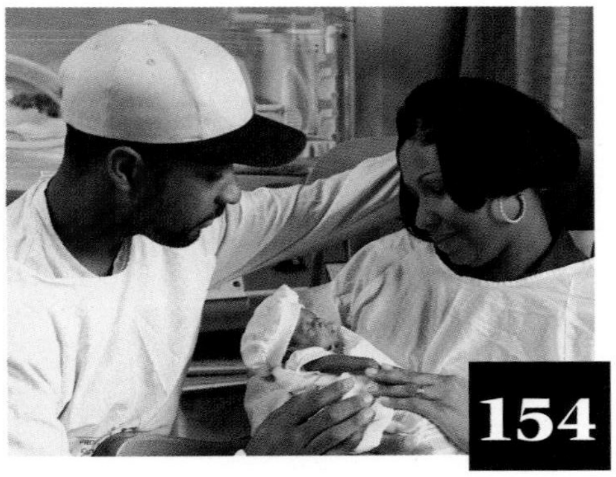

PART TWO

CONTENTS

The area's communications, energy, and transportation firms keep information, power, people, and products circulating inside and outside the Asheville area.

Producing goods for individuals and industry, manufacturing firms provide employment for many Asheville area residents. Research and development activity place the area at the forefront of technology.

Asheville's business, insurance, and financial communities offer a strong base for the area's growing economy.

From law to architecture, accounting to graphic design, Asheville's professional firms are recognized as leaders in their field.

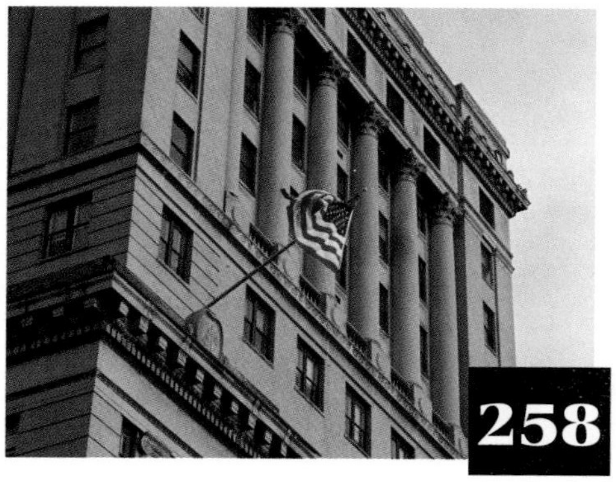

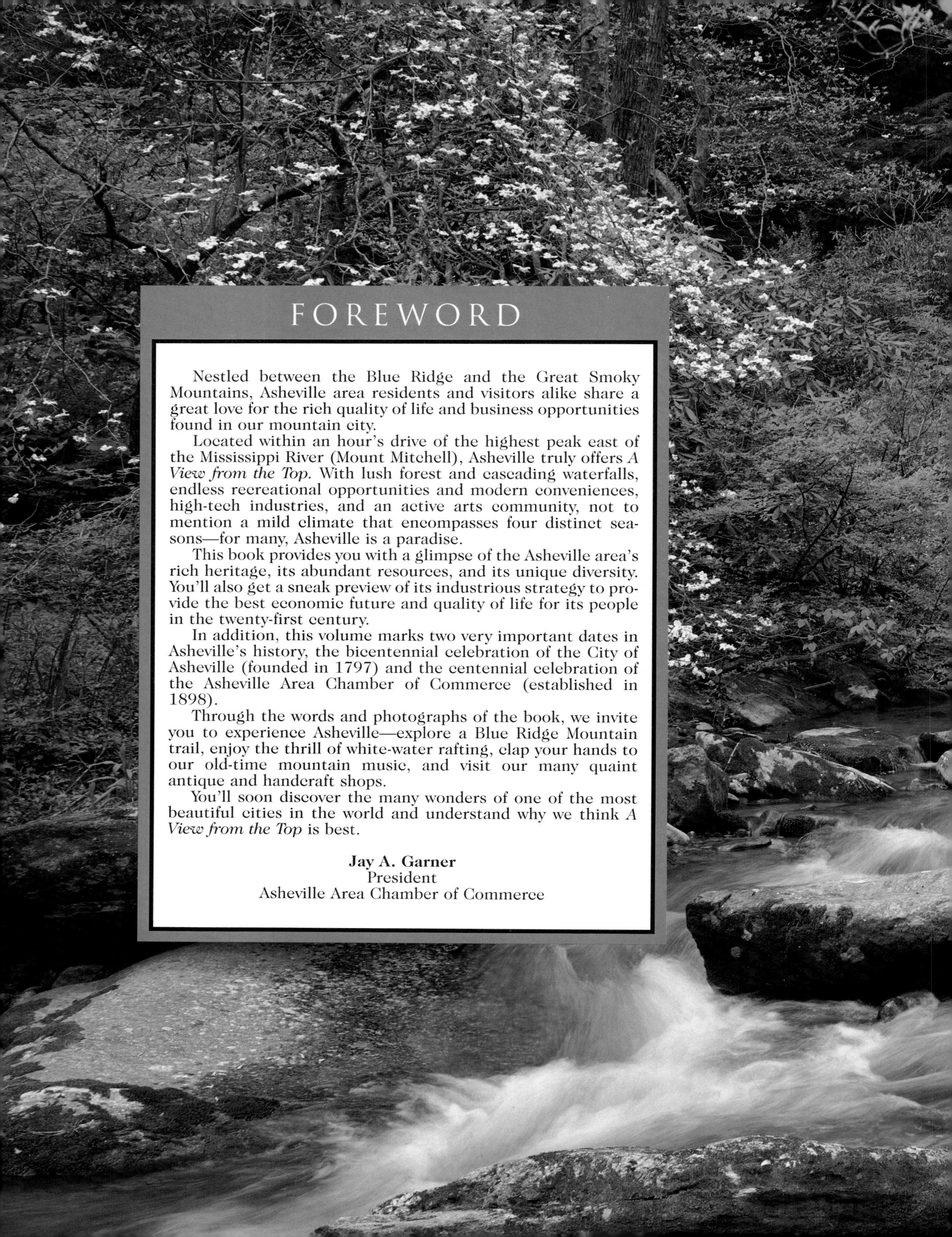

FOREWORD

Nestled between the Blue Ridge and the Great Smoky Mountains, Asheville area residents and visitors alike share a great love for the rich quality of life and business opportunities found in our mountain city.

Located within an hour's drive of the highest peak east of the Mississippi River (Mount Mitchell), Asheville truly offers *A View from the Top.* With lush forest and cascading waterfalls, endless recreational opportunities and modern conveniences, high-tech industries, and an active arts community, not to mention a mild climate that encompasses four distinct seasons—for many, Asheville is a paradise.

This book provides you with a glimpse of the Asheville area's rich heritage, its abundant resources, and its unique diversity. You'll also get a sneak preview of its industrious strategy to provide the best economic future and quality of life for its people in the twenty-first century.

In addition, this volume marks two very important dates in Asheville's history, the bicentennial celebration of the City of Asheville (founded in 1797) and the centennial celebration of the Asheville Area Chamber of Commerce (established in 1898).

Through the words and photographs of the book, we invite you to experience Asheville—explore a Blue Ridge Mountain trail, enjoy the thrill of white-water rafting, clap your hands to our old-time mountain music, and visit our many quaint antique and handcraft shops.

You'll soon discover the many wonders of one of the most beautiful cities in the world and understand why we think *A View from the Top* is best.

Jay A. Garner
President
Asheville Area Chamber of Commerce

PREFACE

When my family escaped the aftermath of a particularly rough Northern winter to settle in Asheville, it was a day to remember: April 13. We left behind dozens of friends and well-wishers and took with us the memories of salty roads and snow plows, bleak spring skies, and having to wait until Memorial Day to plant flowers. Ah, Asheville. My long-awaited return to the South—region of my spirit, soul, and formative years.

Surprisingly, I found that Asheville is not really a Southern city at all. Sure, you can get grits at any self-respecting short order grill, and the locals say “Ashe-ville” with a smooth Southern drawl that melts butter on homemade biscuits. But there’s also a worldliness to this tiny metropolis that’s unlike any other city this size, anywhere in this country.

In doing the research for this book, I discovered why Asheville is unique. Why people from all over uproot themselves and move here to start businesses or to retire. Why tourists keep coming back, year after year, to enjoy our mountains and year-round activities. Why the area’s rich cultural heritage attracts artists and craftspeople in droves. And why George Vanderbilt—one of the wealthiest and most influential men of the late 1800s—chose Asheville as the site for his magnificent Biltmore Estate.

It’s an enchanting place, this mountain mecca for nature lovers, outdoor enthusiasts, and seekers of a “quality of life” that surpasses most places. *Asheville: A View from the Top* is an overview of what makes Asheville so special. Words and pictures can hardly do it justice, but we’ve attempted to capture the magic that’s best experienced in person. Read on; enjoy the photographic “views” from your hotel or living room. Then make the trek from across state, country, or the globe to see firsthand what Vanderbilt called “the most beautiful place on earth.” Asheville, North Carolina.

Lisa Bell
Author

PART ONE

ASHEVILLE

BB&T
VANCE

CHAPTER ONE

LOOKING BACK: A Historical Perspective

Asheville's history unfolds like a patchwork quilt. Exceptionally colorful...pieced together with many decades of determination...and fashioned from a unique blend of cultures that includes Cherokee, European, African-American, and Appalachian. And like the handcrafted quilts this region is so famous for, its heritage grows more precious with age, adding new wrinkles, standing the test of time. In looking back, one gains a greater understanding of what makes Asheville the extraordinary place it is today.

(*left*) Zebulon Vance's birthplace, located on Reems Creek, is the site of a reconstructed pioneer homestead and museum, paying tribute to this popular and distinguished native son. *Photo by Tim Barnwell.*

(*right*) Buncombe native Zebulon Vance spoke out against secession while a member of Congress. Ultimately he supported the Confederacy, serving as governor of North Carolina for three terms. *Photo courtesy of the North Carolina Collection, Pack Memorial Public Library.*

Located at the confluence of the French Broad and Swannanoa Rivers in Western North Carolina, Asheville is surrounded by the majestic Blue Ridge and Great Smoky Mountains. Long before the early colonists laid claim to the area called the "Land of the Sky," her native sons and daughters were the Cherokee. A proud and resourceful people, the Cherokee roamed the expansive mountains, fished abundant streams, and lived in relative harmony with nature and their fellowman. Then came the influx of European pioneers lured by the prospect of prosperity in this rugged, untamed region.

As the French and the British struggled to gain control, the Cherokee joined forces with these white men. First, the Cherokee allied themselves with the French in the French and Indian War in the late 1750s; then they carried a torch for the British against the early colonists in the American Revolution. In each conflict the Cherokee lost ground, figuratively and literally.

With the end of the Revolutionary War and the subsequent Treaty of Paris in 1783, North Carolina frontier territories were officially opened for settlement. A year later a brave and ambitious pioneer, Samuel Davidson, set out from Davidson's Fort (now Old Fort) and built a small cabin at the foot of Jones Mountain along Christian Creek in the fertile Swannanoa Valley. He moved his wife, infant daughter, and a female slave into their new home, making the Davidsons the first white settlers west of the Blue Ridge Mountains.

It was just a few months later that tragedy struck Samuel Davidson; he was killed by a band of Cherokee still daunted by the reality of white encroachment on their lands. It is recorded that Davidson's wife, hearing shots and fearing the worst, quickly gathered up her daughter and slave companion and traveled 15 miles through tangled forest to Davidson's Fort. Bent on revenge, an assembly of Davidson's relatives and friends returned to find his body and take the law into their own hands. A few of the Cherokee were caught and killed;

(above)* In 1797 the rugged settlement of Morristown was renamed Asheville in honor of North Carolina's governor, Samuel Ashe. *Photo courtesy of the North Carolina Collection, Pack Memorial Public Library.

(below)* Built in 1886 by North Carolina banker Colonel Frank Cox, the original Battery Park Hotel attracted the rich and famous. One such visitor was George W. Vanderbilt. *Photo courtesy of the North Carolina Collection, Pack Memorial Public Library.

others fled further west, deeper into the wild and unsettled mountain territory.

Despite Samuel Davidson's calamitous fate, fearless settlers followed, including his twin brother, his sister, their families, and others. By 1792 enough pioneers had arrived to form the new county of Buncombe, named for Colonel Edward Buncombe and referred to as "the state of Buncombe" because of its immense proportion. The area that was to become Asheville was called Morristown.

In 1794 landowner John Burton, later known as "the Father of Asheville," offered 42 lots for sale in an area that is now a part of downtown. Businesses sprang up, including a few places to eat and lodge, planting the seeds of the hospitality industry that would someday blossom. The first school west of the Blue Ridge, Union Hill Academy, was going strong. In 1797 the rugged settlement of Morristown was renamed Asheville in honor of North Carolina's governor, Samuel Ashe. Things were happening in and around Asheville. And yet this picturesque mountain settlement was virtually cut off from the outside world, strangled by its inaccessibility.

The Buncombe Turnpike, completed in 1828, changed all that. Thanks to the hard work and tenacity of David Lowry Swain, a local attorney who was later elected governor of North Carolina, the turnpike became a major thoroughfare linking Asheville with Tennessee and South Carolina. The road was nicknamed the "Drovers Road," accommodating droves of cattle, turkeys, hogs, and horses on their way to market. People came in droves, too, now that their stagecoaches and wagons had more than unrefined trails to travel.

With the burgeoning population, additional counties were established. Buncombe had already lost its Tennessee boundary to Haywood County in 1808; Yancey County to the north was chartered in 1833; and 17 years later Madison County was created from portions of Buncombe and Yancey. "The state of Buncombe" had become a more manageable 660 square miles, down from her original 4,600. As the area was divided geographically, mountain communities maintained fierce independence, true to the Appalachian spirit. So it was no surprise when the War Between the States spawned a war of opposing views between neighbors, friends, and even family.

Slavery was not the main topic of dissension. Buncombe and the surrounding counties had a relatively small population of slaves compared with the rest of North Carolina. Few landholders had the kind of sprawling farms that required the work of many laborers. States' rights was the issue that split public opinion, compelling hardy individualists to support the secession movement while others sought to preserve the Union.

A key Union sympathizer was Buncombe native Zebulon Vance, who spoke out against secession while a member of Congress. Ultimately Vance supported the Confederacy, serving as governor of North Carolina for three terms. Dubbed the "War Governor of the South," Vance was the only governor during the Civil War to uphold the writ of habeas corpus, a Constitutional protection from illegal imprisonment. His birthplace, located just north of Asheville on Reems Creek, is the site of a reconstructed pioneer homestead and museum, paying tribute to this popular and distinguished native son.

Samuel Davidson, the first white settler west of the Blue Ridge Mountains, was killed by a band of Cherokee still daunted by the reality of white encroachment on their lands. *Photo courtesy of the North Carolina Collection, Pack Memorial Public Library.*

The year 1865 marked the end of the Civil War, claiming more American lives to date than all other wars combined. North Carolina was the hardest hit Confederate state, the death toll reaching a resounding 40,275. Now the task at hand was to reunite, rebuild, and reestablish some sense of order in a world turned upside down by the ravages of war. But the world according to Asheville was about to change, slowly at first, then with locomotive speed. The coming of the railroads would set this mountain hideaway on an exhilarating course for the next several decades.

The 1880s were as fast and furious as the "iron horse" responsible for the explosive growth. At the dawn of the decade, Asheville had just 2,610 residents. By 1890 the population leaped to almost 15,000. Real estate boomed. Streets were paved and streetcars rolled. Agriculturally, the focus shifted from tobacco and other crops to the production of milk, butter, and beef. Tourism flourished, due in large part to the Asheville area's worldwide reputation as a health resort for sufferers of respiratory ailments.

Seeking a healthful change of climate, the ailing wife of Cleveland, Ohio, multimillionaire George Willis Pack was referred to Asheville by her physician in 1884. After a short time the Packs decided to stay and built a home

A circa 1886 view of Court Square looks down Patton Avenue from the Buncombe County Courthouse. *Photo courtesy of the North Carolina Collection, Pack Memorial Public Library.*

on Merrimon Avenue. Pack is considered to be Asheville's biggest benefactor, donating various properties to the city and county, including the land now known as Pack Square and the land on which the current Buncombe County Courthouse stands.

To lodge the inflow of well-heeled travelers, the crowning jewel of accommodations was built high atop Battery Park Hill in 1886 by North Carolina banker Colonel Frank Cox. Offering commanding views and equally impressive amenities like indoor plumbing and electric lights, elevators, and orchestra music, the Battery Park Hotel attracted the rich and famous. One such visitor was George W. Vanderbilt, grandson of the late Cornelius "the Commodore" Vanderbilt, railroad magnate and philanthropist.

The youngest of eight children, George Vanderbilt first visited Asheville in the late 1800s with his mother. Awed by the breadth of natural beauty and rural charm, he returned to fulfill his dream of creating a European-style self-supporting estate that would include a magnificent home, working farms, lush forests, and bountiful gardens. Vanderbilt quietly set about purchasing land south of Asheville that was both plentiful and affordable. All told, he amassed 125,000 acres, including Mount Pisgah and the surrounding forest.

Vanderbilt named his estate "Biltmore," derived from "Bildt," the name of the Vanderbilts' ancestral Dutch village, and "more," the Old English word for open, rolling hills. He engaged two of the world's leading professionals, architect Richard Morris Hunt and landscape architect Frederick Law Olmsted, to create the French Renaissance-style chateau and grounds. It took six years and more than 1,000 people to construct the 255-room mansion, a marvel of modern technology boasting comforts like central heat, electric lights and appliances, and the ultimate in luxury—private baths adjoining bedrooms. Opened for privileged guests on Christmas Eve 1895, the house, now the nation's largest private residence, was a showplace for George Vanderbilt's priceless collection of treasured artworks and furnishings. But it was also his home—and later home to his wife Edith and daughter Cornelia.

George Vanderbilt's contributions to the Asheville area are many, including the development of Biltmore Village, The Biltmore Dairy, and Biltmore Industries, an apprenticeship program for traditional handcrafts. Vanderbilt also established the Young Men's Institute (YMI), a community center for the city's black residents; and Edith Vanderbilt founded the School for Domestic Science, which taught housekeeping skills to young women. But according to Vanderbilt's descendants—who still own and operate the Biltmore Estate as a national historic attraction—George Vanderbilt's love of the land was his greatest legacy. As founder of the country's first School of Scientific Forestry, the mild-mannered gentleman farmer from New York made outstanding contributions to land management, forestry, and conservation.

With the turn of the century came the automobile, more sanitariums for the relief of "consumption" (tuberculosis), and more tourists—about 20,000 per year. Some of the most notable included Henry Ford, Harvey Firestone, Teddy Roosevelt, and Thomas A. Edison.

Others came here to live, setting in motion the development of Asheville's first neighborhoods, including Montford, Albermarle Park, Kenilworth-Victoria, and Chestnut Street. Many of the homes were architecturally stunning and reflected the means and status of their original owners. Some are in existence today as private homes; others are experiencing new life as bed-and-breakfasts, apartments, or commercial properties.

When he arrived here from Saint Louis in 1900, Dr. Edwin Wiley Grove, the patent medicine mogul, decided to get in on the real estate boom. Responsible for a number of downtown projects, Grove is best known for The Grove Park Inn Resort, constructed

(left)* Tightrope walkers perform for an amazed audience during an 1887 circus downtown. *Photo courtesy of the North Carolina Collection, Pack Memorial Public Library.

(right)* Asheville respects and honors its Native American traditions. *Photo by Tim Barnwell.

Opened for privileged guests on Christmas Eve 1895, the Biltmore House, now the nation's largest private residence, continues to be a showplace for George Vanderbilt's priceless collection of treasured artworks and furnishings. ***Photo by Tim Barnwell, courtesy of Biltmore Estate.***

Multimillionaire George Willis Pack is considered to be Asheville's biggest benefactor, donating various properties to the city and county, including the land now known as Pack Square. The square is shown here in 1890. ***Photos courtesy of the North Carolina Collection, Pack Memorial Public Library.***

With the turn of the century came the automobile and about 20,000 tourists per year. Some of the most notable included *(left to right)* Thomas Edison, Harvey Firestone Jr., Dr. E. W. Grove, and Henry Ford. *Photo courtesy of the North Carolina Collection, Pack Memorial Public Library.*

Torrential summer rains caused the French Broad and other rivers to spill their banks during the Great Flood of 1916. Property damage ran in excess of $3 million. ***Photo courtesy of the North Carolina Collection, Pack Memorial Public Library.***

The Asheville Royal Giants, shown at Pearson's Park on July 4, 1916, was the area's first black baseball team. ***Photo courtesy of the North Carolina Collection, Pack Memorial Public Library.***

Fire fighters stand ready for call in 1917. ***Photo courtesy of the North Carolina Collection, Pack Memorial Public Library.***

entirely from local granite boulders and completed in just over 12 months. The inn opened in 1913 to rave reviews as "the finest resort hotel in the world" and attracted the likes of Woodrow Wilson, John D. Rockefeller Jr., and F. Scott Fitzgerald.

Situated atop Sunset Mountain, the Grove Park Inn escaped damage during the Great Flood of 1916. Torrential summer rains caused the French Broad and other rivers to spill their banks, taking a heavy toll on Biltmore Village, Riverside Park, and lower-lying parts of Asheville. Only a few lives were lost, but property damage ran in excess of $3 million. It took years to recover.

The city experienced a flood of another sort in early 1917—patriotism. Along with the rest of the nation, Asheville celebrated America's involvement in World War I. Most of Asheville's soldiers served in the 30th Division, known as Old Hickory. At war's end, the city rejoiced again as returning veterans marched down Patton Avenue under a wooden Arch of Triumph.

The Roaring Twenties came in with a bang and went out with a bust. Real estate speculation was at an all-time high. New buildings were constructed: the Jackson Building, the region's first "skyscraper," a new city hall and county courthouse, and three major new hotels (including the new Battery Park Hotel on the razed site of the original). Dr. Grove began construction on the Grove Arcade—one of the nation's first indoor shopping "malls"—but died before its completion.

Colonel Harlan Sanders of Sanders Court on Weaverville Highway was known for his tasty fried chicken. He later went on to become Kentucky Fried Chicken's famous "Colonel Sanders." And the yet-to-be famous Walt Disney worked briefly as a draftsman in Asheville before going on to Hollywood—around the same time that Hollywood came to Asheville to film *Conquest of Canaan* at downtown's Pack Square.

But it wasn't Hollywood that brought almost overnight fame to Asheville—it was one of her own. Thomas Wolfe's first and most famous novel, *Look Homeward, Angel,* was based on the author's experiences growing up in his mother's Asheville boarding house. Although most of the characters' names were changed, many Asheville residents could see themselves in the pages of this very successful but candid book. Written in New York and published in 1929, the book created such a stir that Wolfe did not feel at liberty to look homeward on Asheville again until 1937.

October 29, 1929, signaled the beginning of the end of prosperity. The stock market crash crippled the nation and many of Asheville's wealthy residents. The effects were somewhat delayed, however, until the local Central Bank and Trust Company went bust on November 30, 1930, taking with it $8 million in city-county funds. Asheville and Buncombe County owed about $50 million, more than any other government in North Carolina. Shiny new municipal buildings stood tall, with no way to pay for them. Times were tough. Jobs were scarce. The Great Depression had set in—and didn't budge for nearly a decade.

War was brewing in Europe in 1939, and it was just a matter of time before the United States would jump in,

The Asheville Tourists baseball team poses for a group shot in 1924. *Photo courtesy of the North Carolina Collection, Pack Memorial Public Library.*

which happened following the invasion of Pearl Harbor in December of 1941. Asheville became a hotbed of activity for the United States government, which took over the Grove Arcade, the ground floor of the City Auditorium, four hotels, and other buildings. City Hall and the Asheville-Hendersonville Airport were commandeered to house the weather and communications divisions of the Army Air Corp. The Grove Park Inn was used to confine Axis diplomats until they could be exchanged, then later by United States Navy officers seeking a little rest and relaxation. Even the Biltmore House was called into service. Fearing that Washington might be bombed, the federal government discreetly shipped some of the nation's priceless artwork to Biltmore for storage until the threat had passed.

The year 1945 saw the end of World War II and the beginning of a new era of prosperity. One of the nation's first shopping centers, Westgate Shopping Center, opened for business in the early 1950s. Construction of a new airport began in 1958 and was completed in 1960. Western North Carolina native Billy Graham gained international prominence as an evangelist, bridging the gaps between all people.

The 1960s were trying times for a nation coming to grips with racial issues. Asheville and Buncombe County were more open to the idea of integration than many other areas; and the contributions of several key individuals helped pave the way.

Lucy Saunders Herring was a shining example in the field of public education. The granddaughter of slaves, Herring spent over 50 years in a variety of positions, from teacher to elementary school principal to associate college professor. At a time when most black schools were named for streets instead of people, she was honored in 1961 when the Asheville City School District named a new school the "Lucy S. Herring School."

Asheville residents' love of sports is colorblind. In 1961 Willie Stargell, an African-American outfielder for the Asheville Tourists who hit 22 home runs that year, helped the team take the South Atlantic League pennant. Three years later Asheville native Henry Logan became the first African-American college basketball player in the South, gaining status as a four-time All-American player at Western Carolina College.

Attorney Ruben Dailey, Asheville's first African-American city councilman, was elected for two terms and contributed to numerous civic organizations and served on the National Board of the YMCA. He was a crusader for common sense and cooperation among blacks and whites.

The 1970s and 1980s can be summed up in a word: change. People moved to the suburbs as new residential and retail areas—and the roads to take them there—were constructed. Interstate 240 took shape, leveling stretches of Beaucatcher Mountain in the wake of environmentalist protests. A new Civic Center and Pack Library were added to the downtown landscape. And in an honest-to-goodness "flash from the past," the last of the municipal bonds issued before 1930 were burned in a public ceremony on July 1, 1976, freeing Asheville at last from its 40-year-old debt.

When other cities defaulted on pre-Depression era debt, Asheville persevered. Call it civic pride, mountain spirit, or just doing the right thing, but whatever you call it, the more you get to know about Asheville the more it makes sense. Her history bears testimony to her strength, her courage, and her hope for the future—a future full of promise in this "Land of the Sky" that knows no bounds. ▲

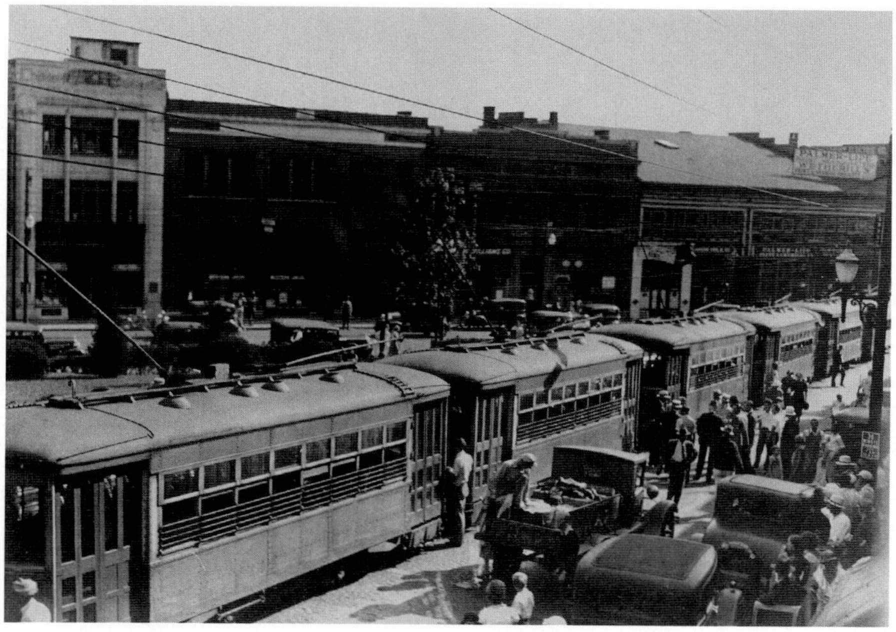

An end of an era—on September 6, 1934, streetcars on College Street were lined up for their last run. *Photo courtesy of the North Carolina Collection, Pack Memorial Public Library.*

The Zebulon Vance Memorial stands out in the view from Patton Avenue in the 1950s. *Photo courtesy of the North Carolina Collection, Pack Memorial Public Library.*

It's a pleasing mix of the old and the new, Asheville's colorful past and prosperous present. The historic Jackson Building is reflected in the Biltmore Building, an I.M. Pei Structure. *Photo by Warner Photography.*

Constructed in the '20s, the Jackson Building was the region's first "skyscraper." ***Photo courtesy of the North Carolina Collection, Pack Memorial Public Library.***

BB&T

CHAPTER TWO

DOWNTOWN: Down-home Hospitality In The Heart Of The City

It all comes together in downtown Asheville—eclectic shopping, interesting sight-seeing, and a world of dining options from tofu to tiramisu, gumbo to gourmet steak and seafood. Downtown is a literal feast for the senses, and not just for the taste buds. Take a walk around town and you'll quickly see what we mean.

(*left*) Asheville's biggest summer celebration is Bele Chere, reputedly the largest street festival of its kind in North Carolina that features music, food, and fun for all ages. *Photo by Tim Barnwell.*

(*right*) Downtown Asheville offers a world of dining options. *Photo by Tim Barnwell.*

Visually you'll be impressed with Asheville's architecture, reflecting a variety of styles ranging from Gothic to Neo-Classical to Art Deco. In fact, Asheville boasts more authentic Art Deco buildings than any other Southeastern city outside of Miami, Florida. As you continue your stroll past a sidewalk eatery, you're likely to smell the aroma of freshly baked muffins and steaming hot coffee. Step inside one of the unique shops and instantly feel the warmth of Southern hospitality as you're greeted by a local shopkeeper, probably the proprietor. Isn't that a swing band playing outside Pack Place? The upbeat music mingles with the sound of children laughing, excited about their field trip to the popular Health Adventure. Over their laughter you can hear someone asking for directions (in French) to the Thomas Wolfe Memorial.

You've just had a taste of what it's like to visit downtown Asheville, the heart of the city and the regional hub for Western North Carolina—a great place to visit, but an even better place to live and work. There's a cosmopolitan influence that you wouldn't expect to find in a city of this size or this location—just slightly off the beaten path in the southern Appalachian Mountains. As exhilarating as it is today, downtown Asheville wasn't always like this.

Like many other towns and cities across the United States, Asheville's downtown area fell victim to the suburban flight that began in the late 1950s and steamrolled in the 1970s. As shoppers took their business to outlying malls, downtown merchants closed their doors. Many beautiful old buildings were left to slowly decay, too expensive to keep up and yet too expensive to tear down.

As fate would have it, the threat of demolishing 11 city blocks is what brought Asheville to her senses. An early 1980s referendum to develop the property into a modern downtown shopping mall and parking facilities was soundly defeated, sparking new interest in historic preservation. Developers took a look around at what downtown had to offer and decided this faded lady could use not just a facelift, but a major overhaul. And that's exactly what she got.

In 1984 Pack Plaza was initiated from 11 jaded buildings, now home to the Pack Place Education, Arts, and Science Center. Breathing new life into the shell of an old department store, developer Robert Armstrong completed the luxurious Haywood Park Hotel in 1986. That same year the City of Asheville established the Downtown Development Office to attract other developers and businesses interested in moving downtown. A group of savvy developers banked on Wall Street's rebirth, and the strategy worked, fueling a "redevelopment fever" that hasn't stopped. Public and private sector expenditures have exceeded $150 million, and downtown occupancy rates have climbed. The next major project is the Grove Arcade, which promises to be one of downtown's most exciting new attractions.

Downtown Asheville is best seen on foot. The Urban Trail is a 1.6-mile walking route through downtown that

In 1984 Pack Plaza was initiated from 11 dilapidated buildings, now home to the Pack Place Education, Arts, and Science Center. *Photo by Tim Barnwell.*

Children of all ages—including grownups—can have fun while learning about the human body at the Health Adventure, located in the Pack Place Education, Arts, and Science Center. *Photo by Tim Barnwell.*

The YMI Cultural Center was commissioned by George Vanderbilt in 1892 as a recreation center for Asheville's black residents. *Photo by Tim Barnwell.*

highlights points of interest and historical significance. Established in 1991, the trail features 27 stations (in various stages of completion) grouped into five themes: the Gilded Age, the Frontier Period, the Times of Thomas Wolfe, the Era of Civic Pride, and the Age of Diversity.

Appropriately, the trail begins at Pack Square, site of two Cherokee crossroads where the city of Asheville was born. Still a crossroads of sorts, Pack Square is a gathering place for locals and tourists, drawn by the popular restaurants, specialty shops, and fine art galleries. Visit Pack Place Education, Arts, and Science Center for a look at some dazzling gems and minerals, significant twentieth-century American art, and interactive health science exhibits. A monument to Buncombe leader Zebulon B. Vance is located in the middle of Pack Square.

Just off the square you'll find the YMI Cultural Center and Mount Zion Missionary Baptist Church, circa 1919, important landmarks in the local African-American community. Commissioned by George Vanderbilt in 1892 as a recreation center for Asheville's black residents, the YMI (Young Men's Institute) was purchased by black leaders in 1906. Most of the land around the YMI is still in the hands of African-American property owners who are board members of the Eagle/Market Streets Development Corporation. Revitalization projects are in the works.

Wandering off the Urban Trail, you enter an area known as Lexington Park, perhaps best known for its wide assortment of antique shops and second-hand stores. Looking for that "one of a kind" antique hall tree to hang your hat on—or perhaps a vintage hat from the 1940s? Chances are you'll find them, plus a variety of other items that once occupied attics and garages. In Asheville's oldest general store, T. S. Morrison, you'll find lots of great items like old-time candy, Victorian greeting cards, and souvenirs of your trip to Asheville.

No visit to downtown is complete without seeing the boyhood home of Thomas Wolfe, who immortalized Asheville in his famous novel *Look Homeward, Angel.* The "Old Kentucky Home," a boarding house run by Wolfe's mother, is a State Historic Site featuring many original furnishings, photographs, and memorabilia. But don't expect a lot of frills—a wealthy woman herself, Julia Wolfe was tight with the dollar and ran the rooming house on a shoestring.

By contrast it feels as if no expense was spared in the redevelopment of the Battery Hill area, primarily the Haywood Park Hotel and Wall Street. You'll feel miles away from the New York financial district as you cruise down Asheville's version of Wall Street, streetscaped with old-fashioned lighting and lots of trees. Specialty shops abound, offering some of the city's most exotic apparel, jewelry, handcrafts, and books. Splurge on a delectable meal at one the neighborhood's fine restaurants—then burn it off with a little exercise at the indoor climbing center. Talk about an "off-the-wall" adventure!

Exploring downtown Asheville is truly an experience all its own. And just when you think you've done it all, a new show or exhibition will breeze into town. There'll be a new nightspot to check out, a new menu to sample, or a lively street festival to attend.

Downtown is home to Asheville's major festivals and celebrations, attracting a diverse crowd of locals and tourists. One of the major events is Goombay!, the city's African-Caribbean festival. The annual Mountain Dance and Folk Festival is the nation's oldest festival of its kind, paying tribute to the toe-tapping tunes of Appalachia.

Things really heat up in the summer in downtown Asheville with ongoing events like Shindig-on-the-Green and Downtown After Five. Started in 1989 as a Friday evening get-together for downtown workers, Downtown After Five now attracts suburban employees and their families, plus a tourist or two. The combination of live music, fabulous food, and your favorite cold beverage will make your workweek worries vanish.

Asheville's biggest summer celebration is Bele Chere, reputedly the largest street festival of its kind in North Carolina that features music, food, and fun for all ages. The three-day annual event brings together well-known entertainers and local performers that range from country and western to alternative and rock. And while you're enjoying the tunes, enjoy the food at one of the dozens of stands serving international cuisine as well as the traditional festival fare like snow cones, hot dogs, and funnel cakes. You'll see why this extravaganza is named "Bele Chere" (French for "beautiful living") when you find yourself living it up, Asheville style.

A monument to Buncombe leader Zebulon B. Vance is located in the middle of Pack Square. ***Photo by Tim Barnwell.***

No visit to downtown is complete without seeing the boyhood home of Thomas Wolfe, who immortalized Asheville in his famous novel *Look Homeward, Angel. Photo by Warner Photography.*

This angel at Park Place was inspired by the monuments carved by Thomas Wolfe's father. *Photo by Tim Barnwell.*

In Asheville's oldest general store, T. S. Morrison, you'll find lots of great items like old-time candy, Victorian greeting cards, and souvenirs of your trip to Asheville. *Photo by Tim Barnwell.*

Things really heat up in the summer in downtown Asheville with ongoing events like Shindig-on-the-Green. Nearly every Saturday evening in July and August, amateurs and seasoned pros join in for fun-filled evenings of mountain music, food, square dancing, and clogging. *Photo by Tim Barnwell.*

Lexington Park is known for its assortment of antique and second-hand stores. *Photo by Tim Barnwell.*

The holiday season is a special time in downtown Asheville, and the Light Up Your Holidays event does just that. Actually, it's a series of events that include the ever-popular *Nutcracker Ballet,* a Christmas parade, tours of historic neighborhoods and bed-and-breakfast inns, and holiday performances by the Asheville Symphony Orchestra and Chorus. The festivities culminate with the observance of Kwanzaa, the African-American celebration of the season at the YMI Cultural Center, and First Night, the no-alcohol, family-oriented New Year's Eve bash. At First Night, the whole family can eat, drink, and be merrily entertained by a variety of performers from jazz musicians to jugglers. And at evening's end you'll be ringing in the New Year with a blast of fireworks that will "Light Up Your Holidays" until next year.

Over a decade has passed since downtown Asheville was reborn in the spirit of historic preservation. Thanks to the efforts of civic leaders, the Asheville Downtown Association, and the Asheville Area Chamber of Commerce, the dream of revitalizing downtown lives on. It is an organized, concerted effort that includes elements like the Asheville Streetscape Plan, which outlines the development of public spaces like parks, squares, and corridors.

As more and more businesses call downtown Asheville home, more people will call it home, too. Today, just under 1,000 people live downtown in a variety of residential units from luxury condos to loft spaces to housing for the elderly. The trend toward living downtown is taking hold, and many developers look to downtown's future with an eye toward multipurpose buildings (commercial, retail, and residential). But whether you live downtown, work downtown, or just visit downtown Asheville, there's always something new and exciting to hold your interest. ▲

Asheville's version of Wall Street is streetscaped with old-fashioned lighting and lots of trees. A group of savvy developers banked on Wall Street's rebirth, and the strategy worked, fueling a "redevelopment fever" that hasn't stopped. *Photo by Tim Barnwell.*

Bele Chere, French for "beautiful living," brings together well-known entertainers and local performers that range from country and western to alternative and rock for this fabulous three-day event. *Photo by Warner Photography.*

Bele Chere offers a sampling of mountain music, food, dance, balloons, clowns, and folkloric storytelling. *Photos by Tim Barnwell.*

The holiday season is a special time in downtown Asheville, and the "Light Up Your Holidays" event does just that. *Photos by Tim Barnwell.*

CHAPTER THREE

MOUNTAIN MAGIC: Your Spirits Will Soar

Picture a stunning sunset on a crisp fall evening in Asheville, mountains ablaze with brilliant yellow, orange, and white against a backdrop of fading blue sky. You can see for miles—as rows of towering peaks pierce the sun-drenched skyline. At sunrise you awake to a completely different horizon. Some of the mountains appear to be floating, engulfed in a wispy smoke that follows the wind. Other peaks have disappeared completely, mysteriously reappearing an hour later. There's something magical about these mountains that is as old as time itself, and the cultures that were born of these ancient mountains are unique and incredibly fascinating.

(*left*) The rushing sounds of water flowing down a mountain create an inner peace and allow the spirit to soar. *Photo by Tim Barnwell.*

(*right*) Mountain magic is a way of life, a spirit, a positive attitude affected by the altitude. *Photo by Tim Barnwell.*

The Cherokee were among the first mountaineers. The mountains were alive to these Native Americans, who paid homage to the great peaks, the rivers, and all things bold and beautiful in Mother Nature's realm. The early European settlers were trailblazers, fearless pioneers who hacked their way through dense forests, over tall mountains, and across rushing waters to call Western North Carolina home. Awed by the area's immense natural beauty and abundance of animal and bird life, ore and minerals, more settlers followed, many of Scotch-Irish and German descent. The pioneer spirit evolved into a sort of mountain fever that still lingers. Highly contagious, mountain fever's symptoms include an insatiable thirst for independence, an uncompromising love of the mountains, and a sincere appreciation of one's home, hearth, and heritage.

Much has been written about the Appalachian culture. The folklore, the traditions. The remote log cabins and split-rail fences. The handcrafted quilts, furniture, and pottery. The folk dance, music, and colorful storytelling for which the region is known. Perhaps romanticized over the years, these things are real, not just figments of a historian's imagination. Many an elder today will give an earful to anyone willing to listen to tales of making birch tea, spotting mountain ghosts, and banjo-picking with the best of them.

Bascom Lamar Lunsford (1882-1973) was considered the "Minstrel of the Appalachians" in his day, picking, fiddling, and strumming his way into the hearts of southern Appalachian folk enthusiasts until the ripe old age of 91. In fact, Lunsford founded America's first (and oldest) folk festival in 1927, the Mountain Dance and Folk Festival, now held each summer at Asheville's Thomas Wolfe Auditorium. The three-day festival is North Carolina's longest-standing event dedicated to mountain traditions and includes over 400 "invitation only" regional performers. Among them are bluegrass bands, fiddlers, shape note singers, storytellers, cloggers, and dulcimer players. Ever hear of the Big Circle Mountain Dance? Rarely performed outside of this festival, the graceful traditional dance of the southern Appalachians involves eight or more couples and a caller. Not to be missed, the Mountain Dance and Folk Festival provides exceptional family entertainment with an emphasis on combining the best of bygone Appalachia with the folk traditions of present day.

If it's festivals you're after, there are more than 200 of these mountain events in the Asheville area that cover all four seasons and a broad range of interests. Most of the major festivals, including the enormously popular Bele Chere, offer a sampling of mountain music, song, food, and folkloric storytelling. The annual three-day "Tell it in the Mountains" celebration is focused entirely on the art

Highly contagious, mountain fever's symptoms include an insatiable thirst for independence, an uncompromising love of the mountains, and a sincere appreciation of one's home, hearth, and heritage. *Photo by Tim Barnwell.*

The Mountain Dance and Folk Festival, an annual three-day festival, is North Carolina's longest-standing event dedicated to mountain traditions and includes over 400 "invitation only" regional performers. *Photo by Tim Barnwell.*

of storytelling, featuring traditional and contemporary performers with a range of experiences.

Some of the most notable events that celebrate mountain folk culture are sponsored by area colleges and universities, including Mountain Heritage Day at Western Carolina University, the Swannanoa Gathering at Warren Wilson College, and the Blue Ridge Old-Time Music Week at Mars Hill College. Mountain Heritage Day attracts close to 60,000 people who come for the music, mountain crafts, and down-home novelties like ax-throwing contests and chain saw demonstrations. The Swannanoa Gathering offers four weeks of courses in traditional music, dance, and storytelling, attracting students from all over the world. The Blue Ridge Old-Time Music Week offers similar instruction, with topics ranging from ballad singing and storytelling, to clogging, and care and maintenance of fiddle and bow. (If you're a clogging enthusiast, don't miss the Bailey Mountain Cloggers from Mars Hill College—they're national champions.)

If you're ready to try out a little clogging yourself, bring your dancing shoes to Shindig-on-the-Green at downtown's City-County Plaza, nearly every Saturday evening in July and August. Amateurs and seasoned pros join in for fun-filled evenings of mountain music, food, square dancing, and clogging.

The annual Lake Eden Arts Festival in Black Mountain features traditional mountain and multicultural folk arts, including storytelling and poetry, a juried handcraft show, activities for children, and workshops in Afro-Cuban, Native American, and contra dance, to name a few. Picturesque Black Mountain is also home of the Black Mountain Folk Festival, held each spring and fall, a Clogging Festival, the annual Sourwood Festival, and the Black Mountain Herbfest.

The annual Mountain State Fair attracts thousands to the WNC Agricultural Center in Fletcher. *Photo by Tim Barnwell.*

With agriculture playing an important role in Western North Carolina's economy, it's not surprising to find a variety of celebrations centered on agricultural products. One of the more colorful (and aromatic) is Waynesville's annual Ramp Festival, a tribute to the onion look-alike that is related to the leek. Western North Carolina is home to a wide variety of herbs, and the largest herb festival in the Southeast—the Herb Days Spring Herb Festival—is held each year at the popular WNC Farmers' Market. The annual Mountain State Fair attracts thousands to the WNC Agricultural Center in Fletcher, site of livestock shows and exhibits, and the new "Down-on-the Farm" musical show for children of all ages. The WNC Ag Center also hosts various horse shows and rodeos throughout the year. Just south of the Ag Center, you'll find historic Hendersonville, home of the North Carolina Apple Festival held each September. A tribute to the area's exceptional harvest, the three-day festival is the largest and most popular event in growing Henderson County.

Apples, mountain cabbage, sourwood honey, and hearty

The North Carolina Apple Festival, held each September, pays tribute to the area's exceptional harvest. The three-day event is the largest and most popular event in Henderson County. *Photo by Warner Photography.*

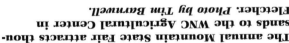

Tasty, home-grown edibles are offered at roadside stands throughout Western North Carolina and the WNC Farmers' Market located in west Asheville. *Photo by Tim Barnwell.*

tomatoes are just a few of the tasty, home-grown edibles offered at roadside stands throughout Western North Carolina. More than 1,200 farmers sell their wares at the 36-acre WNC Farmers' Market located in west Asheville; and you'll find a host of fresh ingredients to concoct those traditional mountain foods like hoppin' John, sweet potato pone, and mountain poke greens. And, if you're hungry for mountain handcrafts, the farmer's market sells a good selection. But don't stop there. Western North Carolina is well-known for its handcrafts, not just in quantity but in quality. A wide variety of crafts can be found off the beaten path at roadside shops, festivals, weekend flea markets, and the downtown areas of Asheville, Biltmore Village, Black Mountain, and the like.

One of the best ways to take in a day of craft shopping is to pick up the guidebook *The Craft Heritage Trails of Western North Carolina,* published by the Asheville-based group HandMade in America. Seven day-long, self-guided tours are outlined in the book, which features about 375 stops, including studios, galleries, shops, and museums in the 21 counties of Western North Carolina. The book also highlights historic inns, restaurants, and other places of interest along the way. The Mountain Cities Trail will take you through Tryon, Saluda, Lake Lure, Hendersonville, and Asheville. Crafts are big business in the area, and HandMade's ultimate goal is to make Western North Carolina the center for handmade objects in the nation.

The region's reputation for outstanding craftsmanship wasn't earned in a decade or even a century. Generations of talented mountain folk have taken up a hewing hatchet, worked at a pottery wheel, and spun yarns of fiber and folklore. The area was, and still is, a literal gold mine of raw materials for craft making—yielding roots and berries for natural dyes, gemstones for jewelry, white oak for baskets, and willows for furniture. Other natural ingredients include clay used for pottery, corn shucks for dolls, and rhododendron wood for caning. Beautiful hardwoods are transformed into useful bowls, spoons, and musical instruments.

With the intention of reviving local interest in mountain crafts at the turn of the last century, George and Edith Vanderbilt founded Biltmore Industries, focused primarily on wood carving and the weaving of woolen

The Qualla Arts and Crafts Mutual, located on the Cherokee Indian reservation, is recognized as the most outstanding Indian-owned and operated arts and crafts cooperative in America. *Photo by Tim Barnwell.*

The Cherokee were among the first mountaineers. The mountains were alive to these Native Americans, who paid homage to the great peaks, the rivers, and all things bold and beautiful in Mother Nature's realm. *Photos by Tim Barnwell.*

A blanket of white covers the mountains.
Photo by Warner Photography.

The region's reputation for outstanding craftsmanship wasn't earned in a decade or even a century. Generations of talented mountain folk have weaved a basket, worked at a pottery wheel, and spun yarns of fiber and folklore. *Photo by Tim Barnwell.*

homespun cloth. The school prospered even after George Vanderbilt's death in 1914. Three years later Fred L. Seely, manager of the Grove Park Inn, purchased the industries and constructed six buildings adjacent to the inn, naming them the Biltmore Homespun Shops. Stop by the Grovewood Gallery, a spacious shop that showcases glass, furniture, jewelry, and other works of some of the Southeast's finest craftspeople. Today you can visit the North Carolina Homespun Museum and see old handmade looms, artifacts, and photos.

The Southern Highland Craft Guild (SHCG) is an active organization with members in nine Southern states. At the guild's headquarters located at the Folk Art Center (Blue Ridge Parkway milepost 382) you'll find a comprehensive collection of folk art literature, traveling exhibits, and periodic craft demonstrations and lectures. The SHCG also operates four craft shops, including Guild Crafts on Tunnel Road in Asheville and the popular Allanstand Craft Shop at the Folk Art Center. One of Appalachia's oldest and best known craft shops, Allanstand sells the work of more than 400 members of the guild. Traditional mountain crafts, furniture, quilts, and pottery are featured alongside more contemporary sculpture, jewelry, handblown glass, and decorative arts. The guild also sponsors dozens of craft workshops for children and adults, and hosts the heavily attended Craft Fair of the Southern Highlands held in the summer, and again in the fall at the Asheville Civic Center.

(left) There are plenty of reasons why people love Asheville—just look around at the surrounding beauty. *Photo by Tim Barnwell.*

For the finest selection of authentic Cherokee crafts, visit the Qualla Arts and Crafts Mutual located on the 56,000-acre Cherokee Indian reservation in the heart of the Great Smoky Mountains. Recognized as the most outstanding Indian-owned and operated arts and crafts cooperative in America, Qualla offers an assortment of handcrafted leather goods, beadwork, and more.

Keeping the mountain spirit alive and teaching new generations how to construct an Appalachian-style rocker, play the hammered dulcimer, or piece together a triple rail fence pattern quilt takes time, mentoring, and training. In music, there's a trend toward "jamming" at informal gatherings—the seasoned picker or fiddler always eager to lend a hand (and an ear) to the novice player. Of course, the local clubs and night spots support the area's rich musical heritage, regularly featuring the best of local bluegrass, folk, dulcimer, and Celtic.

On a more formal level, several instructional programs, some more than 60 years old, deserve mention, particularly in the field of mountain crafts. Two area schools, The Penland School and John C. Campbell Folk School, have been around since the mid 1920s. The Penland School of Crafts in Mitchell County is one of the finest institutions devoted exclusively to craft studies, bringing in more than 130 acclaimed instructors from as far away as Europe to teach classes ranging from glass to metals, weaving to woodworking. The John C. Campbell Folk School in Brasstown offers more than 500 weekend, one- and two-week courses in all sorts of subjects, including blacksmithing, marbling, and mountain music. About 45 miles north of Asheville in Marshall, Country Workshops attracts some of the most distinguished

Western North Carolina is well-known for its quality handcrafts. A wide variety of crafts can be found off the beaten path at roadside shops, festivals, weekend flea markets, and the downtown areas of Asheville, Biltmore Village, Black Mountain, and the like. *Photo by Tim Barnwell.*

woodworkers who travel to this mountain farmstead to attend week-long summer courses in traditional woodworking with hand tools. And if you're looking for a degree program in production crafts, check out Haywood Community College's well-rounded curriculum in four major program divisions: clay, fiber, jewelry, and wood.

The famed Appalachian Trail passes through both the nearby Pisgah National Forest and the Great Smoky Mountains National Park close to the state border. *Photo by Tim Barnwell.*

There wouldn't be mountain magic without the mountains themselves, and the Asheville area has more than you can count. Asheville is nestled between two majestic mountain ranges—the Great Smoky and the Blue Ridge. Named for the smoke-like haze that wafts in and around these lush mountains, the Smokies comprise one of the oldest upland regions in the world and are a part of the Appalachian Mountain chain. It is written that the Blue Ridge Mountains were named by the Cherokee, who called this land Sa-koh-na-gas, which means "blue," referring to the blue mist that rises when warm, humid air meets sunshine and hydrocarbons produced by dense forest cover. Reaching a summit of 6,684 feet, Mount Mitchell in Yancey County is the highest peak east of the Mississippi River and is visible from the Blue Ridge Parkway.

If you've never spent time on the Blue Ridge Parkway, you're in for a treat. Intentionally designed to showcase the best of Appalachia—the rolling pastures and farmlands and the breathtaking overlooks and vistas—the parkway, as its name implies, is a series of parks. Some 6,000 acres have campgrounds, picnic areas, trails, and other facilities, including the popular Pisgah Inn, offering magnificent views from its 5,000-foot elevation at Mount Pisgah in the Pisgah National Forest.

The native rhododendron of Craggy Gardens adds a splash of color to the beauty of the Blue Ridge Parkway. *Photo by Tim Barnwell.*

There's so much to see on the parkway that it's considered a vacation destination in itself. You can hike, bike, fish, or bird-watch. Take in a ranger-narrated nature walk or shop for handcrafts at the Folk Art Center. Visit the North Carolina Mineral Museum or marvel at the twisted trees and native rhododendrons of Craggy Gardens. View vibrant flowering shrubs and wildflowers in the spring and summer, and return for fall's brilliant display of color. Year-round, see the manicured gardens and man-made waterfall at the impressive North Carolina Arboretum. In fact, the 469-mile parkway is the nation's longest scenic attraction and one of the most popular areas in the National Park System. Millions of visitors each year are drawn to the panoramic parkway, a refreshing escape from the billboards and commercial development of other roadways.

Initiated in 1935 as a New Deal project to create jobs, the parkway links the Shenandoah National Park in Virginia with the Great Smoky Mountains National Park in North Carolina and Tennessee. Landscape architect Stanley Abbott was charged with creating a scenic experience for the traveler that depicted a variety of landscapes and appealing snapshots of Appalachia. In turn, this

(*right*) From late September to early November visitors are amazed by the area's legendary display of fall colors. *Photo by Tim Barnwell.*

Water Rock Knob, along the Blue Ridge Parkway, offers breathtaking views. *Photo by Tim Barnwell.*

monumental endeavor would hopefully inspire future generations to protect and preserve the lands in and around this national treasure. (For your information, the parkway is toll-free, and its headquarters are located in Asheville.)

Protecting the lands adjoining the parkway from unsightly or environmentally harmful development is an on-going venture—one that received a boost from the 1996 North Carolina "Year of the Mountains" initiative. This year-long observance set in motion a number of long-range projects designed to protect the region's natural resources, as well as to acknowledge more than 75 mountain cultural treasures and natural heritage sites. Asheville-area mountain parks that made the list, based on their unique geology, flora, and fauna, include Chimney Rock Park, Grandfather Mountain, the Great Smoky Mountains National Park, Mount Mitchell State Park, and the Cradle of Forestry, as well as other historical and cultural sites.

(left)* Chimney Rock towers 2,280 feet above sea level and is estimated to be about 535 million years old. *Photo by Tim Barnwell.

One can only speculate that Chimney Rock was named for its uncanny resemblance to a chimney, towering 2,280 feet above sea level and estimated to be about 535 million years old. The park itself comprises almost 1,000 acres and is located 25 miles southeast of Asheville in scenic Hickory Nut Gorge. On a clear day you can see Kings Mountain, 75 miles to the east beyond the Blue Ridge Mountains.

The park began as the dream of Dr. Lucius B. Morse, a St. Louis physician who had traveled to the area in 1900. Morse and his two brothers pooled their resources in 1902 and purchased the first 64-acre tract that included Chimney Rock and the surrounding cliffs. It was the intention of the Morse brothers to preserve the beauty and heritage of the mountain, while developing the area into a vacation spot that offered lodging, horse trails, golf courses, and the amenities of nearby Lake Lure.

Today's Chimney Rock is still in the hands of the Morse family, more committed than ever to the environmental preservation of the park. Classes, lectures, and school field trips are offered in a range of topics, from wildflower

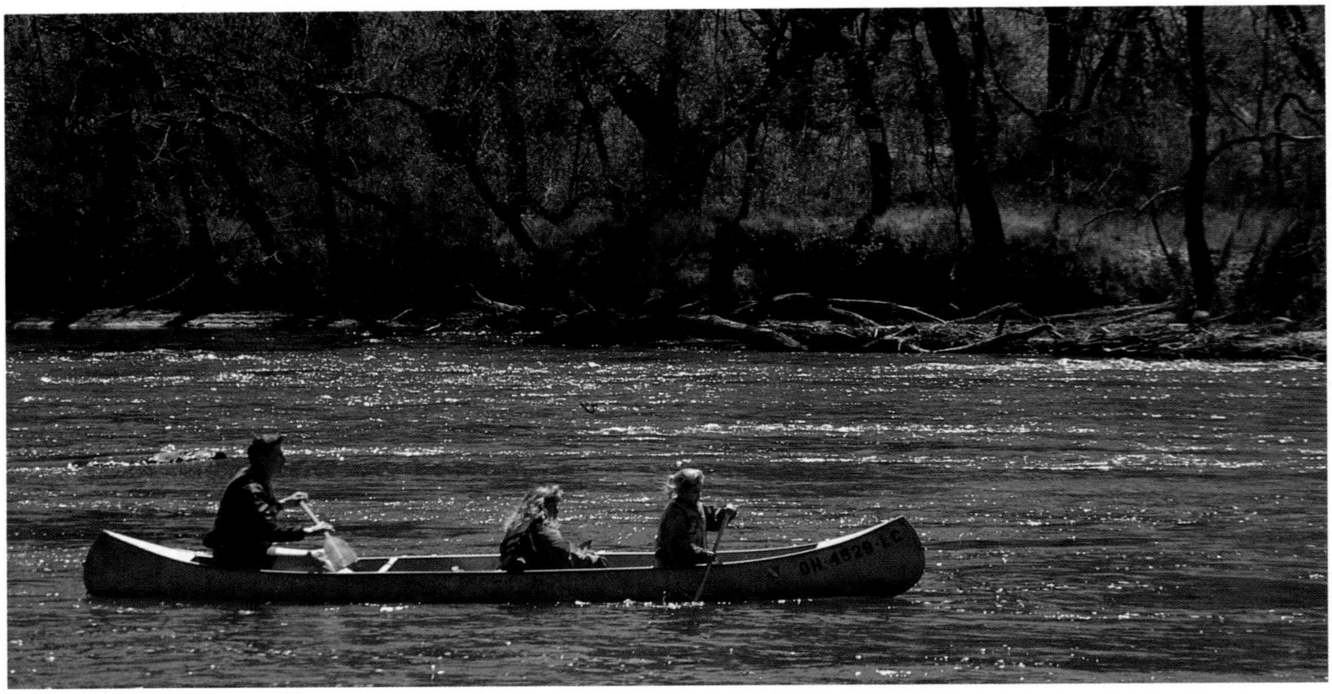

Crisp mountain temperatures inspire visitors to head for the great outdoors. *Photo by Tim Barnwell.*

identification to workshops on the area's bird life. The Chimney Rock Nature Center highlights the abundant natural resources of the park—evident to visitors who explore first-hand the 2.5 miles of beautiful hiking trails that lead to the 404-foot Hickory Nut Falls. Want a breathtaking view from Chimney Rock without an uphill climb? Take the 26-story elevator ride through solid granite to a sky lounge, gift shop, and visitor center. See the exhibit of photo stills and costumes from the 1992 movie *The Last of the Mohicans,* filmed at the park using spectacular locations including Inspiration Point and Hickory Nut Falls.

The highest point along the Blue Ridge Parkway can be found at Grandfather Mountain in Linville. Once there, you'll also find the highest swinging footbridge in America, the Mile High Swinging Bridge, suspending you more than a mile above sea level. Visit the nature museum, visitor center, and wildlife habitats. Spend the day hiking miles of interlaced trails. Stop for a scenic picnic along the way. Privately owned, Grandfather Mountain has been designated by the United Nations as an International Biosphere Reserve, harboring 42 rare and endangered species of plant and animal life.

Talk about biological diversity—the Great Smoky Mountain National Park boasts more than 1,600 different types of wildflowers and more than 140 species of trees. The most visited national park in the nation, this 800-square-mile wonderland extends about 70 miles along the North Carolina-Tennessee border and contains more than 700 miles of rivers and streams, 800 miles of trails, and 200,000 acres of virgin forests. The park is home to several hundred black bears and vanishing species including the red wolf and eastern river otter. Hiking, camping, and fishing are permitted in the park; be sure to stop by the park service office for information and special permits for some activities.

Mount Mitchell is the highest peak east of the Mississippi River and is located off the Blue Ridge Parkway at mile marker 355.4 in the Black Mountains. Mount Mitchell State Park is North Carolina's first state park, established in 1915. The 1,677-acre location offers hiking trails, picnic areas, camping, a restaurant, and a small natural history museum—not to mention the most magnificent views this side of the Mississippi. Temperatures plummet when you reach the summit of Mount Mitchell, so be prepared with jacket in hand, even in the summer months.

Mount Mitchell was named for Dr. Elisha Mitchell, a University of North Carolina science professor who, in 1835, established that the mountain was indeed taller than the then record-holding Clingman Dome in eastern Tennessee. Tragically, Dr. Mitchell fell to his death in 1857 from a cliff above a 40-foot waterfall when he returned to Mount Mitchell to verify his measurements. He is buried at the base of the stone observation tower atop the mountain that bears his name.

To sum it all up, mountain magic means many things to many people. From appreciating the region's boundless natural beauty and striving to preserve it, to remembering our rich cultural heritage and passing it on to our children and grandchildren, to stopping to smell the mountain laurel or sampling a steaming pie made from home-grown apples. It's a way of life, a spirit, a positive attitude affected by the altitude. It's a magic you can feel, whether you're here for a day, a week, or a lifetime. ▲

Fall brings a rainbow of color to the mountains.
Photo by Tim Barnwell.

From winter's soft fallen snow to spring's glorious dogwoods, an abundance of beauty prevails in Asheville. *Photos by Tim Barnwell.*

Asheville is a place with more than its share of dramatic beauty. A good example is Looking Glass Falls in the Pisgah National Forest. *Photo by Tim Barnwell.*

The Blue Ridge Parkway was designed to showcase the best of Appalachia—the rolling pastures and farmlands and the breathtaking overlooks and vistas. *Photo by Tim Barnwell.*

You can see for miles—as rows of towering peaks pierce the sun-drenched skyline. *Photo by Tim Barnwell.*

It is written that the Blue Ridge Mountains were named by the Cherokee, who called this land Sa-koh-na-gas, which means "blue," referring to the blue mist that rises when warm, humid air meets sunshine and hydrocarbons produced by dense forest cover. *Photo by Tim Barnwell.*

There's so much to see along the parkway that it's considered a vacation destination in itself. You can hike, bike, fish, or bird-watch.
Photo by Tim Barnwell.

Many people come to the Asheville area to explore the great outdoors, richly blessed by Mother Nature's hand. *Photo by Tim Barnwell.*

CHAPTER FOUR

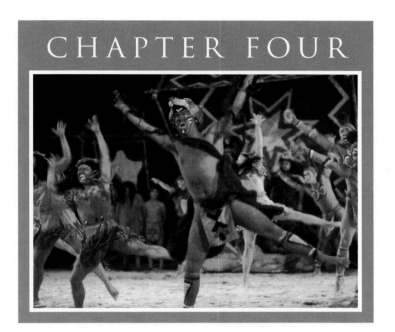

ATTRACTIONS: So Much To See– So Much To Do

Whether you're 8 or 80, a history buff, a shopper, or an outdoor enthusiast, you'll quickly realize that there's no shortage of things to see and do in the Asheville area. In fact, repeat visits are common. It seems that once you get a taste of what Asheville has to offer, your plate becomes so full that you must return at some point for a second helping. From sunup to sundown, winter through fall, you'll be amazed at the smorgasbord of activities and attractions in the Asheville area. But where do you begin to sample them?

(*left*) Visiting the Biltmore Estate is like stepping back a century and across the Atlantic to a sprawling French chateau with glorious gardens. *Photo by Tim Barnwell.*

(*right*) "Unto These Hills" chronicles the history of the Cherokee people—culminating with the infamous "Trail of Tears"—and has been seen by more than 5 million people since its first performance in 1950. *Photo by Tim Barnwell.*

(left)* The Asheville Visitor Center, located just off I-240 downtown at the Asheville Area Chamber of Commerce, is the second most visited center of its kind in the state. More than 130,000 people a year find literally hundreds of brochures on area attractions, accommodations, restaurants, and more. *Photo by Tim Barnwell.

A good place to start is the Asheville Visitor Center, located just off I-240 downtown at the Asheville Area Chamber of Commerce. The second most visited center of its kind in the state, the Asheville Visitor Center attracts more than 130,000 people a year and is well worth the trip. Under one roof, you'll find literally hundreds of brochures on area attractions, accommodations, restaurants, and more. Friendly volunteer staff members will give you the lowdown on favorite festivals, how to get tickets to local events, where to go white-water rafting, and the best places to find authentic mountain handcrafts and food.

Many people come to the Asheville area to explore the great outdoors, richly blessed by Mother Nature's hand. Our mountains have inspired generations of explorers, pioneers, artisans, and dreamers. No visit to the area is complete without catching an awe-inspiring view from the summit of Mount Mitchell, Grandfather Mountain, Chimney Rock, or Mount Pisgah. But the mountains are not our only natural attraction—we've got waterfalls, wildflowers, and white water; birds, black bears, and botanical gardens; and rocks, rhododendrons, and rivers. In fact, Asheville was ranked among the nation's top 10 cities by *Outside* magazine, and the North Carolina Outward Bound School recently moved its headquarters here to take advantage of the area's bountiful backyard.

Enjoying the outdoors on foot is a great way to take it all in, and hikers from all over trek to the Asheville area to pursue this popular pastime. The famed Appalachian Trail passes through both the nearby Pisgah National Forest and the Great Smoky Mountains National Park close to the state border. Trails ranging from easy to difficult can be found in just about every major park in the area and along the Blue Ridge Parkway. Clubs such as the Carolina Mountain Club, Nantahala Hiking Club, and the Sierra Club support local hikers who like to hit the trail on a regular basis.

A mecca for mountain bikers, the Asheville area has been rated by biking publications among the top five United States locations for mountain biking. No wonder, considering the hundreds of miles of trails in the Pisgah and Nantahala National Forests alone. Stop by one of the local bicycle shops for some insider tips on favorite trails, bike excursions, rentals, and other useful information. For an unparalleled on-road adventure, try the beautiful Blue Ridge Parkway. Motorists willingly share the road with experienced mountain bikers, who appreciate the slower driving speeds and absence of stoplights—not to mention the spectacular scenery and challenging elevations. In recent years, Tour DuPont, the country's foremost cycling event, has made its way through Asheville.

For a ride of a different sort, saddle up for some great horseback riding. Western North Carolina has a number of horse farms. Designated riding trails can be found in the Pisgah and Nantahala National Forests, and in the Great Smoky Mountains National Park. A number of Asheville area stables offer trail riding led by experienced guides—day trips as well as multiday rides and pack trips.

Camping in the Asheville area is really a high adventure, considering the elevation of popular camp sites in the Great Smoky Mountains National Park, Pisgah National Forest, and along the Blue Ridge Parkway. You'll awake with your head in the clouds on a cool summer morning, whether you've just emerged from a tent or the controlled comfort of a recreational vehicle. Area campgrounds and facilities are abundant, affordable, and appealing to visitors of all ages.

Children in particular enjoy the sport of rockhounding, whether it's an informal exploration along the trail or a visit to one of the area gemstone mines. Imagine sifting through buckets of dirt to discover rubies, garnets, and riches beyond your wildest dreams. Well, maybe not riches—although a handful of amateur miners have been known to pocket some pretty valuable gems. Nonetheless, the experience alone is worth a lot. To get a glimpse of Western North Carolina's gem and mineral wealth (without getting your hands dirty), visit the Colbern Gem and Mineral Museum at Pack Place, or the North Carolina Mineral Museum on the Blue Ridge Parkway.

A mecca for mountain bikers, the Asheville area has been rated by biking publications among the top five United States locations for mountain biking. *Photo by Tim Barnwell.*

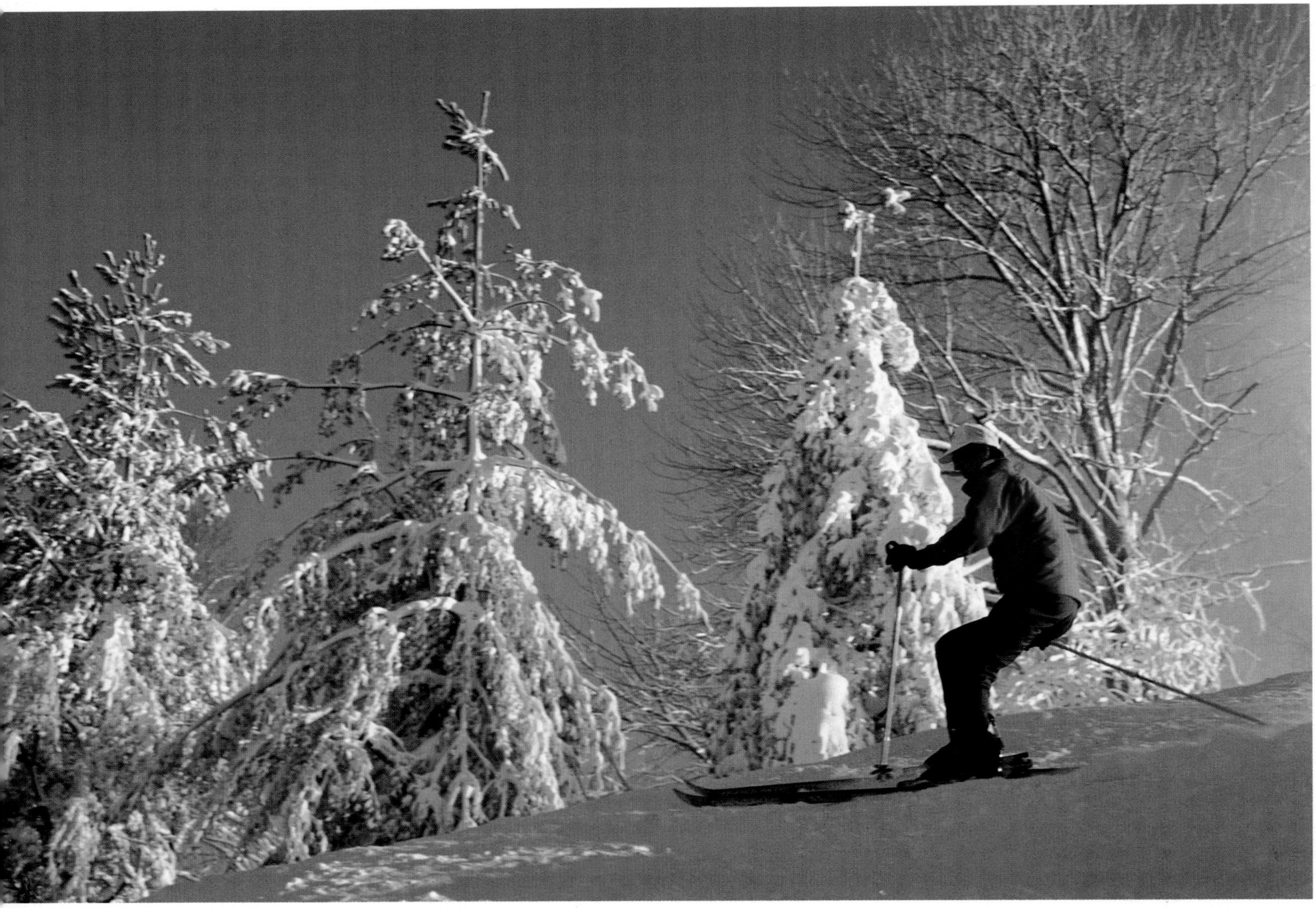

When it's winter, area residents and visitors wax their snow skis and head for the slopes. *Photo by Tim Barnwell.*

Other outdoor adventures include rock climbing, spelunking, llama trekking, hot air ballooning, and hunting. Check with the Asheville Visitor Center for more information and the names of tour operators and outfitters. And then there's the water—and lots of it. Crystal clear lakes, well-stocked rivers, and streams lure fishing, canoeing, and waterskiing enthusiasts by the boatload. Nearby lakes include Lake Julian, Lake Powhatan in the Pisgah National Forest, and Lake Lure, near Chimney Rock. All three are within a 45-minute drive of Asheville and are nice spots to bag that catch of the day. Bring back some bass, bream, or trout at day's end—or a suitable fish story about how the big one got away.

And speaking of big, white-water rafting is one of the area's rapidly growing sports, attracting thousands of thrill seekers each year. Some of the Southeast's best white water can be found in Western North Carolina. Challenging rides can be had on the Nantahala River to the west and south, and the French Broad and Nolichucky Rivers to the north. Contact one of the many area outfitters for a raft, kayak, or canoe excursion that's guaranteed not to leave you high and dry.

Looking for a somewhat calmer way to enjoy a lot of rushing water, without getting wet? Try waterfall watching, popular among hikers, campers, and amateur photographers who, chances are, have more falls to photograph than film. There are literally hundreds of waterfalls in the area stretching from just east of Brevard to just west of Highlands. Nine out of eleven of North Carolina's major falls can be found here in "waterfall country." Looking Glass Falls and Toxaway Falls are two of the most spectacular. The highest waterfall in eastern America is the 411-foot Whitewater Falls, southwest of Asheville off of U.S. Highway 64. If you want to get wet after all, take a slide down Sliding Rock, a 60-foot natural water slide that lands you in a cool, 7-foot deep pond. Located off U.S. Highway 276, Sliding Rock attracts crowds of adventurous plunge takers and spectators in the spring and summer months.

When it's winter, area residents and visitors wax their snow skis and head for the slopes, enhanced with manmade snow for ideal skiing. A number of ski resorts are within a short drive of Asheville; Wolf Laurel and Cataloochee are the closest. Beech Mountain in the

For the adventurists, rock climbing is a thrilling pastime. *Photo by Tim Barnwell.*

Some of the Southeast's best white water can be found in Western North Carolina. Challenging rides can be had on the Nantahala River to the west and south, and the French Broad and Nolichucky Rivers to the north. *Photo by Tim Barnwell.*

Sliding Rock, a 60-foot natural water slide that lands you in a 7-foot deep pond, attracts crowds of adventurous plunge takers and spectators in the spring and summer months. *Photo by Tim Barnwell.*

The waters of Western North Carolina offer thrills for all who love to get wet. *Photos by Tim Barnwell.*

Beaver Lake, near downtown Asheville, is a serene setting for an afternoon outing. ***Photo by Tim Barnwell.***

Banner Elk/Boone region has a peak elevation of 5,505 feet and is the highest ski area in eastern North America. Not far from Beech, you'll find five other ski resorts, including Sugar Mountain Ski Resort. Located in the southern mountains of Cashiers is Sapphire Valley Resort, which offers skiing, plus an array of year-round activities including fishing, golf, tennis, and horseback riding.

Western North Carolina's moderate year-round climate is cherished by tennis and golf players, who have no trouble finding a court or a course on which to indulge themselves. Golf is especially popular, with over 50 courses in the area. The rolling terrain makes for challenging play—plus it's hard to keep your eye on the ball when there's so much beautiful scenery competing for your attention. Asheville area public courses include Asheville Municipal, Black Mountain, Brookwood, Reems Creek, Springdale, and the French Broad Golf Center. Both the Great Smokies Holiday Inn SunSpree Resort and The Grove Park Inn Resort (guests and members only) offer 18 holes of resort golfing, only minutes from downtown Asheville. There are also a number of excellent private golf courses in the area, including those at Biltmore Forest Country Club and the Country Club of Asheville.

If you'd rather be a spectator than work up a sweat, you can still enjoy the sporting life. Basketball is big in the Tarheel State, and Asheville's own UNCA men's team, the Bulldogs, play from November through March on campus and occasionally at the Civic Center. The Asheville Tourists, a Class A farm team of the Colorado Rockies, play professional minor league baseball at Asheville's historic McCormick Field, the oldest minor league field in America. On Friday nights from mid-April through Labor Day, the Asheville Speedway offers NASCAR-sanctioned short track stock car racing. And for NFL football, a quick trip to Charlotte is just over two hours' drive, where you can watch the Carolina Panthers stalk their prey at the new Carolinas Stadium.

You won't find any panthers at the WNC Nature Center, but you will find bobcats, rattlesnakes, red wolves, and other predators native to Western North Carolina. Located in east Asheville, the Nature Center is a living museum where wildlife and wildflowers are showcased in a protected, natural setting—with a few exceptions. The region is home to 22 varieties of snakes, only two of which are poisonous (rattlesnakes and copperheads). Look for them behind glass. Children especially enjoy the Nature Center's hands-on exhibits, the educational farm, and special events such as the annual Farm 'n Fun Day, an old-fashioned frolic with food, crafts, music, and entertainment. Young and old alike enjoy the assortment of fine feathered and furry friends—chickens, lambs, goats, and cows—just waiting to be petted. Local children go "wild" at the Nature Center's Wild Weeks Nature Camp, a series of week-long summer camps that are both fun and educational for young nature buffs.

In addition to the Nature Center, several other outdoor attractions are "must sees." The North Carolina Arboretum in the Bent Creek area features over 3,000 varieties of plants, unique gardens, walking trails, and a man-made waterfall. The Botanical Gardens of Asheville is an impressive 10-acre display of native plants and flowers, located next to the campus of UNCA. Each spring the gardens, UNCA, and the Blue Ridge Parkway sponsor the three-day Wildflower Pilgrimage, a series of lectures, bird walks, and mountain field trips to explore the wealth of wildflowers in the area.

The Blue Ridge Parkway is an attraction not to be missed. There are a number of interesting sites along the parkway in Western North Carolina, including the Linn Cove Viaduct at milepost 304. The final link in the construction of the parkway, the viaduct is considered an engineering marvel and was opened in 1987. Just a mile away at milepost 304, you'll find the exit to Grandfather

A number of horse farms in the Asheville area offer opportunities for horseback riding. *Photo by Tim Barnwell.*

(left)* Western North Carolina's moderate year-round climate is cherished by tennis and golf players, who have no trouble finding a court or a course on which to indulge themselves. *Photos by Tim Barnwell.

On Friday nights from mid-April through Labor Day, the Asheville Speedway offers NASCAR-sanctioned short track stock car racing. *Photo by Roy Rogers.*

Basketball is big in the Tarheel State, and Asheville's own UNCA men's team, the Bulldogs, play from November through March. *Photo courtesy of UNCA.*

The Asheville Tourists, a Class A farm team of the Colorado Rockies, play professional minor league baseball at Asheville's historic McCormick Field, the oldest minor league field in America. ***Photos by Warner Photography.***

(left)* Biltmore Estate is exciting at any time, but especially during the Christmas holidays, when visitors are treated to a feast of Victorian sights and sounds. *Photo by Tim Barnwell.

Mountain, the highest peak along the parkway. Exit at milepost 316.3 to visit Linville Falls, and take U.S. Highway 221 four miles south to the Linville Caverns. You'll see limestone stalactite and stalagmite formations with names like the Frozen Waterfall and the Franciscan Monk. Constant 52-degree temperatures in the deep, dark caverns make for a really "cool" adventure.

If you have the time, stay on U.S. Highway 221 and travel north to U.S. Highway 321 South to get to the legendary Blowing Rock, named for its mysterious winds that have been known to cause snow to fall upside down. On Highway 321 between the towns of Blowing Rock and Boone, the whimsical Tweetsie Railroad theme park offers old-fashioned fudge, a Ferris wheel, and lots of fun for the young-at-heart.

Back on the parkway heading south, you'll pass the Museum of North Carolina Minerals at milepost 331, and the exit for Mount Mitchell State Park at 355.4. At mileposts 363 to 369 the area known as Craggy Gardens offers breathtaking views and colorful "balds"—treeless areas of low-growing plants, grasses, and wildflowers. Giant purple rhododendron and odd-looking gnarled trees add to the unique splendor of Craggy Gardens. The Folk Art Center is right on the parkway at milepost 382 and is a great introduction to the mountain crafts of the Southern Highlands.

The parkway cuts through the beautiful Pisgah National Forest, which spans 12 counties in Western North Carolina and covers more than 500,000 acres of forest land. Mount Pisgah (elevation 5,721) was named for the Biblical mountain of the same name, from which Moses first saw the Promised Land. Sliding Rock, Looking Glass Falls, and the State Fish Hatchery are popular sites in the Pisgah area. The Pisgah Inn at milepost 408 offers "a view with a room," a recommended restaurant, and gift shop. Off milepost 412 you'll find the Cradle of Forestry, a National Historic Site commemorating the birthplace of American forestry and forestry education.

George Vanderbilt started the first planned forestry program in America in 1898 at his Biltmore Estate, which originally included 100,000 acres of Pisgah Forest. Following Vanderbilt's death in 1914, his widow, Edith Vanderbilt, deeded nearly 87,000 acres to the federal government to create the nucleus of Pisgah National Forest. Today's Biltmore Estate spans 8,000 acres and includes the 255-room mansion, restaurants, shops, a winery, and acres of lush landscaping and manicured gardens, designed by Frederick Law Olmsted, creator of New York's Central Park.

Visiting Biltmore Estate is like stepping back a century and across the Atlantic to a sprawling French chateau. There's no other place in America like it, and the house—opened to guests on Christmas Eve, 1895—is the nation's largest private home. George Vanderbilt's priceless collection of furniture, prints, paintings, and one-of-a-kind art objects is on display, not to mention the impressive architecture and ornamental details of the house itself.

Plan to spend a full day at Biltmore; there's a lot to see, and the beauty and opulence of the estate is practically overwhelming. Rent the audiocassette tour for interesting tidbits about the mansion, as you stroll through more than 50 rooms, painstakingly restored to their original splendor. Or take the professionally guided "behind the scenes" tour for even more information, and

The Smith-McDowell House is Asheville's oldest brick residence. *Photo by Tim Barnwell.*

Located just off Highway 64, Dry Falls is one of the area's many picturesque waterfalls. *Photo by Tim Barnwell.*

Tree-lined streets, brick sidewalks, and distinctive architecture give Biltmore Village a special charm, rivaled only by the quality and selection of the merchandise you'll find there. *Photo by Tim Barnwell.*

glimpses of rooms not on the regular tour. Full-color souvenir guide books are available in the gift shops, also featuring Victorian-era gifts, toys, sweets, and the like.

When you've worked up an appetite, take a break for lunch at one of the three estate restaurants, which are known for using fresh, Biltmore-produced ingredients. Then tour the 10 acres of gardens, walk the Woodland Trails, and sample some award-winning wines at the Biltmore Estate Winery, the most visited winery in the nation. Open year-round, Biltmore Estate is a treat any time, but especially during the Christmas holidays and the Spring Festival of Flowers.

Christmas is a special time to visit the Smith-McDowell House, when Asheville's oldest brick residence, c. 1840, is decorated in Victorian holiday splendor. Located on the campus of Asheville-Buncombe Technical Community College, the museum pays tribute to the area's colorful mountain heritage and features restored period rooms and a Victorian gift shop. Guided tours last approximately one hour.

If you're hooked on history, the Asheville area has plenty of historical sight-seeing. A number of sites are listed on the National Register of Historic Places, including Biltmore House, the Smith-McDowell House, and the Thomas Wolfe Memorial, location of the author's boyhood home and the fictional "Dixieland" in his famous novel *Look Homeward, Angel.* The Asheville native is laid to rest in Riverside Cemetery on Birch Street, also the burial place of fellow writer O' Henry.

Downtown Asheville is a treasure trove of significant architecture, including Pack Place (which is actually an amalgamation of several historic buildings) which houses the Asheville Art Museum, Colburn Gem and Mineral Museum, the Health Adventure, and the Diana Wortham Theatre. Douglas Elligton's art deco influence is prolific in the S & W Cafeteria, City Hall, City-County Plaza, and the First Baptist Church at Oak and Woodfin Streets—all listed on the Historic Register. The beautiful Basilica of St. Lawrence (also a historic site) on Haywood Street boasts the largest unsupported dome in North America, designed by Rafael Guastavino in 1909; and the intriguing Grove Arcade is destined for redevelopment in the very near future.

The Grove Park Inn, a crowning achievement of developer Edwin W. Grove, has attracted the rich and famous since its opening in 1913. Eight American presidents have stayed at the inn, as well as numerous celebrities. Look for photos of famous guests in the hallways adjoining the Great Hall.

Listed on the Historic Register, the inn is not just a hotel, but a destination in itself. Guests of the 510-room award-winning resort have access to the 18-hole Donald Ross golf course, nine tennis courts, two pools, and an extensive indoor sports center. The inn boasts generous meeting facilities, programs for children, and year-round special events and theme weekends, such as big band, arts and crafts, and comedy.

Even if you're not staying at the inn, drop by for a dose of rustic romance, as you read the words of wisdom inscribed on the massive stone fireplaces in the monumental Great Hall. Sit out on the big front porch and

The first weekend in December, Biltmore Village transforms itself into a Dickensonian Village, complete with costumed musicians and spectacular holiday decorations. *Photo by Tim Barnwell.*

Linville Caverns offers many interesting formations and extends deep into the mountainside. *Photo by Tim Barnwell.*

rock to your heart's content (there are rows of rocking chairs) as you marvel at the unique granite architecture of this historic haven. Sample some tasty cuisine at one of the fine restaurants, or sip a cold drink on the Sunset Terrace while you enjoy one of Asheville's most spectacular views. And if you dare, ask a hotel employee about the legendary Pink Lady, an apparition that's been the subject of hotel lore for decades.

On the grounds adjacent to the Grove Park Inn, visit the Antique Auto Museum for a glance at life in the slow lane, and stop by the North Carolina Homespun Museum, an interesting collection of antique looms, artifacts, and old photos of Biltmore Industries, the mountain crafts school founded by George and Edith Vanderbilt. To purchase traditional and contemporary crafts, check out the Grovewood Gallery for a splendid selection of handblown glass, furniture, quilts, and other fine handcrafts.

Weaving, open-hearth cooking, and churning are some of the lost arts you can appreciate firsthand at Pioneer Living Days at the Zebulon B. Vance Birthplace in the Reems Creek area. In the spring and fall, this state historic site comes alive with costumed pioneers who demonstrate the skills required for survival without today's modern appliances. Year-round you can tour the reconstructed log home of Vance, "war governor of the South," and visit the museum commemorating this Civil War-era leader, one of the most popular and influential public servants in North Carolina history.

Another historic home to visit is Connemara, the Flat Rock farm of Pulitzer prize-winning author Carl Sandburg. This 263-acre farm is a National Historic Site and was home to Sandburg and his wife for 22 years, until his death in 1967. Take a guided tour through the home, simply furnished and haphazardly adorned with stacks and shelves of Sandburg's many books. Originally a working goat farm managed by Mrs. Sandburg, Connemara comprises several outbuildings, a picturesque lake, and a small herd of goats, descendants of the original Sandburg goats.

Had enough of history and ready for a 90-minute road trip? The mountains west of Asheville, including the towns of Cherokee, Maggie Valley, Waynesville, Bryson City, and Dillsboro, offer a range of activities for all ages. The 56,000-acre Cherokee Indian reservation is located at the North Carolina entrance to both the Great Smoky Mountains National Park and the Blue Ridge Parkway. Here you'll find the fascinating Oconaluftee Indian Village, a replica of a 1700s Cherokee village. Cherokee guides lead you through the realistic village, where you'll see native craftspeople at work—molding clay into pots, chipping flint for arrowheads, and using fire and ax to make a dugout canoe. Go inside the seven-sided Council House for a lively presentation on Cherokee history, culture, and rituals.

Other sites to see around Cherokee include the Museum of the Cherokee Indian, the Cherokee Heritage Museum and Gallery, the Cherokee Cyclorama Wax Museum, and the Pioneer Homestead. There's no shortage of shops selling Indian crafts—you'll find a bevy of bead, moccasin, and leather craft vendors on every corner. The Qualla Arts and Crafts Mutual is a good place to shop and is recognized as the most outstanding Indian-owned and operated arts and crafts co-op in the country.

America's most popular outdoor drama, "Unto These Hills," is performed in the summer months at the beautiful Mountainside Theatre. The story chronicles the history of the Cherokee people—culminating with the infamous "Trail of Tears"—and has been seen by more than 5 million people since its first performance in 1950.

Something new in recent years for adults who visit Cherokee: legalized gambling. The Eastern Band of the Cherokee, the governing body of the Cherokee community, operates three locations featuring tribal bingo, video poker, craps, and blackjack. An $85-million casino and entertainment complex is currently in the works.

For children, Cherokee holds other surprises, like panning for gold and gems at the Smoky Mountain Gold and Ruby Mine and spending the day at Santa's Land Family Fun Park and Zoo. Open May through late fall, the park offers family fun with a Christmas theme. Santa and his elves break away from the North Pole to visit with the children, who delight in riding the rides, powering their own paddle boats, and petting the live reindeer and other animals.

Ghost Town in the Sky is another theme park located east of Cherokee in Maggie Valley. Take the chair lift, railway, or shuttle bus to reach the top, where the Old West comes alive with more than 30 rides and shows, staged shoot-outs on Main Street, and can-can dancing at the Silver Dollar Saloon. It's a mile high and a lot more fun than those old *Gunsmoke* reruns.

If an old-fashioned train ride sounds good to you, get aboard the Great Smoky Mountains Railway and see the mountains from a different perspective. Trains depart from Dillsboro, Bryson City, and Andrews; excursions last from 3.5 to 4.5 hours, depending on the tour you select. Murder mystery evenings and dinner train trips are also available. Highlights of the Tuckasegee River excursion include the train wreck site in the movie *The Fugitive,* and the 836-foot Cowee Tunnel, reportedly haunted by the 19 convict laborers who died in its construction. The Nantahala Gorge tour takes you through the spectacular Nantahala Gorge white-water rafting area, and the Red Marble Gap journey is known as the second highest railroad grade in eastern America.

For those who love to shop, Asheville is home to two major malls—Asheville Mall and Biltmore Square Mall. Shown below, shoppers enjoy the variety of stores at Asheville Mall. *Photo by Tim Barnwell.*

When you've had your fill of sight-seeing and want to shop or grab a bite to eat, there are plenty of places to go. Start with downtown Asheville, the heart of the city and home to more than 100 retail shops and 40 diverse restaurants. Some of the area's most eclectic foods and merchandise can be found in this thriving, downtown district that features fabulous finds at Lexington Avenue antique shops, and a world of wonderful dining and shopping options on Wall Street.

If you'd rather see a familiar chain restaurant or mall store, cruise down Tunnel Road, one of the city's busiest retail areas. Asheville's largest mall, appropriately named Asheville Mall, is on Tunnel Road and has 100 stores, including Belk, Dillard's, JCPenney, Montgomery Ward, and Sears. Innsbruck Mall, a busy shopping center on Tunnel Road, is anchored by Ingles, Brendle's, and Helig-Meyers furniture.

The newer Biltmore Square Mall on Brevard Road houses more than 60 stores, including Proffitt's, Belk, Dillard's, and Goody's department stores. A number of other shopping centers are located throughout the Asheville area and suburbs, and River Ridge Marketplace offers outlet shopping at more than 40 stores.

And speaking of outlets, some of the nation's best off-price shopping can be found in Western North Carolina and the surrounding areas—fashion finds, designer fabrics, furniture, and oriental rugs. The Asheville Visitor

Center has dozens of brochures highlighting outlets within a reasonable drive.

If you don't mind driving a ways, several areas are known for their superb shopping and dining, including Boone, Blowing Rock, and Banner Elk to the north and Bryson City, Dillsboro, and Maggie Valley to the west. Black Mountain, just 15 minutes east of Asheville, boasts a number of antique and furniture shops, as well as handcraft and collectible vendors. South of Asheville in Hendersonville, you'll find a charming Main Street, with an antique shop on every corner, and a nostalgic drugstore that serves sodas and hand-dipped ice cream just like in the good old days.

The most historic shopping district in the Asheville area is just a stone's throw from the Biltmore Estate, and was developed by George Vanderbilt in the late 1890s as a planned community. Today's Biltmore Village is a collection of quaint shops and restaurants, most housed in their original turn-of-the-century buildings.

Tree-lined streets, brick sidewalks, and distinctive architecture give Biltmore Village a special charm, rivaled only by the quality and selection of the merchandise you'll find there. Items like decorative antiques, ceramic angels, vintage dolls, fashionable jewelry, clothing, arts, and crafts are available in large supply. Visit Interiors Marketplace for a cornucopia of stylish furniture, accessories, and original artwork. Then have lunch or dinner at a trendy cafe, or Mexican hot spot. Special activities in Biltmore Village include the annual Village Art and Craft Fair in August, held on the grounds of the historic All Souls Episcopal Church. And you'll have a Dickens of a time the first weekend in December, when Biltmore Village transforms itself into a Dickensonian Village, complete with costumed musicians, refreshments, and spectacular holiday decorations.

No matter what the season, there's something for everyone who ventures into these mountains. Unlimited outdoor recreation, more than 200 area festivals and mountain handcrafts, music, and cultural events await you. If you don't believe it, keep coming back. Chances are, you'll find something that interests you, be it athletic, aesthetic, or academic. Asheville's got it all—and we're eager to share it. ▲

Viewed from the Blue Ridge Parkway, Looking Glass Rock's stark granite face reflects the afternoon sun. *Photo by Tim Barnwell.*

(following page) **Morning mist adds to the magic of Western North Carolina's many mountain lakes.** ***Photo by Warner Photography.***

Located between the towns of Blowing Rock and Boone, the whimsical Tweetsie Railroad theme park offers old-fashioned fun for the young-at-heart. *Photo by Tim Barnwell.*

Ghost Town in the Sky, a theme park where the Old West comes alive, has more than 30 rides and shows, staged shoot-outs, and can-can dancing at the Silver Dollar Saloon. *Photo by Tim Barnwell.*

The town of Blowing Rock offers a quaint and charming shopping experience. *Photo by Tim Barnwell.*

The legendary Blowing Rock was named for its mysterious winds that have been known to cause snow to fall upside down. *Photo by Tim Barnwell.*

The WNC Nature Center is a living museum where wildlife and wildflowers are showcased in a protected, natural setting. *Photo by Tim Barnwell.*

Crystal clear lakes, well-stocked rivers, and streams lure fishers by the boatloads to Western North Carolina. *Photos by Tim Barnwell.*

The Botanical Gardens of Asheville is an impressive 10-acre display of native plants and flowers, located next to the campus of UNCA. *Photos by Tim Barnwell.*

The brilliance of autumn sweeps across the mountains of Western North Carolina. *Photo by Tim Barnwell.*

(previous page) **The Grove Park Inn, a crowning achievement of developer Edwin W. Grove, has attracted the rich and famous since its opening in 1913. Listed on the Historic Register, the inn is not just a hotel, but an attraction in itself. *Photo by Tim Barnwell.***

The Linn Cove Viaduct, opened in 1987, represents the final link in the construction of the Blue Ridge Parkway. *Photo by Tim Barnwell.*

CHAPTER FIVE

THE ARTS: Visual & Performing Arts Abound

Asheville has been called "the Paris of the South," no doubt referring to the charm, sophistication, and cultural diversity the community has to offer. The local arts scene is as impressive as the scenery itself, and many of the area's visual and performing artists agree that there's something about the mountains that gets those creative juices flowing.

(left) The Asheville Art Museum, at Pack Square, features the work of noted artists, many with ties to the Asheville region. *Photo by Tim Barnwell.*

(right) Talented students of all ages participate in Theatre UNCA, the university drama department's season of drama, comedy, and musical theater. *Photo by Tim Barnwell.*

George Vanderbilt thought so, calling Asheville "the most beautiful place on earth." A perfect setting for his beloved Biltmore, the mansion houses innumerable art treasures. But perhaps the most imposing aspect of Biltmore is the structure itself, a venerable work of art and display of superb craftsmanship. In the creation of Biltmore House, Vanderbilt employed skilled artisans and craftspeople from all over the world, including the acclaimed Viennese sculptor Karl Bitter. Although Bitter did not stay on after the completion of Biltmore, others did, including the respected architect Richard Sharpe Smith. With so many talented artists, designers, and skilled artisans in one place, the Asheville area quickly garnered a reputation for exceptional craftsmanship.

Two decades later, in 1912, some of the Italian stonemasons who worked on Biltmore were hired for the construction of the Grove Park Inn. A monument to the art of simplicity, the Grove Park Inn was furnished with functional wicker rockers, oak and leather furniture, and copper lighting created by Arts and Crafts artisans in a movement that flourished from 1895 to 1929. Much of the original furniture was handmade by the Roycrofters of East Aurora, New York, and is still in use today. The inn now boasts the world's largest collection of Arts and Crafts antique furniture, and its annual Grove Park Inn Arts and Crafts Conference draws a crowd of over 2,000 Arts and Crafts enthusiasts from around the country.

The Biltmore mansion houses innumerable art treasures from the collection of George Vanderbilt. *Photo by Tim Barnwell.*

A monument to the art of simplicity, the Grove Park Inn was furnished with functional wicker rockers, oak and leather furniture, and copper lighting created by Arts and Crafts artisans in a movement that flourished from 1895 to 1929. *Photo courtesy of the Grove Park Inn.*

Just as the Arts and Crafts movement was winding down, Black Mountain College (BMC) in nearby Black Mountain was gearing up. From 1933 to 1956 the college thrived as the most innovative educational institution in twentieth-century America. And during a time of social unrest in this country, BMC was one of the first colleges to introduce racial integration. Today Black Mountain College is acknowledged worldwide for its outstanding contributions to the visual arts, music, and literature.

Looking back over the last century, it's easy to see why the Asheville area is deeply rooted in the arts. But what may not be evident to the casual observer is the scope of today's arts community, which includes just about every form of creative expression from glassblowing to traditional Shakespearean theater, to contra dancing and poetry "slams." Few communities the size of Asheville have their own art museum, symphony, numerous theater and dance groups, or chamber music series, much less a science museum, film organization, or public radio station (the Asheville area has two).

At the heart of the arts in Asheville and Buncombe County lies the Arts Alliance, a nonprofit umbrella service organization that represents the interests of about 100 cultural groups. Actively involved in fund-raising and grant allocations, the Alliance was formed in 1993 after the reorganization of the 40-year-old Community Arts Council. The Alliance encourages a spirit of cooperation among the various arts organizations, the business and education communities, and is a leader in community-wide cultural planning.

The Asheville area is also well-known for its fine assortment of mountain

Not enjoyment and not sorrow -
Is our destined end or way -
But to act that each to-morrow -
Find us farther than to-day -
EXIT

handcrafts, including wood carving, weaving, basketry, and quilting. Visit the Folk Art Center and the Grovewood Gallery for an impressive overview of what's available. Pottery is prolific here, ranging from simple stoneware to elaborate one-of-a-kind creations. The tradition for exceptional handmade items lives on, and today's works range from the traditional Appalachian to those with a more contemporary flair. A number of the area's commercial galleries feature furniture, glass, clothing, jewelry, and pottery created by local artisans.

As far as commercial art galleries go, there are over 30 in the Asheville area, from the eclectic coffee shop variety, to the working artist's studio, to the fine arts gallery. Blue Spiral 1 showcases the largest collection of paintings by Will Henry Stevens (1881-1949), a foremost regionalist and modernist of the South. The 11,000-square-foot gallery is constantly changing, featuring sculptures and paintings from established artists as well as new talent. The New Morning Gallery in Biltmore Village showcases a variety of high quality handcrafts, including pottery, fine art glass, furniture, and jewelry.

The Broadway Arts Building, a sort of multiuse arts complex that exhibits both contemporary fine arts and handmade crafts, also hosts avant-garde theater, dance, and music performances. The historic downtown building that was originally a farmer's market has been painstakingly renovated, preserving the original heart pine floors and tin-molded ceilings.

The nonprofit Asheville Art Museum is located in the Pack Place Education, Arts, and Science Center at Pack Square in downtown Asheville. The museum features the work of noted artists, many with ties to the Asheville region, including Kenneth Noland, Josef and Anni Albers, Donald Sultan, and James H. Daugherty.

Housing an impressive permanent collection of twentieth-century American art, the museum also hosts touring

Contra dancing is an offshoot of square dancing, with its two dance lines and directed moves. *Photo by Tim Barnwell.*

exhibits from around the country. And speaking of tours, the museum is a favorite among area school children who enjoy lively age-appropriate guided tours and hands-on studio projects. It's not uncommon to see a group of third graders with both arms stretched high above their heads, representing the direction of vertical lines.

Children of all ages—including grownups—can have fun while learning about the human body at the Health Adventure. Just across the hall from the art museum, the Health Adventure's interactive exhibits include NutriSpace, Bodyworks, Brainstorm, Miracle of Life, and the traveling exhibits of New Adventures. The Creative PlaySpace allows kids under eight to burn off some energy and is especially popular with parents on rainy days.

A visit to Pack Place is not complete without seeing the Colburn Gem and Mineral Museum showcasing a brilliant 229-carat cut blue topaz and a 376-pound aquamarine crystal. North Carolina is considered a geologic paradise, and the museum's display includes minerals and gems indigenous to the region, as well as from around the world.

Just around the corner from Pack Square and a part of Pack Place, the YMI Cultural Center is a national historic landmark and serves as the local resource center for African-American culture, art, and history. Lectures, classes, and performances celebrate the contributions of local and national African-American leaders. Each summer the YMI sponsors the Goombay! Festival, the African-Caribbean celebration, and the annual Kwanzaa holiday festival featuring communal African drumming, storytelling, and poetry based on east African culture. A permanent exhibit of authentic African art and artifacts can be found in the YMI's main gallery. Also on display is the massive bust of the Reverend Martin Luther King Jr., sculpted by Asheville native Wilbur Mapp and dedicated in early 1996.

The Colburn Gem and Mineral Museum showcases the geologic treasures of North Carolina. *Photo by Tim Barnwell.*

Open for special events, shows, and performances, the 500-seat Diana Wortham Theatre is located on the second floor of Pack Place. State-of-the-art acoustics and lighting, a full-size stage, and orchestra pit add to the appeal of this modern facility, used by local, regional, and national companies and touring shows.

The Diana Wortham Theatre is home to the Discovery Series of concerts, presented by the Asheville Symphony Orchestra. The Discovery Series offers concertgoers a different approach to classical music, with its unconventional "from the stage" conversations with the conductor.

The Asheville Symphony Orchestra (ASO) was established in 1958 by a handful of dedicated volunteer musicians. Today the ASO is a professional regional orchestra comprised of local talent from Western North Carolina and out-of-state musicians who travel many miles to perform at the Thomas Wolfe Auditorium with Robert Hart Baker, award-winning music director and conductor. The orchestra features guest artists from around the world and music from classical to popular favorites. A typical season includes six masterworks performances (September through April), holiday and May pops concerts, and a children's concert.

Asheville loves its music, and the variety is somewhat overwhelming. Pick up one of the weekly guides to arts and entertainment, and the list reads like a menu: chamber music, jazz, Celtic, country-western, rock, alternative, gospel, folk, bluegrass, and an occasional opera. There's so much to choose from, be it homegrown talent or touring.

The Asheville Chamber Music Series is one of the oldest in the Southeast, bringing noted chamber ensembles to Asheville for its five-concert season. Warren Wilson College in Swannanoa hosts the Swannanoa Chamber Festival each July, and the Asheville Community Concert Association sponsors an annual concert series that features chamber music, ballet, and other performances. The University of North Carolina at Asheville (UNCA), a progressive public liberal arts college, offers an assortment of concerts, available to the public for a song. Popular night spots like Be Here Now reel in some pretty big names (remember Arlo Guthrie?), and there's almost always some kind of festival or event that features first-rate musical performances. The renowned Brevard Music Center in nearby Brevard hosts North Carolina's premier music festival, held every summer to the delight of packed audiences.

Arthur Murray got his start in Asheville

Each summer the YMI sponsors Goombay!, the African-Caribbean festival. *Photo by Tim Barnwell.*

in the late 1800s, dancing his way into the hearts of the well-heeled guests at the old Battery Park Hotel. Ballroom dancing is still popular in the Asheville area, not to mention jitterbug, swing, shag, clogging, and square dance. Ever hear of contra dancing? An offshoot of square dancing, with its two dance lines and directed moves, contra dancing draws amazing crowds and appeals to dancers of all ages. In keeping with Asheville's rather cosmopolitan nature, workshops and performances in Middle Eastern, African, and Latin dancing—to name a few—are not uncommon.

The professional dance community includes a number of groups such as the Asheville Contemporary Dance Theater, Add Dance, and the JD Project. Local dance schools and university groups add to the talent pool of versatile dancers, who often work together for special performances. Touring troupes from all over the world pirouette, step, tap, and slide their way through the city of Asheville—always a gracious Southern host to the wide variety of guest performers. Mikhail Baryshnikov is a perfect example: the world-famous dancer has performed in Asheville twice.

The theater is alive and well in the Asheville area. That's why big-city ensembles like The Acting Company, America's premier touring repertory company, are drawn to this arts-appreciative community. The community is also very supportive of local theater, which ranges from intimate performances at the funky Green Door on Carolina Lane to the Montford Park Players, who perform Shakespearean drama in the historic Montford area on warm midsummer nights. With attractions like *Hansel and Gretel* and *Tom Sawyer*, the Mockingbird Theatre Company specializes in productions for children and the young at heart. Talented students of all ages participate in Theatre UNCA, the university drama department's season of drama, comedy, and musical theater.

Not long after studying drama at Northwestern University in the 1940s, aspiring young actor Charlton Heston and his wife, actress Lydia Clarke, moved to Asheville in 1947 to serve as artistic co-directors of the newly formed Asheville Community Theatre (ACT). After a nine-month stint and several successful productions, the two returned to New York, and the rest is history. Heston moved to the silver screen and later played Moses in Cecil B. DeMille's epic *The Ten Commandments* and went on to win an Oscar in 1959 for his title role in *Ben Hur.* The Hestons returned to Asheville in 1992 for the dedication of the 468-seat Heston Auditorium at ACT, and to costar in a benefit production of A. R. Gurney's Broadway hit *Love Letters*.

For over 50 consecutive years the Asheville Community Theatre (ACT) has been a shining example of a grassroots community theater. Supported by hundreds of volunteers on and offstage, ACT works year-round to put on six full-scale productions that range from the classics to contemporary comedies. In addition to live stage performances, ACT offers youth acting classes through its Youtheatre program, special student matinees, and the Autumn Players outreach program, produced by, for, and about senior citizens. An offshoot of ACT, Bittersweet

The Asheville Symphony Orchestra is a professional regional orchestra comprised of local talent from Western North Carolina and out-of-state musicians who travel many miles to perform at the Thomas Wolfe Auditorium. *Photo by Tim Barnwell.*

Productions became the first American theater troupe to perform in Kiev, Ukraine, since the former Soviet state gained its independence in 1991. In January 1996, the company produced the stage version of Steinbeck's classic *The Grapes of Wrath* to sell-out crowds in the Ukraine capital.

A little closer to home and just a short drive southeast of Asheville, the well-known Vagabond Players sing, dance, laugh, and cry, all in the course of a typical season of great theater at the Flat Rock Playhouse. Officially named the State Theater of North Carolina, the Flat Rock Playhouse has been rated as one of the top 10 summer theaters in the nation. North of Asheville at Mars Hill College, the Southern Appalachian Repertory Theater features contemporary drama and is one of the longest running repertory theaters in the state.

Asheville loves its music, and the variety is somewhat overwhelming. ***Photo by Tim Barnwell.***

Master fiddler Ralph Blizard teaches a string band class at the Swannanoa Gathering. *Photo by Ben Walters.*

BROADWAY ARTS BUILDING
49

The Creative PlaySpace at the Health Adventure allows kids under eight to burn off some energy and is especially popular with parents on rainy days. *Photo by Tim Barnwell.*

For film enthusiasts, the Asheville Film Society and Cinematique sponsor showings of films that include the eclectic, the international, and the sometimes controversial. And, of course, there's always room on the silver screen for the likes of *Casablanca* and other great American film classics.

As an art form, the written word is perhaps more appreciated here than in many other places. Just count the number of bookstores and libraries to get a feel for the widespread local interest in books of all types, for all ages.

The Asheville area has long been a haven for poets and writers, and literary greats F. Scott Fitzgerald and Edith Wharton spent time here in the early 1900s. Thomas Wolfe, William Sydney Porter (pen name, O' Henry), and Sidney Lanier once called the Asheville area home. Carl Sandburg, the noted Lincoln biographer and poet, purchased a sprawling 1800s farm in Flat Rock in 1945 and spent the last 22 years of his life in creative seclusion at Connemara, now a national historic site.

In more recent years the area has attracted a succession of nationally known authors, many drawn to the area by the reputation of Warren Wilson College's Master of Fine Arts program for writers. Personalities such as John Le Carre, Kurt Vonnegut, and Eudora Welty serve on the advisory board of the independent literary center, the Writer's Workshop, an Asheville-based organization with over 1,000 members. The Writer's Workshop sponsors contests, classes, and scholarships for would-be and published writers.

For poetry enthusiasts, Asheville has its own semi-annual poetry journal, *The Asheville Poetry Review,* and

The Broadway Arts Building, a multiuse arts complex, was originally a farmer's market that has been painstakingly renovated, preserving the original heart pine floors and tin-molded ceilings. *Photo by Tim Barnwell.*

The Asheville Contemporary Dance Theater is just one of the many performing dance groups on the local arts scene. *Photo by David Hildebrand.*

Officially named the State Theater of North Carolina, the Flat Rock Playhouse has been rated as one of the top 10 summer theaters in the nation. *Photo courtesy of the Flat Rock Playhouse.*

The most interesting and unusual form of poetry is called "slamming," which brings new meaning to the phrase "poetry in motion." Slamming is a sort of no-holds-barred competitive event where performers present original poems, sometimes with a mix of theatrics, pantomime, and song. *Photo by Tim Barnwell.*

an annual Poetry Festival sponsored by the Writer's Workshop, UNCA, and Poetry Alive! But perhaps the most interesting and unusual form of poetry is called "slamming," which brings new meaning to the phrase "poetry in motion." Slamming is a sort of no-holds-barred competitive event where performers present original poems, sometimes with a mix of theatrics, pantomime, and song. Slammers compete locally; and members of Poetry Alive! and the Asheville Poetry Slam travel around the country, giving it their best slam. In 1994 the National Poetry Slam brought over a thousand performers to Asheville, a tribute to the local poets who have embraced the art and sport of competitive slamming.

As a dynamic arts community, Asheville not only respects the diverse contributions of its artists, but also welcomes it. Be it offbeat, ethnic, or very traditional, the art that is so much a part of the Asheville area adds to the cosmopolitan flavor of the city. The Alex Paley sculpture outside the federal building downtown is a good example of how art is in the eye of the beholder. Dedicated in 1995, the controversial piece elicits diverse reactions from locals and tourists. Some see gargoyles when they stare at the towering iron sculpture; others see mountain peaks, falling leaves, or jagged-edged feathers. Still others see a jumbled mass of rusted shapes. Entitled "Passages," the work has been explained as a tribute to Asheville's past, present, and future. A sharp contrast to the historic architecture of nearby buildings, the modern sculpture is a celebration of diversity, a reminder of what the local arts community stands for. ▲

For over 50 consecutive years the Asheville Community Theatre has been a shining example of a grassroots community theater. *Photo courtesy of Asheville Community Theatre.*

The Asheville area has long been a haven for poets, writers, and literary greats. William Sydney Porter (pen name O' Henry) and *(below)* Thomas Wolfe once called the Asheville area home. *Photos courtesy of the North Carolina Collection, Pack Memorial Public Library.*

Asheville's arts scene is as impressive as the scenery itself. *Photo by Tim Barnwell.*

The Asheville area is well-known for its fine assortment of mountain handcrafts, including wood carving, weaving, basketry, and quilting. The Folk Art Center has an impressive overview of what's available. *Photos by Tim Barnwell.*

MOUNTAINEER
INN
SKYWAY
MOTEL
ITALIAN
RESTAURANT
IN TOWN
AMOCO
113
125

CHAPTER SIX

CROSSROADS: You Can Get There From Here

From a sleepy little mountain oasis to the regional hub of Western North Carolina, Asheville has always been a crossroads town. A place where ancient Cherokee footpaths crossed...a watering hole for the rough-and-ready men and their mules who came by way of the 1828 "Drovers Road"...the site of the 1880's railroad boom that connected Asheville with the outside world. Once isolated by her rugged terrain, Asheville is easy to get to today.

˄

(left)* Tunnel Road is one of Asheville's busiest retail areas. *Photo by Tim Barnwell.

(right)* The Asheville Regional Airport is fully equipped to handle private, corporate, and commercial aircraft. *Photo by Tim Barnwell.

Located at the junction of Interstates 26 and 40, Asheville is a quick trip from regional hot spots like Knoxville and Kingsport, Tennessee; Greenville and Spartanburg, South Carolina; and Charlotte and Winston-Salem, North Carolina. Currently under construction, the I-26 corridor will link Western North Carolina with a broad corridor to the north connecting I-81 in Johnson City, Tennessee, to Charleston, South Carolina, through Asheville. To points north and south of Asheville, Interstate 85 is only an hour's drive away, providing easy access to Atlanta.

Once in the Asheville area, you'll have 10 well-maintained federal and state highways to get you where you're going. Interstate 240 takes you along the downtown area where points of interest are clearly marked, such as the Asheville Area Chamber of Commerce's Visitor Center, Thomas Wolfe Memorial, and the downtown business district. For a leisurely drive that is scenic as well, take the winding Blue Ridge Parkway. Asheville has four accesses to the parkway—open year-round, weather permitting.

As the hub of Western North Carolina, it's no surprise that Asheville would aim high to provide the best possible air transportation for the more than 550,000 travelers who fly to and from here each year. The Asheville Regional Airport is located just 13 miles south of downtown and is a breath of fresh air for travelers accustomed to the crowds, noise, and faster pace of larger airport facilities. But don't let the small size fool you—it's big on technological improvements. Whether it's resurfacing the 8,000-foot runway or updating the navigational aids, the Asheville Regional Airport keeps pace with the needs of business and leisure travelers. The modern facility is fully equipped to handle private, corporate, and commercial aircraft. The airport is currently served by USAir, Atlantic Southeast Airlines, Comair, Midway Express, and USAir Express. Daily flights, including jet service, offer connections to all major cities through Charlotte, Raleigh, Atlanta, and Cincinnati.

Upon landing at the Asheville Regional Airport, you'll be met with warm Southern hospitality at the airport Welcome Center. You'll find free travel brochures, local news, and entertainment publications and a broad selection of books about Western North Carolina. Not sure about where you're going? Directions and advice are always free. Call a cab, take an airport shuttle, or rent a car. The airport is conveniently located just off I-26, about halfway between downtown Asheville and Hendersonville.

If you'd rather leave the driving to someone else, you can always go Greyhound or Trailways. These national carriers provide bus service to Asheville, as well as transportation from the area to hundreds of cities and towns across the United States. Locally, the Asheville Transit Authority serves the greater Asheville area six days a week with a fleet that includes many modern, wheelchair-accessible buses. Routes include a number of major destinations such as universities, hospitals, and shopping malls.

In the eyes of the local business community, Asheville makes it easy to move freight. Over 70 motor freight

For a leisurely drive that is scenic as well, take the winding Blue Ridge Parkway. Asheville has four accesses to the parkway—open year-round, weather permitting. *Photo by Warner Photography.*

USAir
Flight
Departs
BRITISH AIRWAYS

carriers provide truck service to the area. USAir provides air freight service, and one of the nation's largest railroads, Norfolk Southern, offers piggyback service and daily switching.

For honest-to-goodness shipping, the nearest seaports are found in Charleston, South Carolina (265 miles from Asheville), Wilmington, North Carolina (310 miles), and Morehead City, North Carolina (403 miles). And for the added convenience of Asheville shippers, the North Carolina Ports Authority operates two inland port terminals in Charlotte and Greensboro.

If your shipping needs are limited to an occasional package to Peoria, next-day or standard delivery, count on the services of the United States Postal Service, United Parcel Service, and other national companies, including Federal Express. Several local firms will coordinate small shipping projects, for delivery across town or across country.

As the Asheville area continues its trend of steady growth, look for ongoing improvements to its transportation systems—new roads, new routes, new ways to move people and products. It will be even easier to get to Asheville, but perhaps harder to leave—because you won't want to. ▲

Asheville is a quick trip from many regional hot spots. *Photo by Tim Barnwell.*

One of the nation's largest railroads, Norfolk Southern, offers piggyback service and daily switching. *Photo by Tim Barnwell.*

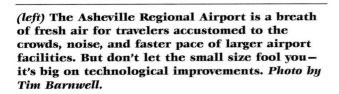

(left)* The Asheville Regional Airport is a breath of fresh air for travelers accustomed to the crowds, noise, and faster pace of larger airport facilities. But don't let the small size fool you—it's big on technological improvements. *Photo by Tim Barnwell.

The Asheville Transit Authority serves the area with a fleet of many modern, wheelchair-accessible buses. Routes include a number of major destinations such as universities, hospitals, and shopping malls. *Photo by Tim Barnwell.*

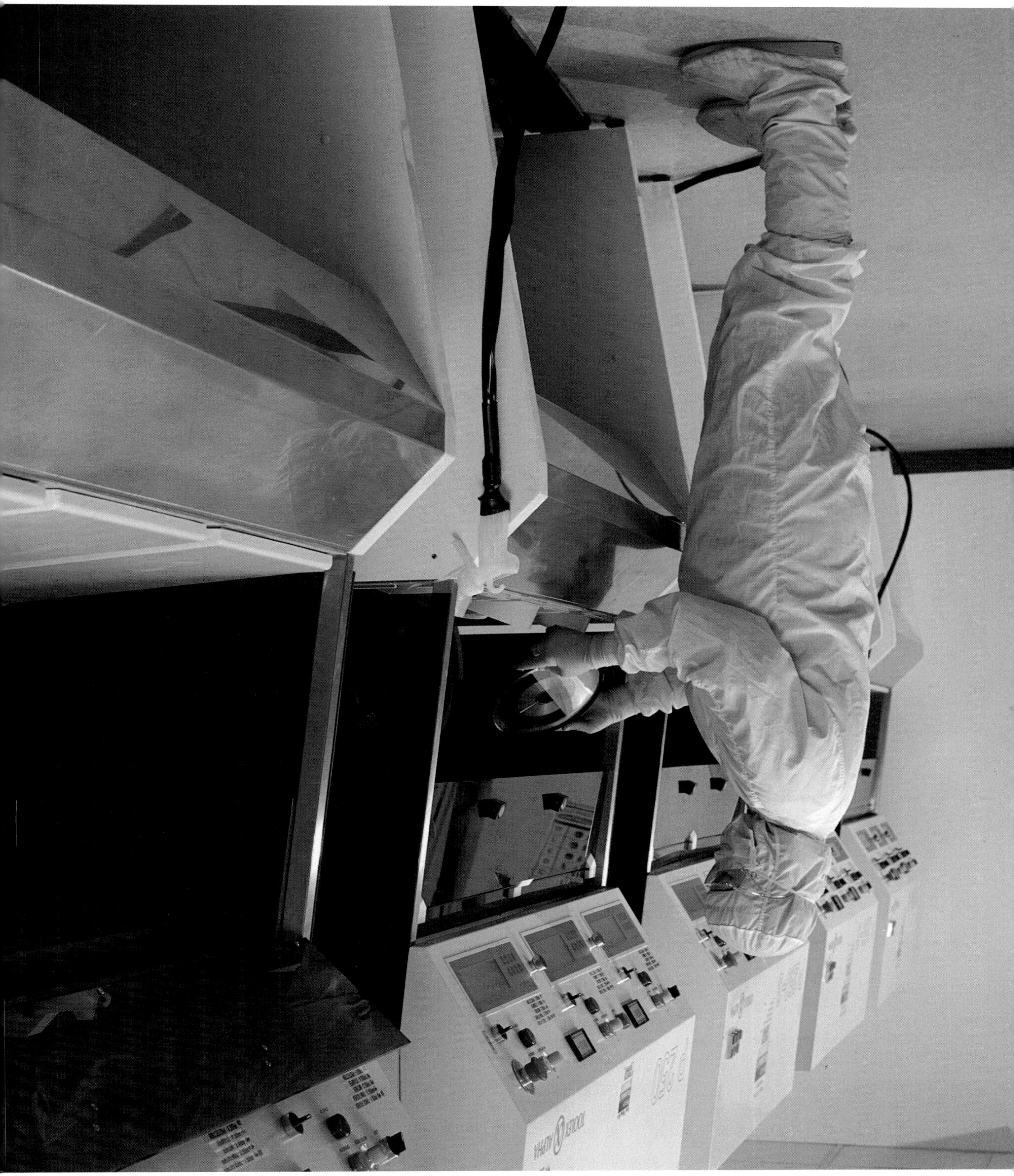

CHAPTER SEVEN

ECONOMIC DIVERSITY: Taking Care Of Business

The ultimate "view from the top" of Asheville can be had via hot air balloon, suspended high above the hustle and bustle of the downtown area, Tunnel Road, and the west Asheville business district. From this vantage point, pockets of enterprise can be seen—thriving retail areas, sprawling manufacturing facilities, historic architectural gems housing a host of shops, services, and professional offices. It's a pleasing mix of the old and the new, Asheville's colorful past and prosperous present. The local economy has always been diverse, from the early days of textiles and tobacco, to tuberculosis care and tourism. Today's economy is just as varied, an exciting blend of the established and the entrepreneurial, the large company and the small.

(left) In many ways it costs less to live in Asheville, which has tremendous appeal to relocating workers accustomed to paying more for some of the basics.
Photo by Tim Barnwell.

(right) The land in and around the Asheville area yields more than just impressive scenery. Top-notch soil conditions, weather, and elevation make the area ideal for the production of various commodities.
Photo by Tim Barnwell.

Asheville has done an admirable job of preserving the past, preferring to substitute creativity for the wrecking ball whenever possible. The downtown area is a case in point—Pack Place, the Haywood Park Hotel, the Jackson Building, and numerous other buildings that once stood vacant are vibrant today. *Photo by Tim Barnwell.*

As the regional hub of Western North Carolina, Asheville takes care of business in a big way, offering advantages that some communities can only dream of. Asheville's per capita tax burden is among the lowest in the nation, and there is no inventory tax. Energy costs typically rank lower than the national average, and when it comes to construction, reasonable costs to build or expand a facility make the area attractive to start-up and growing businesses alike.

It also costs less to live here, which has tremendous appeal to relocating workers accustomed to paying more for the basics like housing, health care, and entertainment.

Of course, the lower cost of living makes for improved quality of life, but it's not the only reason why people love to live here. There are plenty of reasons—just look around at the surrounding mountains and count them. Mother Nature cooperates nicely by providing abundant natural resources and relatively mild weather. Few areas in the nation offer the year-round recreational opportunities found in and around the Asheville area. Consider also the first-rate medical care, solid educational resources, and diverse retail shopping, and it's easy to see why the Asheville area is often cited as a wonderful place to live.

It's a known fact that people are happier at work when they are happy at home. No doubt this contributes to the strong work ethic the region boasts, and employers are pleased to report low absenteeism/turnover rates. Unemployment rates are also consistently low, a good sign that the local economy is stable. Workers' compensation costs are among the lowest in the country, and as a right-to-work state, North Carolina appeals to a broad array of manufacturing and service industries.

The local workforce is also well-educated, a direct result of the excellent network of public and private schools, colleges, and universities. Technical training is receiving increased focus, and institutions like Asheville-Buncombe Technical Community College (A-B Tech) work hand-in-hand with the business community and the public sector to meet the workforce demands of the twenty-first century.

State-of-the-art telecommunication networks, including Asynchronous Transfer Mode (ATM), Synchronous Optical Network (SON), and Integrated Services Digital Networks (ISDN), keep Asheville on top in high-tech communications. High-speed transmission capabilities include fiber optics, microwave transmission facilities, and digital switching services. The University of North Carolina at Asheville's microwave facility links the area with the world-renowned Microelectronic Center for North Carolina at the Research Triangle Park in the Raleigh-Durham area, providing a model for vendor/supplier communications.

High-tech advantages are certainly worth touting, but perhaps Asheville's greatest business advantage is its superb geographic location. Asheville is strategically located within a day's drive of over 150 million American and Canadian consumers, 64 of the nation's top 100 metropolitan areas, and over 60 percent of the United States industrial base. Add to the list at least $500 billion in retail sales—all within a day's drive—and Asheville's location looks even better. Getting to and around Asheville is also a plus, with a sophisticated transportation network that serves the growing needs of Western North Carolina.

For generations, textile-related firms like Beacon Manufacturing and BASF (formerly American Enka) have provided a number of employment opportunities in the manufacturing sector, which accounts for about 25 percent of all jobs in Buncombe County. Other major manufacturers in the area include Champion International (uncoated paper and paperboard), Ecusta Division of P. H. Glatfelter (papers for the tobacco industry), and GE Lighting Systems. Steelcase (wood office furniture) and Square D Company (industrial electrical products) are also among the area's largest manufacturing employers.

The growing automotive industry in the southern United States has created a profitable niche market for automotive products in the Asheville area. There are dozens of suppliers, including ITT Automotive (antilock brakes), Dayco Products (belts and hoses), and Rockwell International (rear truck axles). Expect to see more growth in automotive products as United States and foreign assembly operations look to build or expand automotive plants in the South.

Energy costs typically rank lower in Asheville than the national average. ***Photo by Tim Barnwell.***

The WNC Farmers' Market and numerous roadside stands delight visitors with fresh fruits and vegetables, gift items, and mountain crafts. ***Photo by Tim Barnwell.***

An important part of any community's economic development process is its revitalization of existing facilities, especially those of historical significance. *Photo by Tim Barnwell.*

What do rice cakes, CDs, and earthmoving equipment have in common? They're all produced in the Asheville area, testimony to the diversity mentioned earlier. Quaker Oats, Sonopress, and Volvo Construction Equipment, which has located its world headquarters in Asheville, are companies on the move, with an eye toward expansion that creates new jobs for an eager and educated local workforce.

In the nonmanufacturing sector, education, government, and health care employ the largest number of people, with the Mission + St. Joseph's Health System being the largest nongovernmental employer. Asheville-based Ingles Markets ranks among the largest nonmanufacturing employer; and The Grove Park Inn Resort and the Biltmore Company lead the pack of tourism-related employers. In recent years service operations like Somar (telemarketing) and the J. Crew Group (catalog sales—clothing and telemarketing) have set up shop in the Asheville area, often calling upon the talents of the area's trained and flexible college and retiree workforce.

In-migrating retirees pump millions of dollars into the local economy, and to capture this affluent market, the North Carolina Center for Creative Retirement (NCCCR) hosts the annual Creative Retirement Exploration Vacation Weekend. Participants are exposed to the advantages of Western North Carolina, such as quality of life, housing, health care, and recreation. Many retirees who move to the Asheville area seek active retirements, involving full- or part-time employment, volunteer work, and a variety of outside interests.

It goes without saying that tourism fuels the economy of Asheville and Western North Carolina like dry kindling on a raging mountain campfire—so much, in fact, that the 22-county region takes in an estimated $1.2 billion each year in tourism-related activity. The Asheville area alone attracts over 2 million visitors each year who come for a variety of reasons—to take in the awesome natural beauty, to camp, fish, hike, or go white-water rafting. To hit the links, play tennis, sightsee, or ski at a nearby resort. To visit the Biltmore Estate, a "must-see" attraction. To do some shopping, or just do nothing at all. Whatever the reason or the season that they come, tourists are encouraged to make Asheville their home away from home, and the hospitality industry welcomes them with open arms.

Accommodations in the Asheville area range from the modest campground to the modern chain motel, and from the elegant ambiance of the 36-room historic Richmond Hill Inn, to the rustic charm of the 510-room Grove Park Inn, one of the South's oldest and most famous grand resorts. The conveniently located Great Smokies Holiday Inn SunSpree Resort is a fully remodeled 268-room resort that features an 18-hole golf course, 2 pools, indoor/outdoor tennis, and spacious meeting and convention facilities.

Bed-and-breakfast inns are extremely popular in the Asheville area and offer guests an intimate setting with home-cooked meals and gracious Southern hospitality. Close to 50 bed-and-breakfast inns dot the local landscape, many of them located in the historic Montford area near downtown. For the ultimate in privacy, select a remote country inn or mountain lodge to get away from it all—all except for the crisp mountain air and magnificent long-range views.

Breathtaking scenery and a moderate year-round climate have contributed to the region's growing involvement in the film industry, a high-profile boost to the local economy. On average, 20 commercials a year are filmed in Western North Carolina, pumping an estimated $2 to $3 million dollars into the economy. A major motion picture can generate around $20 million alone, considering all aspects of a film's production: lodging, props, food, local crew salaries, and other services. In recent years, Hollywood blockbusters such as *The Last of the Mohicans, Nell,* and *The Fugitive* were filmed on location in Western North Carolina. Scenes in the comedies *Richie Rich* and *My Fellow Americans* were filmed at the Biltmore Estate and other Asheville locations. The Asheville-based Western North Carolina Film Commission

Close to 50 bed-and-breakfast inns dot the local landscape. *Photo by Tim Barnwell.*

When it comes to construction, reasonable costs to build make the area attractive to new and expanding businesses. *Photo by Tim Barnwell.*

has contributed significantly to North Carolina's ranking among the top five states in the nation for film and video production.

The land in and around the Asheville area yields more than just impressive scenery. Top-notch soil conditions, weather, and elevation make the area ideal for the production of various commodities, including fruits and vegetables, dairy products, beef cattle, and mountain trout. Western North Carolina is well-known for its production of the world's finest Christmas tree, the Fraser fir, in addition to other popular species and a variety of ornamentals.

To get a first-hand look at agribusiness in Asheville, visit the North Carolina Arboretum, a 426-acre research facility bordering the Pisgah National Forest that features unique horticultural exhibits, a state-of-the-art greenhouse complex, and National Native Azalea Repository. Then stop by the WNC Farmers' Market at the intersection of I-40 and I-26 to pick a peck of peaches, plums, or other locally grown produce. Over 1,200 farmers sell at this state-owned wholesale and retail facility, which includes a restaurant and garden center. The market attracts more than a million visitors a year who are delighted to find not only the freshest fruits and vegetables around, but also some pretty interesting farm gift items and mountain crafts.

Although technically hundreds of years old, the handcraft industry in Western North Carolina is receiving renewed focus from an economic development standpoint. And well it should, with an annual contribution to the economy that exceeds $122 million. The numbers make sense, considering the fact that the area has the fourth largest concentration of craftspeople in the nation, based on membership figures of the American Craft Council.

Recognizing the enormous potential for future growth of the handcraft industry, in 1993 the Asheville Area Chamber of Commerce created the nonprofit organization HandMade in America. Now a thriving organization of its own, HandMade brings craftspeople, educators, businesspeople, and community leaders together in support of a common goal: to make Western North Carolina the acknowledged center of handmade objects in the United States.

Artisans and craftspeople who have flocked to the Asheville area to start or expand a business are a part of a group loosely referred to as "lone eagles," mobile entrepreneurs, or risk takers—individuals who can pick and choose where they want to live—and they chose Asheville. Small retailers, independent consultants, and professionals are included in this group of savvy, quality-of-life-seeking folks who, like George Vanderbilt, may have searched the world over and decided to settle here.

Eighty-five percent of the membership of the Asheville Area Chamber of Commerce comes from the ranks of small business owners and entrepreneurs. The on-going Advantage Asheville! campaign is dedicated to helping small businesses expand and prosper, in addition to focusing on workforce preparedness and developing sites and buildings for industry. To attract new business to Asheville, the Chamber's Economic Development Department uses a combination of prospect visits, trade show participation, and award-winning print and audiovisual materials to

It's a known fact that people are happier at work when they are happy at home. *Photo by Tim Barnwell.*

Elegant ambiance is a feature of the 36-room historic Richmond Hill Inn. *Photo by Tim Barnwell.*

The handcraft industry in Western North Carolina is receiving renewed focus from an economic development standpoint with an annual contribution to the economy that exceeds $122 million. ***Photo by Tim Barnwell.***

market the unique advantages of Asheville. There's even a home page for the Asheville Chamber on the World Wide Web, providing economic developers and entrepreneurs with instant information on Asheville's quality of life, demographics, and business opportunities. As a boost to the tourism industry, the web site also includes Asheville Convention and Visitors Bureau information on things to see and do in the area. Roughly 50 percent of the Internet "visits" are from prospective tourists.

The Chamber also works closely with a number of local, regional, and state organizations to advance the economic growth of Asheville and the region. These include the Buncombe County Economic Development Commission, the City of Asheville, area colleges and universities, and regional organizations like Advantage West and the Land of Sky Regional Council. The North Carolina Department of Commerce's regional office is based in Asheville; its mission is to support existing businesses as well as to attract new business to Western North Carolina.

In support of minority business development, local groups include the African-American Business Task Force, the Black Business and Professional League, the YMI Community Development Corporation, and the Cherokee Business Development Center. The Asheville area has attracted its share of women entrepreneurs, and organizations like Women Mean Business, TWIN (Tribute to Women in Industry), and the Western Carolina Women's Coalition sponsor programs and training sessions designed to help women start, run, and expand their businesses.

An important part of any community's economic development process is its revitalization of existing facilities, especially those of historical significance. Asheville has done an admirable job of preserving the past, preferring to substitute creativity for the wrecking ball whenever possible. The downtown area is a case in point—Pack Place, the Haywood Park Hotel, and numerous other buildings that once stood vacant are vibrant today. The Preservation Society of Asheville and Buncombe County targets endangered properties for renovation, then sells them to private concerns for new life as offices, hotels, and apartments. The Richmond Hill Inn and the Manor on Charlotte Street are a couple of shining examples.

An aggressive revitalization project known as RiverLink is making waves along the French Broad River. Started in 1987, RiverLink is a nonprofit, public-private partnership dedicated to the economic and environmental rehabilitation of the French Broad River and its watershed. With the support of the business community, local government, and hundreds of volunteers, RiverLink has made steady progress. Stroll along the beautifully landscaped French Broad River Park; then visit a working artist's studio in a nearby historic riverfront building. The best is yet to come. RiverLink's long-range plans feature a riverfront restaurant and shops, an outdoor performance area, and additional fishing, boating, and picnic sites.

Exciting things are happening in the Asheville area, thanks to a stable economy, abundant resources, and dedicated local leaders who realize that economic development is the lifeblood of Asheville's future. Lower business operating costs translate into higher potential for success, and that alone puts Asheville over the top. Combined with all the other advantages that the area has to offer, it's easy to see why the Asheville Area Chamber of Commerce proudly proclaims, "altitude affects attitude." ▲

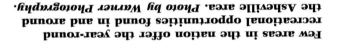

Few areas in the nation offer the year-round recreational opportunities found in and around the Asheville area. *Photo by Warner Photography.*

In support of minority business development, local groups include the African-American Business Task Force, the Black Business and Professional League, the YMI Community Development Corporation, and the Cherokee Business Development Center. *Photo by Tim Barnwell.*

Asheville boasts a strong work ethic, and employers are pleased to report low absenteeism/turnover rates. *Photo by Tim Barnwell.*

As the regional hub of Western North Carolina, Asheville takes care of business in a big way, offering advantages that some communities can only dream of. Pictured is the Jackson Building. *Photo by Tim Barnwell.*

Local government supports the economy of the area by providing a strong foundation for the business community. ***Photos by Tim Barnwell.***

A project of RiverLink, the French Broad River Park is a beautiful setting for a relaxing stroll. ***Photo by Tim Barnwell.***

EXIT

CHAPTER EIGHT

EDUCATION & HEALTH CARE: Nurturing Mind and Body

Good schools and access to quality health care are important to every community, large or small. The Asheville area has both, and not just the basic services. As the hub of Western North Carolina, Asheville leads the region in learning resources and health care.

(left) From the beginning, the Asheville medical community has been larger and more advanced than would be expected for a city its size. *Photo courtesy of Mission + St. Joseph's Health System.*

(right) The local workforce is well-educated. *Photo by Tim Barnwell.*

The Asheville City School System is a case in point: in 1995 the district ranked number one in high school SAT scores in the state of North Carolina. And with 75 percent of the Asheville High School seniors taking the exam—higher than the state or national percentage—the ranking is certainly one to be proud of. Also ranked among the 10 best high school fine arts centers in the nation, Asheville High boasts state-of-the-art facilities for classes in art, music, drama, dance, and video production.

With over 80 percent of Asheville High School graduates continuing their formal education, an aggressive program involves college visitations, guest speakers, and job fairs designed to help students make solid career choices. Students in the Tech Prep Program receive counseling specifically geared to vocational/technical, whether they plan to enroll in a technical school or enter the workforce upon graduation.

In addition to a first-rate high school, the Asheville City School System has six elementary schools (kindergarten through fifth grade), Asheville Middle School (sixth through eighth grade), and an Accelerated Learning Center for students with special needs. Total district enrollment exceeds 4,500 students. The Asheville City Preschool is one of the oldest in North Carolina and has been recognized as one of the best in the state.

Ever hear of the term "magnet school"? Like a magnet, students are drawn to an area of interest, such as classical studies or math, science, and technology. The Asheville City School District is unique in North Carolina: all six of the elementary schools are magnet schools, centered on a particular theme. Of course, the standard core curriculum—reading, writing, and arithmetic—doesn't fall by the wayside. Introduced in 1990, the magnet school program is popular with parents and students who like the idea of choosing an elementary school based on an individual student's interests, needs, and abilities.

The Asheville City School District is surrounded by the six districts of the much larger Buncombe County School System. Thirty-six schools serve in excess of 24,000 students, in kindergarten through twelfth grade. In recent years Buncombe County has placed a high priority on expansion and modernization of its schools; and to keep pace with the school system's growth, the county has constructed new schools when warranted, most recently Avery's Creek Elementary in south Buncombe.

On the elementary level, Buncombe County Schools go beyond the traditional academic experience with an emphasis on developing positive character traits. One south Buncombe elementary school gives new meaning to the three "Rs" with its motto "respect, responsibility, and reasonable thinking." Good advice for future citizens who get daily reinforcement from teachers, administrators, and signs posted in the school hallways.

Becoming a productive member of society starts early in Buncombe County Schools, thanks to programs sponsored by Junior Achievement, field trips to local businesses, and guest speakers who educate and motivate elementary and middle school students to think about the future. Once they reach high school, students in

Education is a high priority in Western North Carolina. *Photo by Tim Barnwell.*

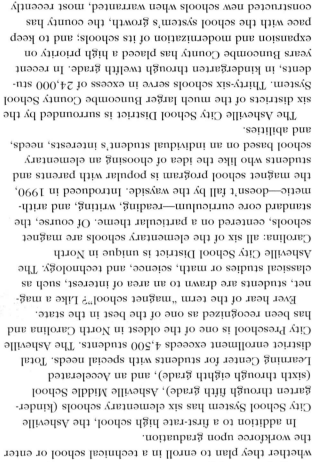

Buncombe County have been exposed to a variety of educational experiences, so the transition to high school is surprisingly smooth. Buncombe County also participates in a tech prep program, career expo/job fair, and apprenticeship and internship programs. For "at risk" students in grades seven through twelve, Buncombe Community School serves students from both the county and city school systems.

The Asheville Area Chamber of Commerce is actively involved with the city and county schools to foster a spirit of cooperation between the schools and the business community. The "Partners in Education" program, sponsored by the Chamber, pairs area employers with nearby schools to share resources and ideas. Not just a vo-tech partnership, the program has brought a spectrum of specialists to the classroom, including television journalists, mineral researchers, and animal habitat management experts.

There are a number of private schools in the Asheville area that offer quality instruction from pre-kindergarten to college preparatory. Some of the larger private schools include Carolina Day School, The Asheville School, Christ School, and Asheville Christian Academy.

Higher education in the Asheville area is diverse, affordable, and well-respected. Programs of study range from the arts and humanities to business administration and vocational/technical, and then some. There's also a community-wide focus on continuing education that gives area residents exposure to subjects like desktop publishing, foreign languages, watercolor painting, and small business start-up.

The University of North Carolina at Asheville (UNCA) serves close to 5,000 students enrolled in the undergraduate, graduate, and North Carolina Center for Creative Retirement programs. A premier public liberal arts university, UNCA offers students a private liberal arts education at a state school price. The prestigious *Fiske Guide to Colleges* named UNCA a "best buy" and one of the top 10 public liberal arts schools in the nation.

UNCA's undergraduate programs include humanities, natural and social sciences, pre-professional and professional, and interdisciplinary studies. Unlike most universities, UNCA

places a heavy emphasis on undergraduate research, allowing students to prepare and present research projects in their individual fields of study. UNCA is nationally recognized for conceiving the annual National Conference on Undergraduate Research, which brings together close to 2,000 undergraduate student researchers from across the country.

On the graduate level, UNCA is the site of the Asheville Graduate Center, a part of the University System of North Carolina. Students can obtain master's degrees from participating universities, including UNCA, North Carolina State, UNC-Chapel Hill, UNC-Greensboro, and Western Carolina University. Programs range from education and health sciences to liberal arts and business administration.

UNCA's Center for Creative Retirement is certainly that—creative. Nationally known for its innovative programs, the purpose of the center is two-fold: "to promote lifelong learning and community service for retirement-age individuals." Active seniors are given the opportunity to take courses of interest, teach courses in their areas of expertise, and trek all over the world on some pretty interesting field trips. Plus, they become an integral part of the community through an extensive volunteerism program that impacts local schools, businesses, and other seniors.

Preparing students for the workplace is the primary thrust of Asheville-Buncombe Technical Community

The Asheville City School District is unique in North Carolina: all six of the elementary schools are magnet schools, centered on a particular theme. *Photo by Tim Barnwell.*

The importance of a good education is recognized early in Asheville. ***Photo by Tim Barnwell.***

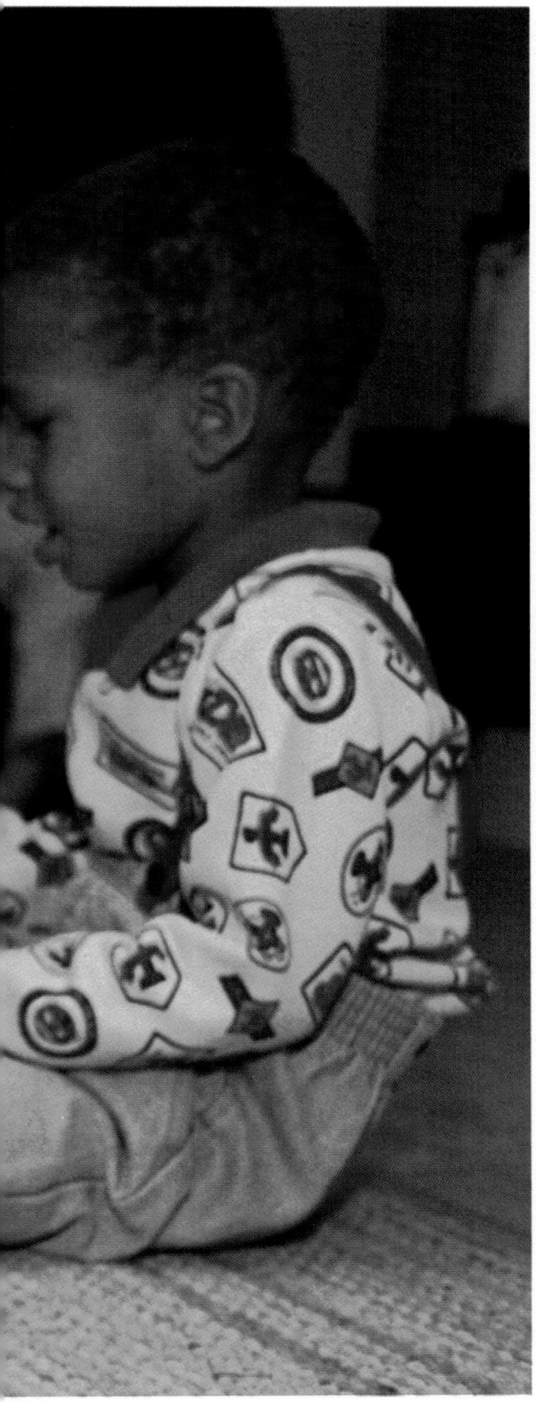

College (A-B Tech). A two-year public institution, A-B Tech offers associate degree programs through three divisions: allied health and public service education, business, and engineering and applied technology. A student who plans on transferring to a senior college or university can also earn an associate in arts or associate in science degree at A-B Tech.

Continuing education programs at A-B Tech benefit not only the part-time student who wants to learn Spanish or folk art painting, but the business community as well. The Center for Business and Industry works closely with the Asheville Area Chamber of Commerce, and other groups, on an array of economic development programs. These include Focused Industrial Training, designed for skilled and semiskilled workers in the manufacturing segment; occupational programs; and a quality program that includes all phases of ISO 9000 implementation. The Small Business Center addresses the needs of small businesses, and customized training programs are available for new and expanding industries in the Asheville area.

Founded in 1894 as the Asheville Farm School, Warren Wilson College in the beautiful Swannanoa Valley is not your typical private liberal arts college. Students can earn a bachelor's degree in any of 15 major and 19 minor subjects, or an MFA in creative writing, considered to be among the best programs in the nation.

In addition to carrying a full course load, the 585 students also carry a load that could include logs, mulch, or hog feed, or papers to be filed in the school office. Each student is required to work 15 hours a week on the 1,100-acre campus, which includes a working farm, sawmill, and archeological dig. Named one of the "best buys" in higher education by *Barrons* and *Money* magazine, Warren Wilson College receives high accolades for its character-building approach to work and community service, and for its outdoor leadership and environmental studies programs.

About 15 miles east of Asheville lies the picturesque little town of Montreat, home of Montreat College. A four-year coed, liberal arts college affiliated with the Presbyterian Church (USA), Montreat offers four-year degrees in majors and minors ranging from business administration, to Bible and religion, to environmental studies. There's also an off-campus School of Professional and Adult Studies offering BBA and MBA degrees with classes held in Asheville, Charlotte, Marion, and other locations. Total enrollment for Montreat College exceeds 850.

Other institutions of higher learning in the area include Cecil's College and Shaw University, both in downtown Asheville; Mars Hill College in Mars Hill; Western Carolina University in Cullowhee; and Brevard College in Brevard. Community/technical colleges within a 30-mile radius of Buncombe County include Blue Ridge Community College in Flat Rock, Southwestern Community College in Sylva, and Haywood Technology Community College and Regional High Technology Center, both located in Clyde.

Newcomers to Asheville are often surprised to discover the breadth of health care resources right here in their

A well-rounded student's education extends beyond the boundaries of a classroom. ***Photo by Tim Barnwell.***

Founded in 1856, Mars Hill College emphasizes the importance of reaching for individual goals, fulfilling spiritual needs, and serving the community. ***Photo by Tim Barnwell.***

In 1995 Asheville High School ranked number one in SAT scores in the state of North Carolina. ***Photo by Tim Barnwell.***

own backyard. As the regional hub for health care in Western North Carolina, the Asheville area is home to four hospitals, over 400 physicians, and more than 100 dentists.

Asheville's medical community boasts a long history of excellence and cooperation among providers. This is most evident in the creation of the Mission + St. Joseph's Health System in December 1995. This health system, which brought together Asheville's two regional medical centers in a precedent-setting partnership, was created to contain health care costs, improve the quality of health care in the region, and improve access to care, particularly for the uninsured.

Preparing students for the workplace is the primary thrust of Asheville-Buncombe Technical Community College. ***Photo courtesy of Asheville-Buncombe Technical Community College.***

The partnership, which was the first of its kind in North Carolina and one of the first in the nation, is widely supported by other hospitals in the region, as well as the communities and businesses of Western North Carolina. Under the terms of the partnership, the two hospitals maintain their identities—Memorial Mission as a not-for-profit community hospital and St. Joseph's as a not-for-profit Catholic hospital—but they are no longer friendly competitors.

The Mission + St. Joseph's Health System serves an estimated 143,000 outpatients on an annual basis. Another 78,000 receive emergency room care, and more than 41,000 surgeries are performed annually in the award-winning facilities. In 1994 Memorial Mission was named a Top 100 Hospital by *Modern Healthcare* magazine, and in 1995 St. Joseph's was awarded the North Carolina Quality Leadership Award.

Named one of the "best buys" in higher education by *Barrons* and *Money* magazine, Warren Wilson College receives high accolades for its character-building approach to work and community service, and for its outdoor leadership and environmental studies programs. *Photo by Tim Barnwell.*

Through the Mission + St. Joseph's Health System, residents of Western North Carolina have access to the full range of health care services. At Memorial Mission they include the Catherine and Charles Owen Heart Center, the Helen Powers Women's Center, and the Ruth and Billy Graham Children's Center.

At St. Joseph's they include programs in urology, orthopedics, and psychiatry. Other specialized services offered through the health system include cancer care, a genetics center, Neuro Trauma Intensive Care Unit, WNC Poison Center, MRI centers, a community health information hotline, addictions recovery, industrial medicine programs, and MAMA (Memorial Mission Air Medical Ambulance), which transports critically ill or injured patients to Asheville for care.

The Asheville area has other premier health care facilities, including the Asheville VA Medical Center, a 535-bed facility that specializes in cardiovascular and thoracic surgery. Thoms Rehabilitation Hospital, an 80-bed hospital, offers inpatient and outpatient rehabilitation services to patients with physical, cognitive, and developmental impairments, including strokes and brain and spinal cord injuries. Charter Asheville Behavioral Health System is a 100-bed general psychiatric hospital offering adult inpatient treatment, a children's inpatient unit, and treatment for drug and alcohol abuse.

Staying healthy is a way of life in the Asheville area. Call it "mountain motivation." It's hard not to get off the couch and participate in some kind of outdoor activity with so many opportunities at hand. The area hospitals, schools, and health clubs offer a variety of outdoor and indoor exercise programs ranging from mountain biking to aqua aerobics and yoga. Wellness programs abound, including smoking cessation, weight reduction, and stress management. There's also a range of alternative health care options in the area, from Chinese acupuncture and herbology, to macrobiotics and esoteric healing.

The Asheville area's reputation as an excellent retirement location has attracted thousands of senior citizens to the area. Naturally, a number of domiciliary-care facilities and nursing homes have been established to meet the needs of this growing segment of the population. Adult day care is gaining in popularity, as seniors and their family members seek life-enhancing experiences with an element of personal care.

As the Asheville area continues to grow, expect to see positive changes in education and health care services. Not that we're lacking in these areas, mind you. It's just that the Asheville mentality is one of optimism, hope, and support for the resources that strengthen the mind and body. ▲

A four-year coed, liberal arts college affiliated with the Presbyterian Church (USA), Montreat College offers four-year degrees in majors and minors ranging from business administration, to Bible and religion, to environmental studies. *Photo courtesy of Montreat College.*

THE HUMAN
TRAGEDY
ANATOLE FRANCE

Western Carolina University's various academic disciplines seek to incorporate regional outreach activities into its curricula, making the school a leader in providing training and assistance for mountain residents. *Photo by Tim Barnwell.*

The prestigious *Fiske Guide to Colleges* named UNCA a "best buy" and one of the top 10 public liberal arts schools in the nation. *Photo courtesy of UNCA.*

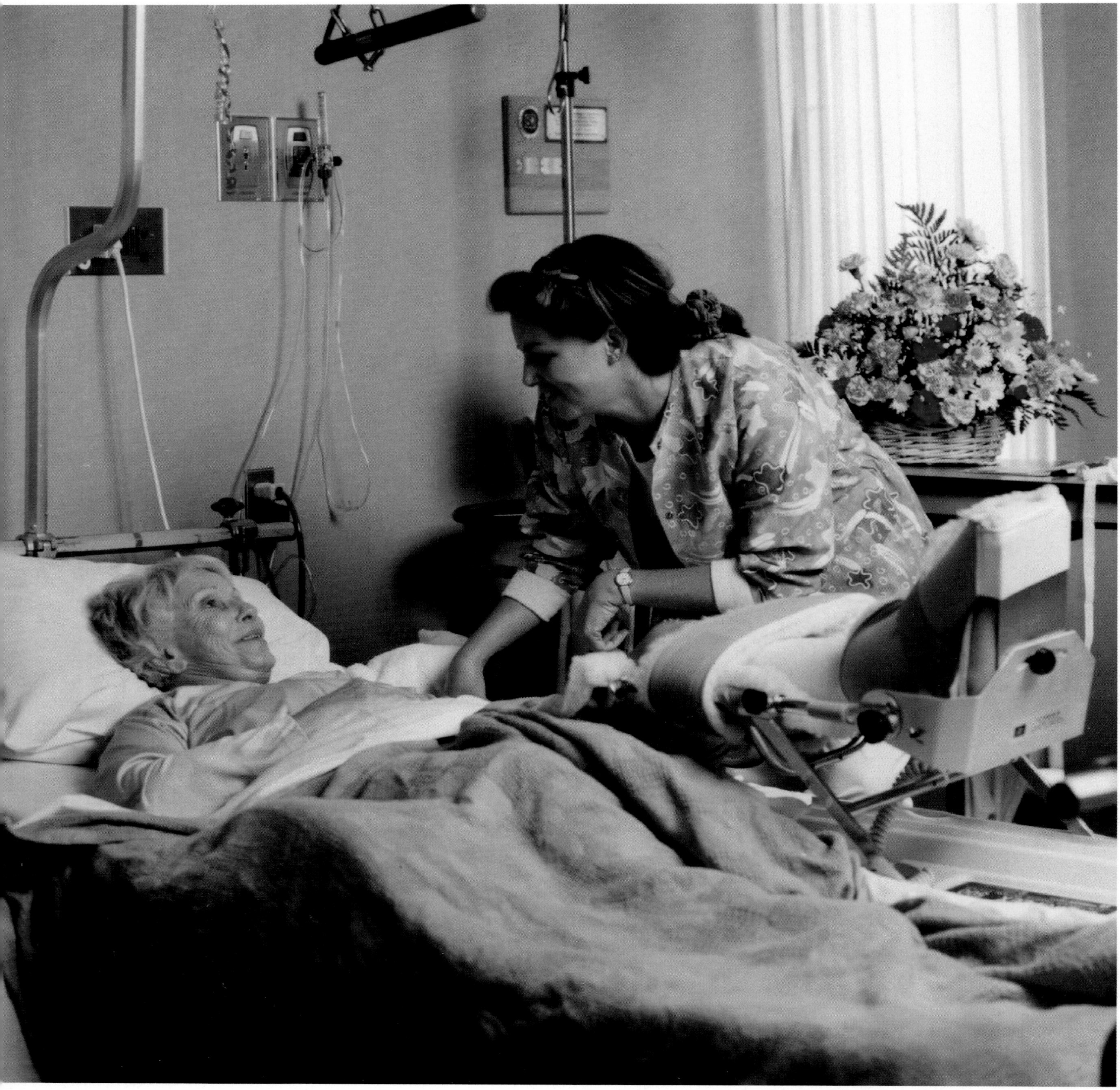

The orthopaedics center of Mission + St. Joseph's Health System provides compassionate treatment to patients with bone and joint problems.
Photo courtesy of Mission + St. Joseph's Health System.

The Asheville area's reputation as an excellent retirement location has attracted thousands of senior citizens to the area. *Photo by Tim Barnwell.*

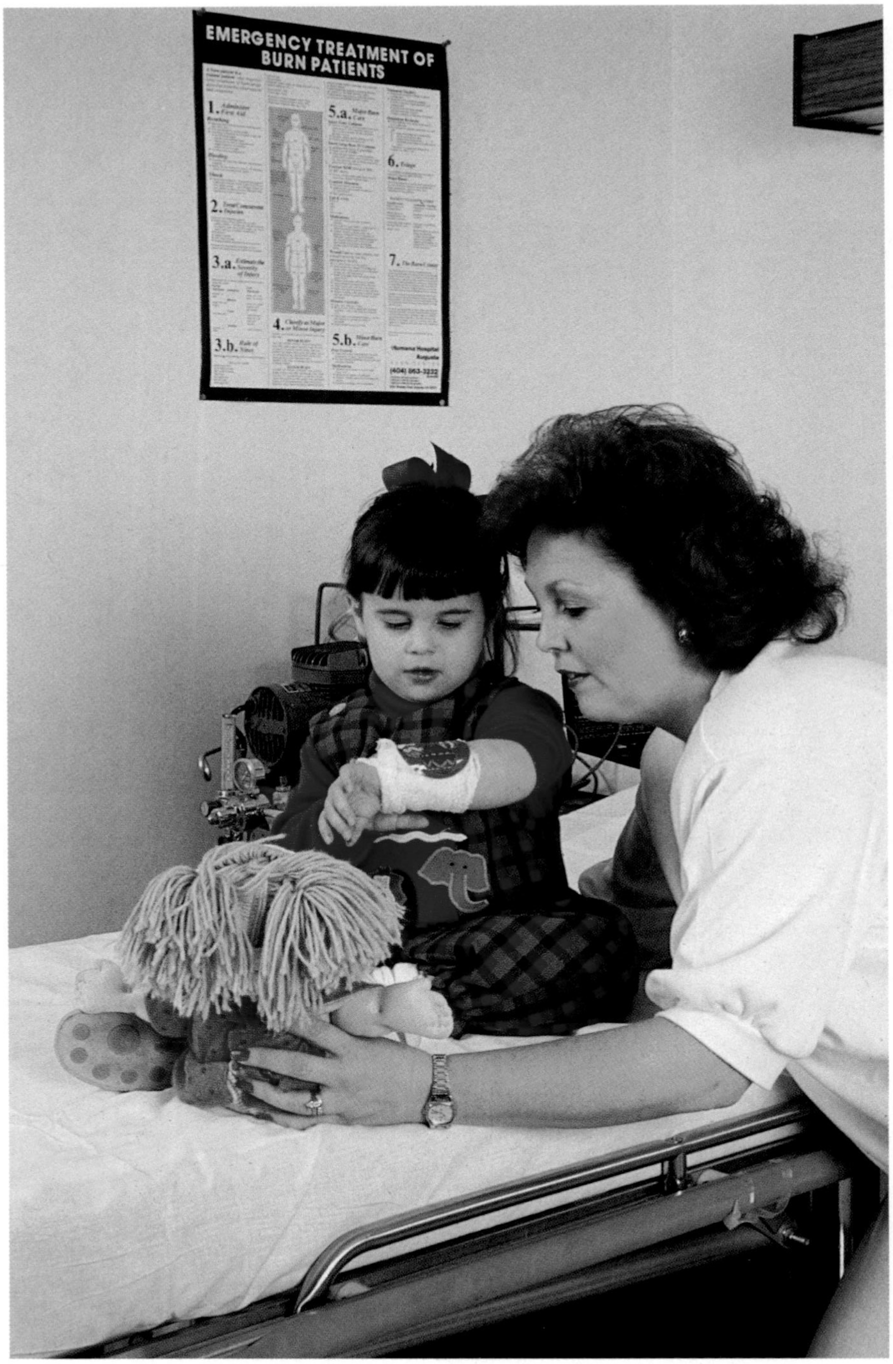

Care is available around the clock for all levels of illness and injury. *Photo by Tim Barmwell.*

Thoms Rehabilitation Hospital offers inpatient and outpatient rehabilitation services to patients with physical, cognitive, and developmental impairments. *Photo by Tim Barnwell.*

The creation of the Mission + St. Joseph's Health System in 1995 brought together Asheville's two regional medical centers in a precedent-setting partnership. *Photos by Tim Barnwell.*

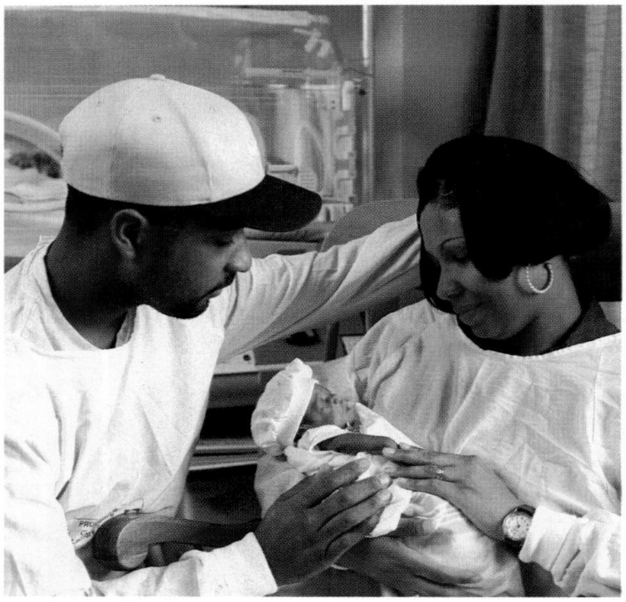

Even the smallest patient gets quality care in Asheville. *Photo courtesy of Mission + St. Joseph's Health System.*

The Medical Center For Western North Car
Mission
EMERGENCY

CHAPTER NINE

IT'S BETTER UP HERE: Altitude Affects Attitude

Ask a dozen residents of Asheville why they live here, and you may find their answers to be surprisingly similar. Breathtaking mountain scenery, abundant outdoor recreation, cultural diversity, and small town "feel" with big city amenities. A lot of things combine to make the Asheville area a wonderful place to live—important things like excellent education and health care resources, a good mix of job opportunities, affordable cost of living, and relatively low crime rates.

(*left*) Asheville is an enchanting place, a mountain mecca for nature lovers, outdoor enthusiasts, and seekers of a "quality of life" that surpasses most places. *Photo by Warner Photography.*

(*right*) Altitude truly does affect one's attitude. *Photo by Tim Barnwell.*

In numbers, the Baptist and United Methodist denominations lead the way, with more than 150 churches combined in the area. But there's a following for almost every type of faith. ***Photo by Tim Barnwell.***

Even the weather cooperates nicely, by blessing the area with four distinct seasons—winter's mild temperatures with distant snowcapped mountains, spring's renewal and explosion of green, summer's lush forests and fragrant blossoms, and fall's glorious color and cool autumn air. No wonder, then, that the *Rand McNally Places Rated Almanac* consistently rates Asheville as one of the best places to live in the nation, among metropolitan areas with fewer than 250,000 people (The Asheville MSA consists of Buncombe and Madison Counties and has close to 200,000 residents).

Visitors and newcomers alike are enchanted by Asheville's unique blend of Southern and mountain influences, coupled with a healthy dose of cosmopolitan culture from all over. You'll hear a few "y'alls" mingled with accents from the four corners of the earth—whether you're visiting Biltmore House, mingling in the lobby of Pack Place, sipping espresso at a downtown cafe, or enjoying a neighborhood picnic.

Asheville's neighborhoods come in all types and sizes, and range in age from the turn-of-the-century Montford and Albermarle Park in North Asheville to the newer communities high atop Town Mountain, such as Peach Knob and Trail Ridge. The 1920s real estate boom gave birth to several sought-after north Asheville neighborhoods, including Grove Park, Lakeview Park, and Sunset Parkway. Gracious Kimberly Avenue adjoins the Grove Park Inn's manicured golf course, and is a favorite stretch of sidewalk for strollers and joggers.

Downtown Asheville offers historic rental apartments, luxury condominiums, and affordable multiunit housing. Asheville's downtown renaissance isn't over—look for an increase in the number of residential units in the years to come. Several older structures have been targeted for rehabilitation.

South Asheville also boasts the old and the new, with some of Buncombe County's finest homes. Historic Kenilworth is conveniently located near Memorial Mission and St. Joseph's Hospitals, and offers older homes in various price ranges. Biltmore Forest is an affluent community of homes situated on land once owned by George Vanderbilt. You'll find 1920s mansions interspersed with the occasional newer home, most on heavily wooded and oversized lots. Other popular south Asheville neighborhoods include Oak Forest, Ballantree, and Park Avenue. New upscale developments include Biltmore Park and Blake Mountain Estates. Suburban growth has taken south Buncombe County by storm, and popular subdivisions like Coventry Woods, Glen Arden Heights, Brookwood, Glen Crest, and White Oak Plantation are considered real estate hot spots.

East Asheville is not just an active commercial area; it's also home to some great neighborhoods, including the upscale Silverstone and Sondley Estates. Well-kept, moderately priced homes sell fast in the Beverly Hills, Botany Woods, and Thorn Ridge communities, to name a few.

West Asheville is an established area of older, medium-priced homes. With the widening of Leicester Highway, a major thoroughfare in west Asheville, look for new residential development in once rural areas.

You don't have to travel far to be in the country, if it's country living you seek. In all four directions you'll find rural areas remarkably close to the city. Horse farms, charming old farmhouses, and mountain hideaways can be found in picturesque valleys or tucked away on mountain hillsides. Quaint little towns like Weaverville to the north, Fletcher to the south, and Black Mountain to the east offer worlds of opportunity for country living, just minutes from downtown Asheville.

No matter where you choose to live, it's almost assured that you'll be welcomed with open arms. Asheville is an exceptionally friendly town—the kind of place where people wave at perfect strangers, chat in the grocery line, and take the time to help stranded motorists. And it doesn't stop there. The Asheville area has an enormous talent pool of volunteers, who give countless hours of their time to worthy causes that benefit area residents. A surprising number of senior citizens are vigorously involved in volunteerism, many of whom are affiliated with the nationally recognized North Carolina Center for Creative Retirement at UNCA.

Western North Carolina has become a mecca for retirees, and many of these relocating seniors are active, well-educated, and relatively affluent members of the community. Buncombe County alone has a high number of retirees per capita, a whopping 16 percent. To accommodate this growing segment of the population, area retirement communities offer a range of amenities, from clubhouses and planned activities to assisted living services. A number of support services for seniors are also provided by the local hospitals and groups like the Land of Sky Regional Council and the Buncombe County Council on Aging. Each year the city of Asheville sponsors the Asheville-Buncombe Senior Games, a fun-filled series of sporting and arts-oriented competitive events for seniors.

If competition's your thing, the YMCA, City of Asheville, and Buncombe County offer competitive and instructional sports for residents of all ages. Baseball and soccer are especially popular. If you'd rather not compete, join a special interest club. Whatever your hobby or interest, chances are there's a local club for it, be it sports, health, or arts and crafts-related.

Taking care of the elderly, children in need, the disadvantaged, and disabled rank high on Asheville's list of priorities. The United Way of Asheville and Buncombe County supports a number of local agencies, including the American Red Cross, Salvation Army, the Manna Food Bank, and the Rape Crisis Center. Programs offered by the YMCA and the YWCA benefit all ethnic and age groups, and include not only recreational programs, but also continuing education, health-related summer camps, and outreach programs for "at risk" youths. An active Big Brothers and Big Sisters organization matches children in need with caring adult role models.

The more than 300 religious institutions in Asheville provide outreach, education, and spiritual guidance for area residents. In numbers, the Baptist and United Methodist denominations lead the way, with more than 150 churches combined in the area. But there's a following for almost every type of faith.

Western North Carolina is home to a number of religious-oriented conference centers, including Ridgecrest, founded by the Southern Baptists, and the Lake Junaluska Assembly, owned by the Southeastern Jurisdiction of the United Methodist Church. At the Billy Graham Training Center, "The Cove," participants attend a variety of Christian seminars that focus on the teachings of the Bible, interpreted for everyday living. The Cove was founded by the world-renowned Reverend Billy Graham, a native of nearby Montreat. In May of 1996, all eyes were on the Reverend Graham and his wife, Ruth, when they were awarded the Congressional Gold Medal, the highest United States civilian honor, for their "outstanding and lasting contributions to morality, racial equality, family, philanthropy, and religion."

Breaking down racial and ethnic barriers has always been a part of the Billy Graham ministry, and his local roots serve as an inspiration to today's community leaders. Efforts to foster a spirit of cooperation among all groups are on-going and welcomed. The YMI Cultural

Affordable programs, like the YWCA Day Camp, offer fun and education for area preschoolers. ***Photo by Tim Barnwell.***

Center, local churches, and civic groups have banded in recent years to strengthen ties among Asheville's diverse population. Events such as the annual Asheville Martin Luther King Prayer Breakfast, UNCA's "Opening Doors" program, and the 1996 Greater Asheville Multi-Ethnic Crusade help continue this united effort.

Keeping the public informed is the job of a responsible, fair media—and the Asheville area is well served by nine daily and weekly newspapers, four television stations, and several radio stations. The area's largest daily newspaper is the award-winning *Asheville Citizen-Times,* covering a 19-county area and known for its special sections and in-depth reporting of local news. The weekly *Mountain Express* is a gold mine of information featuring arts and entertainment, the inside scoop on local government meetings, and some of the most candid movie reviews you'll find in print. *Out 'n About,* also a weekly, offers a convenient day-by-day entertainment calendar of things to see and do in Western North Carolina. Other local publications, many of which are free, cover topics including business, real estate, parenting, senior living, shopping, and African-American interests. Published twice a year, *The Old Asheville Gazette* reprints local news items from another era–an interesting look back at Asheville's boom period of the 1920s.

With the advent of cable, the Asheville area receives a number of stations, too numerous to list. As the cable companies expand their services, expect new stations to be added in the near future.

Local broadcast stations include Western North Carolina's ABC affiliate WLOS, located in Asheville near the Grove Park Inn. WLOS provides up-to-the-minute coverage of local news, features, sports, and weather. Northeast Georgia and South Carolina's upstate are also covered by WLOS. WFBC features a "no news" format with sports and syndicated programs. Designed to compete locally, a new Asheville-based station, WHNC, is currently on the drawing board. Greenville-based Fox affiliate WHNS covers Asheville, Anderson, Greenville, and Spartanburg. Two other South Carolina stations, CBS-affiliate WSPA and NBC-affiliate WYFF, cover upstate South Carolina, northeast Georgia, and Western North Carolina.

When you're scanning your dial for a radio station in the Asheville area, you'll find a range of formats including country (WKSF-FM), country and news/talk (WWNC-AM), adult-oriented rock (WZLS-FM), talk (WSKY-AM), religious/public affairs (WFGW-AM; WMTT-FM), nostalgic (WISE-AM), gospel (WKJV-AM and WLFA-FM), and public radio (WCQS-FM and WNCW). Greenville, South Carolina, Waynesville, and Black Mountain stations can also be picked up, depending on whether you're driving through a valley or looking down on one from the top of a mountain.

Whatever your perspective, rest assured that Asheville is on top when it comes to planning for the future. Spearheaded by the Asheville Area Chamber of Commerce, the Asheville "Visioning" project launched in 1996 is designed to help the city and county become more competitive by the year 2010 in six key areas: education, quality of life, infrastructure, economic development,

The Basilica of St. Lawrence boasts the largest unsupported dome in North America and is listed on the National Register of Historic Places. ***Photo by Tim Barnwell.***

Asheville's neighborhoods come in all types and sizes. *Photos by Tim Barnwell.*

private-sector leadership, and government. Action steps are in place, supported by the local governing bodies, the Asheville City Council and Buncombe County Commissioners. An array of other civic groups are involved, including the League of Women Voters, the Council of Independent Business Owners, Leadership Asheville, and the Community Foundation of Western North Carolina. It's a strategy that makes sense—a hope, a blueprint for the future that involves strategic growth, not just something that happens.

The year 1997 marks Asheville's year-long bicentennial celebration, "Yes, You Can Come Home Again." Two hundred years of prosperity and progress, set in motion by the city's founding fathers, who instinctively knew they'd stumbled upon a special place. And in 1998, the Asheville Area Chamber of Commerce celebrates its centennial as one of the oldest Chambers of Commerce in North Carolina. As we acknowledge Asheville's achievements with fanfare, let it be with the notion that it's better up here—altitude truly does affect one's attitude. And it all adds up to a quality of life that rivals most places. ▲

(left)* Western North Carolina is home to a number of religious-oriented conference centers, including Ridgecrest, founded by the Southern Baptists. *Photo by Tim Barnwell.

(right)* The Cove was founded by the world-renowned Reverend Billy Graham, a native of nearby Montreat. *Photo by Tim Barnwell.

Western North Carolina has become a mecca for retirees, and many of these relocating seniors are active, well-educated, and relatively affluent members of the community. ***Photo by Tim Barnwell.***

More than 300 religious institutions in Asheville provide outreach, education, and spiritual guidance for area residents. *Photo by Tim Barnwell.*

Rand McNally Places Rated Almanac* consistently rates Asheville as one of the best places to live in the nation. *Photo by Tim Barnwell.

In the foreground of downtown's Saint James AME Church, the Martin Luther King Jr. Memorial stands as a testimony to the work of the great civil rights leader. *Photo by Tim Barnwell.*

No matter where you choose to live, it's almost assured that you'll be welcomed with open arms. Asheville is an exceptionally friendly town. ***Photo by Tim Barnwell.***

PUBLIC SERVICE COMPANY
PUDDNUCKERS
PUBLIC SERVICE COMPANY
SAUCES RESTAURANT
PUBLIC SERVICE COMPANY
ALA KART
CAROLINA WILDERNESS
VANCE
Lite

PART TWO

ASHEVILLE'S ENTERPRISES

CHAPTER TEN

NETWORKS

The area's communications, energy, and transportation firms keep information, power, people, and products circulating inside and outside the Asheville area.

WWNC and WKSF

On Monday, February 21, 1927, Calvin Coolidge was president. Al Jolson and Greta Garbo were the year's most popular actors. The average three-bedroom home sold for just under $5,000. And live from an eight o'clock dinner program at Asheville's elegant George Vanderbilt Hotel, WWNC, a broadcasting legend, was born, as it paid tribute over the airwaves to its namesake: Wonderful Western North Carolina.

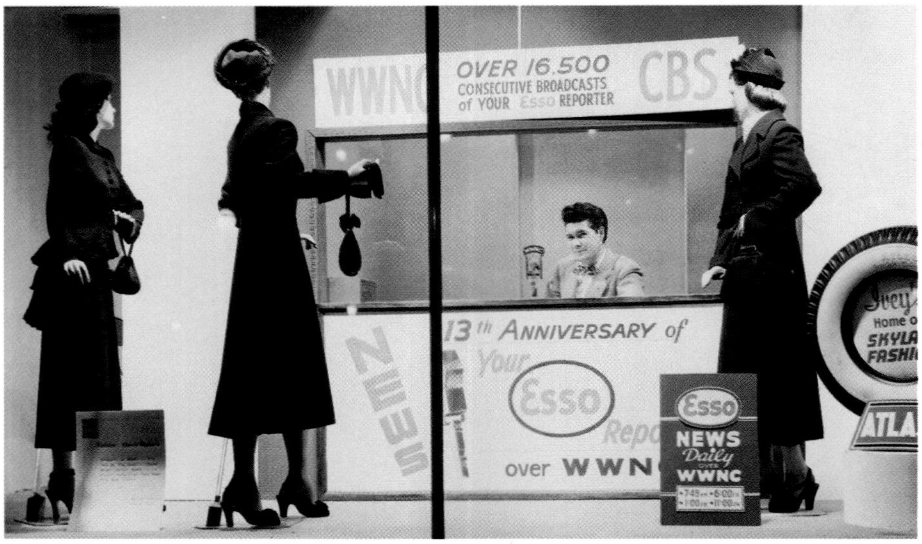

Through the years, WWNC has maintained it's high news profile. Pictured here in earlier days, WWNC's Esso Reporter announces the news live from a downtown Asheville storefront.

Seventy years later, after the 1927 debut that had charmed local residents as well as listeners from as far away as Canada and Texas, the enchantment that first sprang up between the fledgling radio station and its audience continues. Through changes in ownership, ranging from the *Asheville Citizen* newspaper in 1929, to Osborn Communications Corporation, the station's current owner, one thing has remained constant: WWNC's unswerving commitment to its family of listeners and the communities of Western North Carolina.

In response to that commitment, the station has enjoyed the loyalty of generations of area residents. For most of his 41 years on the air, WWNC's Scotty Rhodarmer, a broadcasting legend in his own right, has been easing sleepy listeners out of bed and off to work with a unique blend of music, weather, and timely down-home information. As much a part of the morning routine as coffee and toast, few Asheville area families miss the pleasure of sharing breakfast every day with "Scotty In the Morning."

WWNC is one of the last full-service radio stations in America. In addition to a satisfying mix of current and traditional country music, each day's programming includes news, up-to-the-minute weather reports by the only broadcast meteorologist in the market, traffic and stock market reports, *ABC Network News,* and *Paul Harvey News and Comment.*

In addition to WWNC's daily programming, the station is never a more welcome voice than during an emergency. "Especially in a weather emergency," notes Promotion Director Carol Whiting. "People may not have power or TV or a newspaper, but they do have batteries and a radio—and they tune in to WWNC first because they know we'll be broadcasting the information they need." Twenty-four hours a day, station personnel keep listeners in constant touch with road conditions, weather updates, and weather-related closings. "During a bad storm," Whiting says, "our air staff actually sleeps and eats at the station, so that, even in the worst conditions, we're there for people."

Reflecting on the WWNC tradition, Vice President and General Manager Bill McMartin adds, "People are comfortable with us because we make them feel good. Over and over again, when people are describing WWNC, you hear words like 'dependable' and phrases like 'there when you need it.' That's a big responsibility for us. One we're proud to accept and take very seriously."

WWNC also offers special programming that reflects the lifestyle of the community. As the only broadcast source in the market to air the complete NASCAR racing schedule, WWNC broadcasts an average of 90 races a year. In addition, when UNCA approached the station about broadcasting their basketball games, the station

Western North Carolina's favorite radio personality, Scotty Rhodarmer, has broadcasted on WWNC for over 40 years. *Photo by Evelyn Graham.*

responded to the challenge of giving the team the local presence they needed by nearly quadrupling game attendance in a single season.

"WWNC has a tremendous history," says McMartin. "And with a tradition of owning and operating other legendary radio stations like WWVA in Wheeling, West Virginia, it's easy to see why Osborn Communications is proud to have WWNC as a part of its broadcasting family."

With Osborn Communications' acquisition of historic WWNC, however, came red-hot sister station WKSF-FM. In a daring move just weeks before the purchase of the two stations was finalized in 1994, new owner Frank Osborn made the decision to flip WKSF's contemporary hit format of over a decade to hot country. Research had indicated an overwhelming local desire for a Western North Carolina FM country station, and according to Osborn at the time of the change, "Everybody's response is that's what is needed." His gamble paid off. Big. The new KISS Country became the highest debuting radio station in the history of Arbitron, the National Radio Rating Service.

With a powerful 24-hour-a-day signal blasting into six Southern states from Mount Pisgah, 6,000 feet above sea level, KISS Country concentrates on a simple, but serious, mission: to have lots of fun playing plenty of great music. Fifty minutes of every hour is devoted to the hottest new country hits. Weather, time, and hard-hitting 99-second morning headline updates are also featured. Exciting giveaways and zany stunts are added to reinforce the high energy "let's not take ourselves so seriously" image of KISS Country. Morning show hosts Dale Mitchell and Nikki Thomas set the blistering pace of the day, and hit after hit, the tempo never slows down.

From atop beautiful Mount Pisgah, Kiss Country transmits a powerful signal that reaches into six states. *Photo by Tim Barnwell.*

Fully equipped remote vehicles allow WWNC and Kiss Country to broadcast live from events throughout Western North Carolina.

Like her older, more traditional sister station, KISS Country shares a strong commitment to Asheville and the surrounding communities. Both radio stations play high profile roles in major regional events—everything from Christmas parades to celebrity golf tournaments, the Bele Chere Festival to Thirsty Thursday at the ballpark. Through hourly public service announcements, sponsorship of events, and public appearances at virtually dozens of charitable events each year, WWNC and KISS Country are recognized as indispensable keys to success by many local agencies and organizations. "It's fair to say," says McMartin, "that, in the course of a year, WWNC and KISS Country help raise hundreds of thousands of dollars for a variety of charities. Over the history of the two stations, millions of dollars have been raised for this community."

That strong presence in the community has also been an important contributing factor in bringing in country superstars like Reba McEntire, Alan Jackson, Vince Gill, Brooks and Dunn, and Tim McGraw, who now view Asheville as a country concert venue of ever-increasing significance. In conjunction with Osborn Entertainment, the parent company's concert promotion division, these relationships with the stars are constantly being strengthened, making it possible for residents of Western North Carolina to enjoy top-caliber entertainment without having to travel to Atlanta, Knoxville, or Charlotte.

Jointly commanding a local radio listenership of nearly 200,000 people, WWNC and KISS Country take the impact they have on the community seriously. "We operate with a strong awareness of our responsibility," McMartin affirms. "People have listened to these stations for so long, invested so much loyalty, they feel a sense of ownership. And we couldn't agree more. It's a high standard, and we're committed to living up to it every day." ▲

Asheville Regional Airport

An estimated 20,000 additional jobs and more than $1 billion in annual sales are generated for the region as a direct result of the airport's presence. *Photo by Tim Barnwell.*

The *New York Times* quoted a visitor to Asheville as saying, "The Asheville Regional Airport was a pleasant surprise." But it is no surprise to Director Jim Parker—for almost a decade he has overseen the development of the Asheville Regional Airport into a major air transportation facility serving the needs of Western North Carolina. Today this newly renovated and efficient airport is the fourth largest airport in North Carolina.

The airport is actually home to two distinct facilities. The first and more familiar is the main terminal for public travelers taking advantage of the commercial flights offered by major airlines. The second is the Asheville Jet Center, a general aviation, fixed base operation adjacent to the main terminal. Both services share the same runway but otherwise operate separately. "We have a total facility here," states Parker, "that can serve whatever air travel the customers need, whether for business, pleasure, or corporate."

While it is impossible to top the beautiful views of the Blue Ridge Mountains surrounding the 900-acre grounds, the main terminal offers a warm, light-filled interior that says welcome to its guests. That's right, guests. Travelers here receive true Southern hospitality in a comfortable and accommodating environment. Parker and his staff of 25 consistently look out for and meet their needs. "Our bosses are the people who use these facilities," Parker emphasizes.

Hundreds of thousands of customers are served each year by national and regional airlines operating daily jet and turbo-prop service to four major hub cities—Cincinnati, Atlanta, Charlotte, and Raleigh. From these hub cities the traveler can continue on to virtually anywhere in the world. As more and more business leaders discover Asheville as a branch office or corporate relocation site, the sophistication of the airport plays a key role in their success. Tourists also find that the centrally located airport makes Asheville the ideal jumping-off point for exploring all of Western North Carolina.

The newly renovated and efficient Asheville Regional Airport is the fourth largest airport in North Carolina. *Photo by Tim Barnwell.*

An impressive list of amenities at the airport includes second level boarding with boarding bridges that make a comfortable transition between the terminal and aircraft. The efficient baggage claim area is adjacent to a cluster of rental car companies, shuttle services, and ground transportation options. Convenient "close-in" public parking adjacent to the terminal provides customers long-term and short-term parking with short walking distances between parking and aircraft boarding. A spacious and well-stocked welcome and information center presents travelers with literature and advice on the abundant opportunities for fun and relaxation at nearby destinations. And a full-service travel agency in the terminal building can assist with future travel plans. In addition to concession tenants like the full-service restaurant, the airport also hosts the offices of the Western North Carolina Regional Economic Development Commission (Advantage West) and the North Carolina Department of Commerce, Western Region. These prestigious tenants are another indication of the central role Asheville and the airport play in the region.

Asheville Jet Center has operated the fixed base operation at the airport since 1991, when the facility was enlarged and completely renovated. All private aircraft—large or small—receive a first-class welcome at the Jet Center, which offers 24-hour, full-service aviation fuel services, aircraft maintenance, and flight training. Corporate travelers are invited to take advantage of these services whether they are here for a stopover, a longer stay, or as home base. Aircraft storage is available for large corporate and small private aircraft, including individual T-hangars. As Asheville grows in popularity with the corporate and private traveler, the Jet Center has expanded its services to include rental cars, hotel reservations, and the sale of tickets to area attractions. More

Hundreds of thousands of customers are served each year by national and regional airlines operating daily jet and turbo-prop service to four major hub cities. *Photo by Tim Barnwell.*

and more pilots' associations, for example, are selecting Asheville as a site for their annual fly-ins because of the beauty of the mountains, abundance of golf courses, nationally recognized attractions, and professional services available to them. "We get many letters and comment cards that this is one of the nicest FBOs they have flown into," states Joel Barker, president of the Asheville Jet Center.

The Asheville Regional Airport has been in its present location since 1961. Just 15 miles south of Asheville and 8 miles from Hendersonville, it is directly accessible to I-26 and nearby I-40. Five hotels share the same interstate interchange, and a wide selection of area hotels are close by. Several hotels offer courtesy vans.

Airport facilities such as the landing strip, air freight/air cargo, and fixed base operation are open 24 hours day. The 8,000-foot-by-150 foot runway is capable of handling any size commercial or corporate aircraft. It has a Category 1 Approach Lighting System, with precision instrument approaches on both ends, and features an FAA control tower on-site.

The airport's economic impact on nonaviation businesses is substantial. An estimated 20,000 additional jobs and more than $1 billion in annual sales are generated for the region as a direct result of the airport's presence. Other benefits include the number of lives saved thanks to air ambulances and the swift transport of time-critical medical supplies and donor organs. The quality of life is enriched by the convenient and reliable transportation the Asheville Regional Airport affords.

Parker reports that in the last several years more than $30 million has been spent to make the airport what it is today. This reflects a strong commitment by the Asheville Regional Airport Authority, the governing board, to continue to provide safe and efficient facilities for anyone living in or coming into the area and to continue to pursue additional commercial service, whether from existing or new carriers. To accomplish that, Parker states that new plans are always underway. "The terminal, parking, airfield—we have a lot of projects in mind for these facilities. We will continue to develop and expand the airport to meet the demand placed on it. We are committed to serve our customers with facilities that meet their needs now and in the future." ▲

The Asheville Jet Center, located at the Asheville Regional Airport, is a general aviation, fixed base operation adjacent to the main terminal.

Telephone Systems of Asheville

"Hello" and "Good-bye" used to mark the purpose of a connection between two telephones, a simple conversation. In Asheville, just as around the world, chips and computers have spawned a mind-boggling potential for communications and information management systems. "Those people who learn to ride the waves of change in today's business environment will be successful, and, the ones who can't keep up are going to be left behind," says Bill Arledge, president of TSA, a broad-based communications service headquartered in Asheville. "Increasingly, businesses will find themselves isolated if they don't have the capabilities to communicate and manage information using, not just the telephone, but FAX, computer E-mail, the Internet, and direct links for things like video teleconferencing and data connectivity. That's why we're so committed to service and helping people grow into the next level of high-tech communications solutions."

(Left to right) Bill Arledge, president of TSA, and Jeff Lowdermilk, TSA vice president, provide the leadership for a broad-based communications service.

Known simply as TSA, Telephone Systems of Asheville, Inc. has grown to be the largest private telephone company in Western North Carolina from a start back in 1982 as a division of M. B. Haynes Corporation, one of the area's major construction and electrical contracting companies. "We got started back before the big telephone monopoly breakup, when it was really tough to earn business away from the big boys," says Jeff Lowdermilk, TSA vice president. "I started here as a salesperson, and we had to provide more service than anybody else just to get our foot in the door. Fortunately, we still have that attitude, and it's helped us know people's needs better, so we can help them keep up with the latest technology."

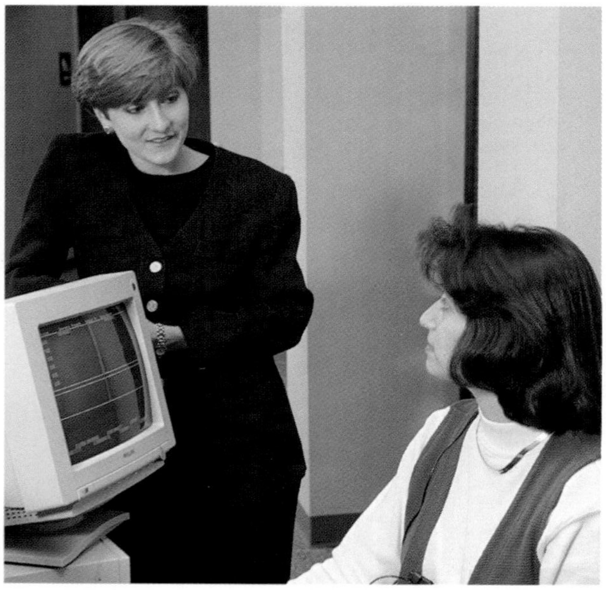

The capability to combine computers and telephone communications is called Computer Telephone Integration, or CTI. *Photo by J. Weiland.*

Herb Kelleher, CEO of Southwest Airlines, speaking of his lack of expertise in technology, was quoted in *USA Today* as saying, "If they do away with number two pencils, I'm really incommunicado." That just points to how rapidly things have changed. We used to go to work at a desk. More and more personal computers have helped us create "work stations." Now, in order to share files, printers, or other peripherals, we've needed to tie users together with "networks."

"We've all heard about the information superhighway. I guess you could call us the traffic engineers in a way. So many options and innovations make choices confusing sometimes, and we're able to help people sort out their needs, then make sure the system they install gives them what they need for today as well as preparing for the future," says Lowdermilk. "We've seen the changes coming for a long time. Now, it's important to find the best ways to use the new technology in business applications. That's where our staff really shines."

Noting the capabilities for combining computers and telephone communications, Arledge continues, "They call it CTI. That stands for Computer Telephone Integration, and it's the wave we're all riding right now." He notes it includes internal and external networking, known as LANS and WANS (Local and Wide Area Networks), voicemail (with or without automated attendant), and, of course, the latest technology in wiring systems, whether Category 5 unshielded twisted pair, the current standard in the industry, or fiber-optic backbones. "We help our customers know what's available, so they can make better choices."

"We know we can't be all things to all people, but we are specialists in anything to do with telephones and communications. We offer our customers true one-call service for all their telecommunication needs: telephone equipment, BellSouth voice and data services, LCI long-distance service, and computer networking as well." Lowdermilk says, "When it comes to telecommunications, we can handle anything our customers need, including placing orders with service providers like BellSouth when a change in service or a new line is needed. We call this one-contact approach Telemanagement."

Known simply as TSA, Telephone Systems of Asheville, Inc. has grown to be the largest private telephone company in Western North Carolina. *Photo by J. Weiland.*

"One of the most frustrating things that can happen in business is losing your telephone, whether it's a single phone or an entire system; then when you try to call to get service, you can't figure out who's responsibility it is, whether it's the line provider or the equipment vendor. We've solved all that," says Arledge. "With Telemanagement, in conjunction with our all-inclusive service agreement, we make sure that people get back in business quickly if things do go wrong. We even promise you how long it will take us to do it. And we back up our promises with a money-back guarantee."

Mitel, one of the nation's leading manufacturers of PBX telephone systems, recently hailed TSA as a leader in the industry with a number one ranking and award for service to its customers. The award recognized TSA as being number one in the Southeast and fourth in the entire USA and Canada in customer satisfaction. A national research firm, TD Marketing Research, Inc., Santa Clara, California, surveyed telephone system customers across North America and rated TSA's performance in initial installation and long-term service and support in the selection for the award. "We appreciate being recognized for the service we provide," says Lowdermilk.

"You can't imagine how satisfying it is to be able to be a part of the growth in this business community the way we are," he continues. "There are hundreds of customers who've been with us for years, and we've been able to watch them grow. Some of them have moved several times to larger facilities, and we get to grow with them. But we've also been privileged to be a part of many new businesses coming to the area. It's exciting to see the free enterprise system at its best, like it is in Western North Carolina. We're enjoying it and are eager for the challenges ahead as we help people grow their own businesses." And Bill Arledge says, "You bet! Riding the waves of change in business is a lot of fun, when you do it right and have great customers like ours." ▲

In Asheville, just as around the world, chips and computers have spawned a mind-boggling potential for communications and information management systems. *Photo by J. Weiland.*

United States Cellular® Wireless Communications

First there were two-way radios. Then pagers were developed. Now cellular phones are leading the way in wireless technology. United States Cellular® Wireless Communications is revving up the drive for information technology by giving its customers the opportunity to transmit information from anywhere. Technological advances in laptop computers, wireless phones, and facsimile equipment make mobile offices a reality.

"Today you have to get information to people as quickly as possible," states Debra C. Kasey, branch manager for the Western North Carolina region. "We have so much information at our fingertips, and now, because of the wireless industry, you can get it a lot quicker—anywhere, anytime."

Founded in 1983, Chicago-based United States Cellular Corporation is one of the pioneers in the wireless industry with customers in 143 markets and is the seventh largest cellular company in the United States. In 1987 United States Cellular installed the first cellular antennae in Western North Carolina. Since then the company has experienced remarkable growth, making it not only the first but also the largest cellular provider in the region with the broadest local calling area.

Debra C. Kasey (right), branch manager for United States Cellular's Western North Carolina region, poses with the Mirheli family in front of their home built with proceeds from the annual United States Cellular Invitational Golf Classic. *Photo by Tim Barnwell.*

Customers enjoy one-on-one service in United States Cellular's many stores throughout Western North Carolina. *Photo by Tim Barnwell.*

But it is not just the number of antennae that makes the difference. The engineering behind them also is the key. Western North Carolina is known as a "problem terrain" because of the mountains, which can make it difficult to successfully and consistently transmit cellular phone calls. United States Cellular's talented and well-trained personnel make sure their system delivers. "We have a very well-engineered system," Kasey stated. "Our engineers have done an excellent job of placing the antennae so we can optimum service."

The company's extensive outreach program includes a minimum of 75 events a year, most notably the annual United States Cellular Invitational Golf Classic to benefit the Asheville Area Habitat for Humanity, which builds a home for a local family each year. United States Cellular takes part in other community activities, including Tour DuPont and Bele Chere, and donates airtime and phones to the American Red Cross and DARE, as well as sharing equipment with executives on loan to the United Way Campaign so they can keep in touch with the campaign as well as their offices. United States Cellular is the largest capital supporter of March of Dimes WalkAmerica in the area.

When disaster strikes, United States Cellular's outreach extends to the entire region. The company maintains a well-organized disaster plan with a company manager on call 24 hours a day, 365 days a year in case of an emergency like the Blizzard of '93. A bank of phones is strictly reserved for disasters so they will always be on hand and ready, and Kasey states that more can be made available if necessary.

This commitment to the community is as reliable as United States Cellular's technology and service. "We have an exclusive budget just for community services," Kasey states, "and we will be here for them next year and the next and the next. Our philosophy is the community has been very good to us, so we want to give back to them. And I believe they know that about our company."

This remarkable United States Cellular technology is not for the well-financed executive only. A telephone once priced as high as $2,500 now costs only $40. Mothers at soccer matches, senior citizens traveling, even teachers on field trips have all appreciated the convenience of cellular telephones, turning the once luxury tool into a mass market product. The increased customer base has helped to reduce prices, which, in turn, stimulates the market.

As a result of the rapidly expanded market, growth figures are off the charts. In fact, the size of United States Cellular's system is growing so fast, Kasey hesitates to state a figure. What is accurate one day may be drastically different a week later. From 1993 to 1994 the company grew at a rate of 52 percent; from 1994 to 1995 that figure increased to 54 percent, each year building on the last. Unprecedented growth coupled with technological advances means United States Cellular is constantly training its staff to continue as the wireless experts in Western North Carolina. "We owe it to our customers," Kasey adds. "After all, the tools we use today may not be the tools we need tomorrow."

Kasey is committed to service, not just for the company but for the entire community. "As a corporate citizen we believe it is our duty to be part of the community. We live here. Our kids grow up here. We want to make sure all our employees are proud of who they are working for. We don't just write checks to organizations—we get involved, we sponsor their events, we donate equipment. We want to help them do something for themselves." ▲

Wireless technology allows your mobile office to be anywhere you are.

DARE officers (left to right) Lieutenant Gloria Nock and Lieutenant Ricky Bishop display cellular phones donated by United States Cellular.

Carolina Power & Light Company

CP&L operates three generating plants in Western North Carolina. Of the three, the Skyland Steam Plant is the largest. It began operation in 1964 and consists of two coal-fired units. When operating at full capacity, the plant consumes 3,700 tons of low-sulphur coal a day—or 37 railway cars' worth—to produce 392,000 kilowatts of electricity.

The remaining two plants are hydroelectric, each unique in its own way. The Walters Plant, located on the Pigeon River near the Tennessee border, is unusual because it sits about six miles from the dam. A concrete-lined tunnel channels rushing water through solid rock from the reservoir to the plant. Built in 1930, the Walters Plant can produce 105,000 kilowatts of electricity. The Marshall Plant, built in 1908, has the distinction of being the smallest in CP&L's entire system, a reminder of the early days of electricity when plants of its size dotted the banks of the region's rivers. The flow of the river's current through the plant's turbines generates up to 5,000 kilowatts.

The electricity produced by each of these plants is interconnected with the rest of CP&L's 16 coal, nuclear, gas, and hydroelectric plants located throughout the Carolinas. The size of the system provides customers a source of reliable and dependable electric energy.

About 250 CP&L employees call Western North Carolina home. They work in a diverse range of capacities, from the technicians at the generating plants who transmit the electricity to the line and service crews who make sure it is delivered.

CP&L lineman Ronald Scott performs routine line maintenance high above the city of Asheville. Service reliability is a source of pride for the company and comfort for customers. Even in severe weather emergencies, CP&L personnel work around the clock to restore power to all customers as quickly as possible.

A horn blasts, and the band takes five. As the electric lights flicker and fail, the dancers disperse to the corners of the room to sip cool lemonade. Soon the dance hall is dark except for the glow of a few hastily lit candles. Then, with another blast of the horn, in comes the band, on come the lights, and the dancing resumes.

That's how it was in 1900 with the dawn of electric power in Western North Carolina. A horn alerted people when the hydroelectric generator at the outskirts of Asheville lost pressure and again when pressure was restored. The records of a local electric company for that year show that it supplied power to 100 street lights and 5,000 light bulbs—not customers—light bulbs.

Today, another story has unfolded, one in which Carolina Power & Light Company (CP&L) plays a major part. At night, the lights of Asheville form a bright constellation, and the days are just as alive with electric power, from the hum of computers to the whir of automated machinery on factory floors. As a company, CP&L strives to meet the energy needs of this thriving city and contributes to its future prosperity and well-being through support of area education, economic development, and the environment.

Like many other communities at the turn of the century, Asheville received its first electricity from several small rival companies. Eventually these companies were consolidated into Asheville Power & Light Company, which merged with Carolina Power & Light Company in 1926. CP&L was formed in 1908 through a similar consolidation in the eastern part of the state.

CP&L sales representatives, like (left) Nancy Thompson, advise customers on the best SafeShine outdoor lighting options for private homes as well as businesses.

(Left to right) CP&L account manager Gary Hamrick and Quaker Oats plant manager Jim Kloman discuss plant electrical needs. CP&L provides energy efficiency consultations to help customers save money, strengthening their businesses.

Employee volunteers complete a pedestrian walkway in the summer mists of Mount Mitchell. Part of CP&L's innovative Adopt State Parks program, this project is one of the many park improvements completed through CP&L's service area each year.

CP&L has a long tradition of partnership with the area's business community. According to Western Region Vice President Fred N. Day, the company is eager to carry this partnership into the future. "We work with existing industrial and commercial customers to provide solutions for their energy needs as well as with new customers," he said. To help customers decrease energy costs, CP&L offers consultations on energy-efficient lighting, electrotechnologies, and other improvements.

But electricity is not the only resource CP&L provides local industry. In addition to a strong relationship with the Asheville Area Chamber of Commerce, the company has been a major supporter of such economic development efforts as the Asheville Initiative and Advantage Asheville and an original backer for CarolinaWest, a regional marketing organization. From the recruitment of industry to the area to programs promoting workforce preparedness and expansion of local businesses, CP&L demonstrates its belief in the power of building a brighter future.

CP&L also offers homeowners advice on building energy-efficient homes and improving the efficiency of existing homes. Safety is an important educational focus for the company, too. A CP&L program called TreeSmart advises homeowners, businesses, and municipalities on how to select the right tree for the right place when landscaping, decreasing the chance that the tree will cause an interruption in service.

"CP&L is committed to providing the very best possible service to our 120,000 customers in Western North Carolina," Day said. "And our employees are committed to the communities they serve." By supporting CP&L's Project Share, which assists low-income customers experiencing weather-related crises, and spending thousands of volunteer hours with such organizations as the United Way and Habitat for Humanity, CP&L employees make a difference in Asheville.

Through the company's Adopt State Parks program—the first of its kind in the country—employees volunteer for projects like clearing trails and building picnic tables. In Western North Carolina, CP&L employees have adopted Mount Mitchell, working to improve the grounds for the enjoyment of all park visitors.

With each of these programs CP&L extends its commitment to the community. And while much has changed between those early days of flickering electricity and today, when our hands do not hesitate in their reach for a light switch, one thing has remained constant: CP&L's dedication to the quality of life in Asheville and Western North Carolina. ▲

CHAPTER ELEVEN

MANUFACTURING, DISTRIBUTION, AND TECHNOLOGY

Producing goods for individuals and industry, manufacturing firms provide employment for many Asheville area residents. Research and development activity place the area at the forefront of technology.

Southeastern Container, Inc.

Located in Enka, just west of Asheville, is the headquarters of Southeastern Container, Inc., one of the largest plastic beverage bottle manufacturers in the world. Southeastern Container opened in 1982, when a group of small Coca-Cola bottlers decided to try self-manufacturing as a means of reducing their bottle cost. They hired Richard W. (Dick) Roswech, who had plastic bottle manufacturing experience with the plastics division of Owens-Illinois, to start a production plant manufacturing two-liter plastic beverage bottles. The company is structured as a cooperative, which means that the customers (Coca-Cola bottlers) are also the owners of the business.

Southeastern Container was never expected to grow to its present size. Dick and key managers that contributed to the plant start-up used to joke about "manufacturing a few bottles and playing a lot of golf." The demands of company growth have allowed little time for golf.

Expansion of the business has occurred at a rate far greater than anyone in the company ever anticipated. Many things have contributed to this growth; however, major factors include the company's ability to attract highly skilled key managers, a commitment on the part of management to forge partnerships with important suppliers that have resulted in tremendous advances in technology, and a willingness on the part of the owners to take the risks offered by management that would allow the company to stay ahead of other bottle manufacturers.

The process for manufacturing a plastic beverage bottle begins with small pellets of PET, or polyester terepthalate, a polyester similar to the polyester used in fibers. The PET is injection molded into a test-tube-shaped product with a threaded top ("finish") that looks like the top of a Coke bottle. This part is called a "preform." The preform is then heated and blown ("blow-molded") into the familiar shape of a Coke bottle.

Southeastern Container senior management includes (seated left to right) Cathy Phillips, vice president manufacturing services; Dick Roswech, president and CEO; Henry Pinto, vice president and division manager; Michelle Yanik, vice president human resources; (standing) Charles Capp, vice president finance; and Tom Francis, executive vice president and division manager.

Southeastern Container is one of the largest plastic beverage bottle manufacturers in the world.

In 1982, when the company opened, Southeastern Container operated only the blowmolding process for the production of two-liter bottles. The blowmolding machines were Cincinnati Milacron machines that produced about 3,600 bottles per hour. Word of the company spread to other bottlers who then joined the co-op, and in 1984 production of 16-ounce and three-liter bottles began. The company also purchased their first rotary blowmolding machine, a Sidel SBO 10 that produced 5,000 two-liter bottles per hour.

Southeastern Container worked to develop a close working relationship with Sidel, a French company, that resulted in the ability to create high-speed, efficient blowmolding equipment using the process knowledge contributed by Southeastern and the equipment design expertise of Sidel. The Sidel SBO 10 that was purchased in 1984 was the first of many Sidel machines to be brought into production. An SBO 10 is a rotary blowmolder with 10 mold stations that normally produces about 5,000 bottles per hour. The next machine to be purchased by Southeastern was an SBO 24, which had 24 mold stations and produced approximately 15,000 per hour. This machine was first designed to produce small, single service (16-ounce and 20-ounce) bottles. There was a significant improvement in efficiency when, in 1986, an SBO 24 that produced two-liter bottles was delivered. In 1990 another significant efficiency increase occurred with the installation of the SBO 40, a blowmolding machine with forty molds that produces in excess of 40,000 bottles per hour. As with the SBO 24, the initial machines were designed for single-service production. The first SBO 40 producing two-liter bottles arrived in 1991. The SBO 40 is now the standard blowmolding machine for Southeastern Container. There are other machines in use, but they are primarily designed

Sidel, a French company, has developed high-speed, efficient blowmolding equipment for use in Southeastern Container's production operation.

for production flexibility to produce bottles that are used in lower quantities by the bottlers than the high-demand two-liter and 20-ounce bottles.

Similar growth and development have occurred in the injection molding process. Preforms, in the early 1980s, were produced primarily on 16-cavity injection molding machines (this means that the machine could produce 16 performs at a time, or in one "shot.") When Southeastern bought their first injection molding machines in 1983, they purchased equipment from a Canadian manufacturer, Husky, and requested machines that could produce 32 preforms in a shot. As with Sidel, Southeastern Container worked at developing a close relationship with Husky, and contributed process knowledge that allowed development of higher cavitation injection molding machines. In the mid '80s, 48-cavity two-liter machines were used, and 72-cavity machines were created for the single service bottles. By 1990, 96-cavity machines were in development, and currently, every injection machine at Southeastern Container, with one exception, is a 96-cavity machine. The number of injection machines has also grown dramatically. In 1984 the injection molding department consisted of four 32-cavity two-liter injection machines. There will be 24 injection molding machines in the Enka plant by the end of 1996, with an equal number in the Winchester facility. Both plants have the flexibility to run a variety of sizes.

The development of higher cavitation, more efficient injection molding and blowmolding equipment has brought benefits to the company other than simply more production output. The owners of the company, acting upon the recommendations of top management, have been unusually willing to reinvest savings from increased efficiencies back in to the company. This has allowed Southeastern to maintain state-of-the-art injection and blowmolding equipment. In addition, there have been opportunities to both reduce bottle weights and increase the strength of the bottle due to increased technical knowledge and machine capabilities. These savings have also been reinvested to help maintain Southeastern Container's position as an industry leader.

In addition to the development of more efficient production equipment, the company has also experienced tremendous physical growth. The Enka plant was built in 1982 and has been expanded four times—twice for major manufacturing additions (in 1984 and 1985), and twice for added warehouse space (in 1989 and 1996). There have also been numerous minor changes and additions to allow the building to keep up with production and shipping demands.

The company expanded to Florida in 1988. Located in the heart of Orlando is a manufacturing facility that serves all of the Florida Coca-Cola bottlers and also services bottlers in Alabama and Georgia on a regular basis. This plant is a blowmolding facility only, and receives all of its preforms from the Enka location.

Southeastern's partnership relationship with Sidel has resulted in machines that are computer touch-screen controlled for ease of operation.

In 1991 a major plant was built in Winchester, Virginia. This plant is similar in size to the Enka plant and produces both preforms and bottles. In addition to allowing the company to ship to more bottling locations, the addition of a second injection molding facility brought the flexibility and security of having a second plant with preform production capability. The plant ships to many Coca-Cola bottlers in the mid-Atlantic and Midwest regions, and at times ships into the northeastern United States.

Hudson, New Hampshire, was the location of the next production facility, in 1993. This plant is a blowmolding plant only, receiving its preforms from the Virginia location. Due to the high population concentration in the Northeast, the production from this plant is virtually dedicated to the Coca-Cola bottlers from New York to Maine.

The injection molding department at Southeastern utilizies state-of-the-art molding machines developed by Husky Injection Molding Systems, Ltd. Automatic guided vehicles (AGVs) move the finished product from the injection machines to a staging area for warehousing or shipment to other plants.

The most recent expansion of Southeastern Container occurred in 1995. When the plant was opened in Effingham, Illinois, bottles became available for shipment to the Midwest and western United States. As with the Florida and New Hampshire operations, this plant is a blowmolding facility. The preforms are shipped to Illinois from the Enka production operation.

The product mix at Southeastern Container has grown and changed over the years, in response to the needs of the member bottlers. The two-liter bottle was the first product to be produced in 1982, and 16-ounce and three-liter bottles were added in 1984. Production of one-liter bottles began in 1989, and 20-ounce containers were added in 1991. The Coca-Cola Company modified the design of the 20-ounce bottle to reflect the "contour" shape of the old glass bottles, and production of this new design began in 1994. In 1995 the one-liter bottle was modified to a contour shape, and the 20-ounce and one-liter Sprite bottles were introduced with the "dimple" design that is similar to the original glass packaging. The 16-ounce container was dropped from production at the end of 1995. As design changes occur, Southeastern will continue to meet the needs of its owners.

Southeastern Container employees are trained to operate many different types of production equipment.

The mission of Southeastern Container is to meet the packaging needs of its Coca-Cola bottler/owners by supplying high-quality PET beverage containers while optimizing quality, service, and price. The company strives to meet this mission by maintaining a corporate culture that focuses every employee on the importance of improving quality, reducing costs, and increasing productivity.

Southeastern Container holds regular partnership meetings and seminars with their member bottlers to encourage frequent communication between Southeastern's plants and the bottling operations. The bottlers are encouraged to discuss any issues that arise, and dialogue is encouraged on ways to improve Southeastern's products or processes. At times, focus teams are formed to address items that are global in nature and require in-depth analysis.

Customer service engineers are available to visit and assist bottlers at the production facility. Bottler opinions are surveyed frequently, and information from the surveys is used to evaluate total customer satisfaction.

The "downstream" is the area where all of the finished bottles are stacked, strapped, wrapped, and staged for storage in the warehouse.

Meetings are held periodically between bottling plant employees and employees of Southeastern Container to keep lines of communication open at all levels.

Southeastern Container has established networking relationships with companies in the plastics industry in many parts of the world. It is not unusual to see visitors from Europe, the Far East, or Australia taking a tour of the plant and meeting with employees. Contacts are maintained that allow Southeastern to keep abreast of technical developments that occur globally.

In addition to maintaining communications between Southeastern Container, member bottlers, and plastics industry representatives worldwide, the company also encourages a high level of interaction between the different production facilities. Staff meetings are held monthly that include General Managers from all locations. In addition, technical meetings involving maintenance, engineering, and quality control personnel from each plant are held monthly. These meetings focus on injection molding or blowmolding developments, and often include representatives from Husky, Sidel, or other appropriate suppliers. An important goal of these meetings is to be sure that process improvements are shared among all locations so that quality, cost, and efficiency are optimized company wide.

Southeastern Container is committed to team management. This concept has been introduced "grass roots" at the Virginia, New Hampshire, and Illinois facilities. In Florida and Enka, the concept has been one of gradually changing management styles to encourage employees to become more active in the daily operation of the production process. This is a long-term commitment of the company that should provide benefits to both the owners and the employees of Southeastern Container.

Southeastern Container recognizes that recycling and reuse of the PET container are important issues. Southeastern participates in the National Association for Plastic Container Recovery (NAPCOR) at a board level. In 1988 a full-time staff member was hired to encourage the growth of recycling programs and help develop local markets to purchase collected plastic. In 1989 the company started the first local recycling center that accepted recycled plastic from small regional collection sites. This provided an opportunity for groups collecting relatively small quantities of plastic to sell the plastic and return it to the recycling stream. Southeastern Container's ultimate goal was to develop local markets so that they could buy and sell recycled plastic profitably. This goal was achieved, and the groups that were selling plastic to Southeastern's recycling center were redirected to local organizations that purchased the collected plastic. Southeastern Container continues to remain very involved in the recycling effort.

Southeastern Container's dedication to technical excellence and commitment to optimize resources have served the company well in their first 14 years of growth. The company has achieved a world-class position in the plastics industry, and looks forward to continued improvement in the years to come. ▲

The warehouse at Southeastern Container's Enka facility has a capacity of over 15 million bottles. Finished pallets are shipped out in full truck-load quantities.

Sonopress

President and CEO Michael Harris points out, Sonopress has secured its lead in the industry by adjusting its schedules to match the timetables of its customers.

Off U.S. Highway 25-70 in Weaverville, just north of Asheville, Sonopress bustles with the activity of a manufacturing plant that has not stopped to catch its breath in more than 10 years. Cassettes stamped with the name of John Grisham's latest courtroom drama glide down a conveyor belt. Compact discs gleam with a metallic lustre as they spin freshly minted off the press. And in a nearby room, workers assemble the boxed kits of discs, manuals, and warranties that make up a CD-ROM encyclopedia. Across the plant, engineers mix and master sounds, printers run off glossy cassette inserts, and technicians develop screens for artwork that will decorate both compact discs and their cases.

Sonopress Weaverville manufactures "storage media"—a catch-all term that includes spoken word and music cassettes, compact discs, and CD-ROMs—for clients who range from book publishers to music and computer companies. In the multimedia industry, where the current moves swiftly and success often depends on how soon orders reach the shelves, Sonopress has stayed strokes ahead of the competition by producing quality products at speeds measured to the seconds.

Sonopress is part of the German-based entertainment company Bertelsmann. The second-largest media conglomerate in the world next to Time-Warner, Bertelsmann is composed of more than 300 companies and 50,000 employees. It obtained the Weaverville facility in a 1986 acquisition of RCA Records, which had opened the plant two years before for the production of music cassettes. In 1988 the facility was folded from the RCA division into Bertelsmann's audio manufacturing subsidiary, Sonopress.

Nine production facilities placed in international hubs such as Hong Kong, Dublin, and Mexico City serve as gateways to major markets and give Sonopress access to service and distribution networks that traverse the globe. The Weaverville facility, currently the company's only manufacturing site in the United States, is no different. To RCA, and in turn to Bertelsmann, Weaverville represented the perfect location for production: it was close to the populous East Coast market, which cut shipping times and costs, yet the price of land and labor was substantially lower than in cities farther north.

The choice of locale paid off in a strong, reliable workforce that continues to meet the challenge of the company's rapid expansion into new services and technologies. With 100 million cassettes shipped from the facility each year, Sonopress Weaverville has become the largest cassette manufacturer in the country. But the biggest change for the facility came in 1993 when it began to produce compact discs and CD-ROMs. Within three years the workforce doubled from 400 to 800 employees, while a series of expansions tripled the size of the facility to 475,000 square feet. Today, Sonopress Weaverville ranks as a leading manufacturer of discs for both the music and computer industries, with annual shipments of more than 165 million.

Off U.S. Highway 25-70 in Weaverville, just north of Asheville, Sonopress bustles with the activity of a manufacturing plant that has not stopped to catch its breath in more than 10 years.

At Sonopress, a run of Whitney Houston compact discs for Arista one day may be followed by a run of Beethoven symphonies for BMG Classics on the next. Because what is being manufactured fluctuates order by order, the company has no inventory of finished products on which to draw. As a result, Sonopress Weaverville must depend on lightning turnaround in every step of its operations. And while rushing to complete an order, not only must plant employees juggle an ever-changing crop of master recordings, but they must also match these recordings with artwork and packaging specifications that change with each client.

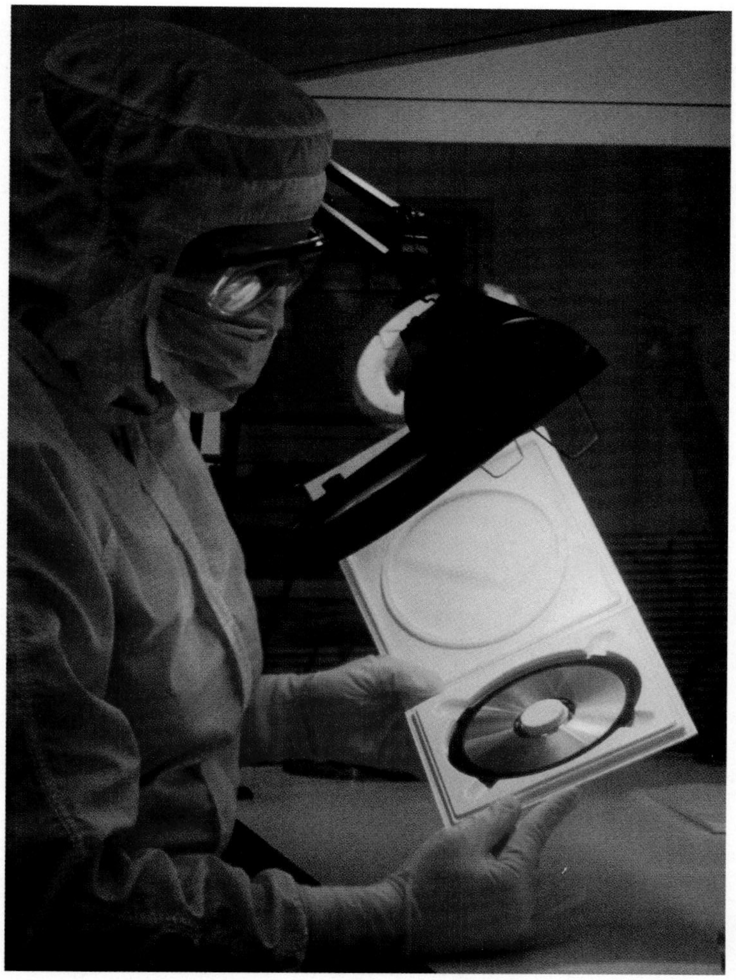

Sonopress has stayed strokes ahead of the competition by producing quality products. Final inspection of the stamper takes place in a Class 1,000 clean room to ensure the highest quality sound.

To succeed in a competitive market, Sonopress has given a service-driven edge to its manufacturing process. For example, turnaround time is usually five days for a new release and three days for a reorder. But, as President Michael Harris points out, Sonopress has secured its lead in the industry by adjusting this schedule to match the timetables of its customers, even when that means working six and seven days a week. "If it's a good customer of ours and they say that they need an order shipped by tomorrow morning, more often than not we will ship it tomorrow morning," he explains. "We try to be very responsive to our customers."

The manufacture of cassettes, once the company's mainstay, still plays a vital role at Sonopress Weaverville. In addition to production of music cassettes for sister companies in the Bertelsmann family, such as BMG, RCA, and Arista, the company counts Disney, Soundmakers, and Northword as customers. Sonopress is also one of the largest producers of books on tape, with clients that include Bantam Audio Publishing, Harper & Row, Simon & Schuster, and Random House.

The whirred rustle of spinning reels announces the area of the plant where cassettes are made. Here an original recording is duplicated onto what looks like old-fashioned movie reels called "pancakes." A single pancake can hold many copies of the same recording, usually 40 or more—the exact figure varying, of course, with the length of what's being duplicated. After being tested for quality and sound, the pancakes are moved into a loading area where the tape of the reel is broken back down into individual duplications and loaded into cassette cartridges. Through a series of automated steps, these cartridges are printed on and then packed into plastic cases in which the glossy inserts that form the cassette cover have already been placed. Once assembled, the cassettes are shrink-wrapped and stacked into boxes, ready to be shipped.

This production line is clearly not under the auspices of the Dewey decimal system: a reading of a Western by Louis L'Amour may come hard on the heels of a horror story by Stephen King. But quality checkpoints help to guarantee that no mix-ups occur, such as, for example, a recording of rap music being mistakenly switched for one of children's programming. "I can say confidently that there are few audio manufacturers who strive to the extent that we do to minimize those types of errors," states Harris.

As an audio manufacturer, Sonopress Weaverville is dedicated to replicating the sounds of original recordings with flawless clarity. But its pursuit of quality goes far beyond sound fidelity. For instance, having noticed that

When the Weaverville facility began to manufacture compact discs in 1993, it borrowed technology developed by a Sonopress plant in Germany. The engineers at the German facility created a machine known as a Sonoliner that presses compact discs with the precision of a diamond cutter.

Sonopress completes on-time distribution of the customer's final product.

The Sonopress facility is complete with a sound studio for critical listening of a master tape.

books on tape often had blurry printing on the sides of the cassette, a team of engineers and machine operators reworked the production process until the finished print was sharp and clear. It is meticulous attention to details such as these, notes Harris, that adds polish to all of the plant's operations.

As music lovers know, compact discs deliver a peak in sound experience. From a blues musician's murmured aside to the pealed notes of an opera diva, CDs capture it all. When the Weaverville facility began to manufacture compact discs in 1993, it borrowed technology initially developed by a Sonopress plant based in Germany. As pioneers in the art of CD-manufacturing, the engineers at the German facility created a machine known as a Sonoliner that presses compact discs with the precision of a diamond cutter.

A Sonoliner is a complete manufacturing cell, responsible for all of the steps necessary to transform raw materials into a compact disc ready to be played. It fuses quality with speed. A CD is completed every 5 seconds, a time that is continually being pared down to remain among the lowest in the industry. And because the disc is not being moved from machine to machine, the risk of damage is decreased and the process easily controlled and monitored.

The first step in the Sonoliner is the most critical: the disc, formed from a clear polycarbonate, is clapped between two metal pieces shaped like cymbals. During the short seconds that follow, audio is stamped onto the disc by injection molding. Once the disc is released, it rotates along the Sonoliner to be metallized and lacquered. Now a familiar silver, the disc's face is printed by rollers hooked to robotic arms that draw up colors from three ink trays housed in the machine. The disc is then ejected from the Sonoliner and, after a run is completed, taken to another part of the factory for packaging.

The 40 Sonoliners at the Weaverville facility also produce CD-ROMs. A medium that blends text and animated graphics with sound, CD-ROMs represent one of the fastest-growing markets in the multimedia industry. And with Microsoft, America Online, and IBM/Lotus already included as clients, Sonopress Weaverville is positioned to grow with it.

Obviously the manufacture of CD-ROMs demands space-age technology to transfer intact all the bits of data—from speech to moving pictures to song—on the disc. Less obvious is the amount of manufacturing that goes into the CD-ROM kit that comes with the discs—a sheaf of manuals, brochures, and warranties as thick as the discs are slim.

Sonopress Weaverville has always integrated the printing and packaging needs of its customers with production, beginning with the fold-out inserts that come inside a cassette case. With compact discs, these inserts, and the packages in which they're placed, have become increasingly elaborate. Boxed sets, for example, have discs configured in special patterns alongside a booklet that chronicles the history of the musician. Or CDs for children might come with a cardboard cutout of a character like Mickey Mouse and a read-along story book.

CD-ROMs take the complexity of these packaging requirements one step further. Not only are the manuals for the discs bigger than story books, but they are also accompanied by piracy protection mechanisms such as holograms and watermarks. Serial-numbered certificates enclosed with the discs can be logged and tracked by Sonopress to further protect its customers from counterfeiters. All of these components must come together in a package that attracts the sophisticated eye of the computer aficionado.

Computer companies are eager to outsource all of the services associated with production, explains Harris. As a result, Sonopress Weaverville should grow in coming years as it increases the volume of its production while expanding its printing and assembly division to cater to its newest clients. While many of these packaging innovations can be automated, many more cannot and will depend on a large pool of employees to assemble the kits by hand.

While growth has been courted by the company, it has brought its own challenges. Change has touched every inch of the facility, from what's being produced to how many employees it takes to produce it. As a result, Sonopress has embarked on a quality assurance program to ensure that all of its products continue to meet the highest requirements set worldwide. Quality engineers measure the plant's performance daily, placing equal emphasis on both the product and the service with which it's delivered. "When you deal in large volumes like we do, it's imperative that every cog of your operation runs smoothly," states Harris. "We want to be sure that when we run into a problem, we attack it at its roots."

Automated packaging of CDs and graphics ensures a better quality product and reduces the risk of damage to the final product.

The company's whirlwind expansion has been welcomed by the Weaverville community and the surrounding area, where Sonopress is seen as a progressive and people-oriented employer. A competitive compensation and benefits package, which includes annual profit sharing, is matched with a dedication to keeping employees informed and involved in all aspects of the business.

But Sonopress's popularity in the community extends beyond the realm of economic development. The company is a generous supporter of local organizations and events. Each year, Sonopress is involved in such festivals as Bele Chere and Shindig on the Green and lends support to groups like the United Way and YMCA. Not surprising in a manufacturer of music, the company is also a patron of Asheville's thriving arts community through its donations to WCQS, Asheville Community Concerts, and the Arts Alliance. It just goes to show that whether it be at home or abroad, Sonopress Weaverville is a company bent on delivering the best in sound. ▲

Original recordings are duplicated onto what looks like old-fashioned movie reels called "pancakes" to produce a cassette. A single pancake can hold many copies of the same recording.

Fishburne International

Frank Fishburne Jr. looks you straight in the eye when he says his company is like family. This is no front-office hype, just a way a life, the one he inherited from his father. Since 1948, when Frank Fishburne Sr. founded Fishburne International, this family business has been designing and manufacturing tobacco presses known the world over for reliability and performance.

But the family Frank Jr. refers to extends well beyond bloodlines. It includes the 102 employees of Fishburne International, 28 of whom have been with the company 10 years or more. "We care about our employees," Frank Jr. states. "We are invited to their weddings; we attend their family funerals. They are the most important asset of this business."

Under the leadership of (left to right) David Felts, vice president of sales and Frank B. Fishburne Jr., president and chairman of the board of directors, Fishburne products have continued to improve.

Being family makes a difference. Because turnover is virtually nonexistent, Fishburne International reaps the benefits of an educated and dedicated workforce. As a result, the company has earned 80 to 90 percent market share of all tobacco presses built in the world. "While in Czechoslovakia a few years ago a tobacco plant manager told me that Fishburne is the Mercedes of the tobacco presses," Frank Jr. muses. "A year and a half ago in China a man told me Fishburne is the Rolls Royce of tobacco presses. And in Zimbabwe it isn't called a tobacco press; it's a Fishburne. Money can't buy that kind of reputation."

What gave them this edge? "My father's genius," Frank Jr. answers without a moment's hesitation. "He was a brilliant engineer and designer, and we're still building on that genius." It seems Frank Sr. had quite a reputation as an engineering wizard, and in 1948 he was asked to solve a problem that would revolutionize the industry. In those days tobacco was packed into straight-sided wooden barrels called "hogsheads." The leaf had to be packed from below to ensure that oil leakage of the ram cylinder would not contaminate it. (A single drop of hydraulic fluid can ruin an entire thousand pound hogshead). Trouble arose when a tobacco processor in Asheville needed to install a tobacco press in a facility along the banks of the Swannanoa River. The shallow bedrock and water table ruled out conventional up-packing presses that required a deep pit below the factory floor to house the machinery. It didn't take a genius to see that the only solution was down-packing. It did take a genius to design a down-packing cylinder that successfully prevented fluid leaks. And while he was at it, Frank Sr. built in a few other bonuses—the new process reduced the time to pack the hogshead and enhanced the quality of the packed leaf.

Over the years Fishburne products continued to improve, and word spread. In 1960 their first Fishburne press went to Canada. Thirty-five years later Fishburne machinery is installed in 55 countries, placing Fishburne International among the top 20 exporting companies based in North Carolina. As the growth markets for tobacco extended into developing nations, Fishburne established a strong presence in Brazil, Zimbabwe, and China, to name a few.

In keeping with the family tradition, Frank Jr. invests in the future by providing opportunities for the ambitious. "Ambitious people are your best employees. We have a nice opportunity path here. I think that's why people stay with us. Someone can come here not knowing anything and sweep the floors. Then he can learn to weld; he can learn to read blueprints; he can learn to fit materials to make machinery. If he is reliable and honest, he can start doing some field work for us at higher

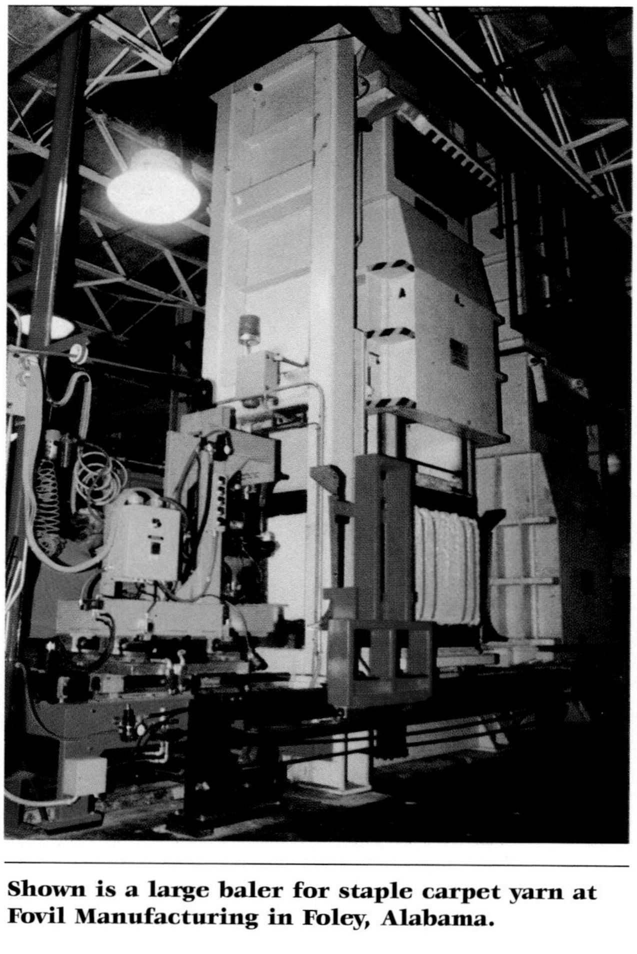

Shown is a large baler for staple carpet yarn at Fovil Manufacturing in Foley, Alabama.

A welder is grinding a weldment smooth in Fishburne shops.

rates and a per diem. And if he works in the field long enough, he'll learn about hydraulics and the electrical aspects of our business. He can become a service person who could travel to installations all around the world making good money."

Fishburne's reputation comes from a combination of product excellence and unparalleled service. Their products are based entirely on customers' needs. "We engineer solutions for our customer—and from the solutions come the equipment," states David Felts, vice president of sales. "We are in a position to provide their exact needs." Each customized press is a major undertaking—a specific design for a specific machine for a specific task. And all equipment is built with the possibility of expansion in mind. In fact, one of the company's original presses from 1958 is still running today.

As new trends develop, the company is diversifying beyond its historic tobacco roots into synthetic fibers and cotton. Ten years ago when DuPont and Celanese needed very large textile balers, they called on Fishburne ingenuity to create a fully automatic operation. In 1994 Fishburne introduced a baler to the cotton ginning industry. Its sophisticated design and state-of-the-art systems have created a near insatiable demand ever since.

To accommodate these new directions, Fishburne International recently expanded its manufacturing operations to a 63,000-square-foot facility in the Vista Industrial Park. The move provided a safer environment for its employees and increased production capabilities.

Diversification into fiber baling calls for increasingly heavier components. Tobacco presses, for example, require 40 tons of pressure and cotton presses up to 500 tons.

Frank Jr. sees to it that the family connection extends beyond the workplace. Employees are encouraged to coach Little League baseball and soccer, and each department has its own budget for contributions to employees' favorite charities. The company takes its role in the community seriously. Frank Jr. is committed to their support of the Chamber of Commerce's Economic Development Commission working to attract high-paying manufacturing jobs and assisting existing industries in their needs to grow.

Fishburne's policy of innovation and reward keeps the future bright. "We have some very creative people around here with unique design capabilities," Frank Jr. states. "Right now we are in tobacco, cotton, and synthetic fibers. But that is not to say we cannot do a project for anyone else, too, if we see a future market unfolding." ▲

Fishburne International is among the top 20 exporting companies based in North Carolina. Shown is a single ram extrusion baler for tobacco at P. T. Djarum in Kudus, Indonesia.

Knight Manufacturing

Ask Thomas Finger, president of Knight Manufacturing, about his company, and he enthusiastically lists off its attributes. It takes both hands. "We're new, progressive, aggressive, efficient, dependable, and innovative. We have the most modern computerized machinery making state-of-the-art-equipment." Actually, he is being humble. His manufacturing of dental chairs, stools, lights, and delivery systems (systems for delivering air and water to dental instruments) can also boast rapid growth, remarkable turnaround time, consolidated ordering, and easy maintenance.

With 40 percent of its business international, Knight Manufacturing and its complete line of products are respected worldwide. With so many languages and cultures to serve, it is committed to shipping uncomplicated, reliable products that are simple to maintain and repair. Replacement parts are easily accessible, and all Knight products are value priced. Its equipment comes with the features and benefits of more expensive products but only at a mid-range price.

Knight's reputation for innovation is unparalleled—in the past three years it has introduced 20 new products. "This is almost unheard of in the industry; companies can take seven years to develop one product. We have a fantastic research and design department that seems to hit the nail on the head every time. And we are able to bring these designs to market quickly." Stool designs, for example, are based on research into physical stresses on the body and incorporate features that make the doctors and assistants more comfortable. Knight also developed a new light that allows the doctor to see better, increasing efficiency and cutting down on eye strain.

Because no other company in the United States manufactures more parts in-house, it can deliver its products within two weeks. That, too, is almost unheard of. Industry averages range from 6 to 16 weeks, depending on the time of year and the number of orders. The company's proficiency also benefits from five sister companies that handle metalworking needs such as electroplating, heat treating, painting, and polishing.

Knight's reputation for innovation is unparalleled—in the past three years it has introduced 20 new products.

Finger is quick to credit his employees for his company's quality products and service. "Everyone who comes here from around the world comments on our friendly atmosphere. That's because people feel part of the team. They share in the profits through bonuses and a lucrative retirement program. This creates a better workplace and, as a result, a better product. We very seldom have anyone leave." When Finger purchased Knight Manufacturing in 1987, there were only 12 employees; today that number has skyrocketed to 125, and Knight Manufacturing has grown from a non-entity to one of the largest manufacturers of dental equipment in the United States in eight years.

Knight's corporate office sales team has helped the company grow to become one of the largest manufacturers of dental equipment in the United States.

Finger exudes an obvious affection for the community he lives and works in. He has recently donated two complete offices of equipment (stools, chair, delivery system, and lights) to the Billy Graham Mobile Dental Unit and another two offices to Asheville Buncombe Community Christian Ministry Clinic. And when he can, he names a product after the region, like his new Biltmore Chair, so named due to the proximity of Knight Manufacturing to the village of Biltmore.

As for the future, Finger sees the expansion continuing. "We are in a rapid growth mode with new products coming out all the time. We are on a roll." ▲

T.L.F., Inc.

Last year when Thomas Finger was named North Carolina Small Business Person of the Year by the United States Small Business Administration, he won top honors due to his extraordinary success with not one, but five companies.

"We have a family of metal finishing companies under one umbrella—T.L.F., Inc.," Finger states, "which enables us to provide our customers unparalleled service. They hand us their product, we take away all their shipping and receiving worries, and return to them a finished product. We take pride in meeting our customers' needs, which is exactly why we acquired these companies."

It all began in 1983 with Asheville Metal Finishing, Inc. specializing in difficult electroplating jobs in the automotive, medical, and recreational fields. Six years later the 20,500-square-foot Dotson Metal Finishing, Inc. was acquired to handle a variety of finishes, from anodizing to zinc. In 1991 Southeastern Heat Treating, Inc., with its 14,000-square-foot plant, added electroplating processes, annealing, vacuum brazing, and hardening, to name a few. In 1992 buffing and polishing needs were met by Charlotte Metal Finishing, Inc, the only T.L.F. facility outside the immediate region. Asheville Paint and Powder Coat, Inc., the newest company, is a fully automated operation opened in 1996.

Tracking the processing of mirror brackets for the Ford Motor Company provides a good example of how these companies work together. "We heat treat the bracket at Southeastern Heat Treating, polish and copper-nickel-chrome plate it at Asheville Metal Finishing, and then put a clear coat powder paint on it at Asheville Paint and Powder. We are a one-stop shop for metal finishing services."

In 1991 Southeastern Heat Treating, Inc., with its 14,000-square-foot plant, added electroplating processes, annealing, vacuum brazing, and hardening. Shown here is the auto belt furnace.

Savings of time and money are considerable. Rather than cutting individual orders for three to five different companies, their customers cut only one order. Internally, T.L.F. handles everything and ships them a finished product. This integrated process also cuts down on the time from when they ship to T.L.F. until they receive it back. "Say a customer needs all these functions," Finger explains. "They do not cut five individual purchase orders; their inside personnel don't have to keep up with five different companies; they don't have to ship it and receive it five times, and they don't have to inspect it five different times. On our end, we don't have to handle five different invoices. From shipping to accounts payable to receiving it saves a lot of money. Our marketing research shows that it costs $75 to cut the typical purchase order. That can mean a $300 savings just in placing the order."

T.L.F. serves customers in the automotive, aviation, construction, medical, and recreational fields, and can custom plate based on any specification. It meets all military, industrial, and medical specifications. And this dynamic team contributes to the success of Finger's other business, Knight Manufacturing, maker of dental equipment.

Efficient and cost-effective, these companies today are manufacturing 20 times what they were in 1983.

Asheville Paint and Powder Coat, Inc., a fully automated operation which opened in 1996, is the newest company in the T.L.F. family. Pictured here is the auto spray booth.

BASF Corporation

For almost 70 years the community of Enka has played a key role as part of a large international corporation of fiber producers.

Today, the BASF Corporation Enka site is part of the Fiber Products Division, a leading global producer of nylon fibers and intermediates. The division maintains major integrated production facilities and market presence in the NAFTA Region, Europe, and the Far East. The BASF Group, with headquarters in Germany, is one of the world's largest chemical companies and conducts business in more than 170 countries.

Basofil fibers are used in fire blocking and heat insulating fabrics, protective apparel, and high temperature filtration. Fire fighters wear Basofil-based fire suits.

The BASF Enka site was established originally in 1928 as the American Enka Company, by the Netherlands Artificial Silk Company of Arnhem, Holland, to open the North American market for rayon products. The company purchased 2,200 acres of farmland west of Asheville, known as the Hominy Valley, and built their first United States plant to produce rayon yarns. The bed of Hominy Creek was changed to circle the plant site, and a large area was flooded to create an artificial lake, now known as Enka Lake, to serve as a reservoir. In addition to plant construction, a cafeteria, clubhouse, stores building, post office, and village with houses for workers were built nearby. The community became known as Enka, and the post office and nearby middle school and high school still carry the name.

The name Enka comes from the Dutch pronunciation of "N.K.," the initial letters of the parent company, Nederlandsche Kunstzijdefabriek, which later changed its name to A.K.U. In 1954 the Enka site added nylon production and became the first United States producer of fine denier Nylon 6. Over the years, production increased and the plant supplied fibers for everything from high-priced fine apparel and hosiery to tire cord and other high-strength fibers for military applications, as well as nylon carpet yarns. The company enjoyed its greatest growth period during the 1960s.

BASF purchased American Enka Company in 1985. Today, the BASF Enka site is composed of manufacturing facilities, a research and development center, and a multistory office building that houses corporate engineering and other corporate and regional offices.

Under the leadership of General Manager Jack Dellinger, the Enka site manufactures products for use both internally within BASF and externally to worldwide markets. Millions of pounds of washed and dried Nylon 6 chips, no bigger than a slice of spaghetti, are produced at Enka and shipped to BASF's state-of-the-art Clemson, South Carolina, facility, where they are melted and extruded to produce a variety of carpet yarns.

Also produced at Enka is the Resistat® fiber collection, one of the most diverse in the world, which includes melt spun polyester, melt spun nylon, and carbon suffused nylon conductive fiber products.

A $17-million antistatic fibers plant began manufacturing at Enka in 1993. Designed for the carpet industry, the antistatic fiber eliminates static shock. This fiber is shipped to the BASF Clemson and Anderson, South Carolina, and Arnprior, Canada, plants.

In 1993, BASF's conductive fibers operation relocated to Enka, and the process has been in continuous expansion. This carbon-coated fiber is used in carpet applications, clean room garments, and by manufacturers of copy machines such as Xerox to reduce static and for other industrial applications. In addition to sales within BASF, conductive fibers are shipped throughout the United States, Europe, and Asia.

The world's first commercial plant to produce Basofil® heat and flame resistant fiber started production in mid-1996 at Enka. Basofil fibers are used in fire blocking and heat insulating fabrics, protective apparel, and high temperature filtration. Applications for Basofil fiber include the fire-blocking layer in aircraft seating, which reduces the flame spread during a crash, allowing passengers to exit safely.

These plants are in the process of achieving ISO 9002 certification, assuring customers that they conform to quality standards and practices accepted throughout the world.

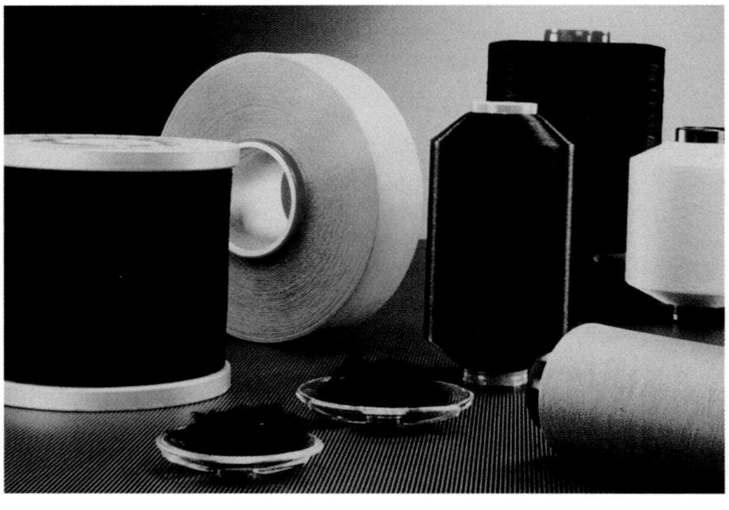

Resistat conductive fibers are used in carpet applications, clean room garments, and by manufacturers of copy machines.

The BASF Corporation Enka site is part of the Fiber Products Division, a leading global producer of nylon fibers and intermediates.

Another major partner at the BASF Enka Site is the Fiber Products Division Research and Development Center headed by Otto M. Ilg, vice president of technology. A diverse and highly skilled group of chemists, engineers, and technicians are organized into project teams in support of all division business units and sites. Assisted by research and development work, the division as a whole has enjoyed improvements in all areas of the fiber manufacturing process, cost, and in fiber quality. New products introduced recently as a result of research and development projects include fibers with excellent stain resistance, reduced flammability, fibers for static control in garments, carpets, and industrial end-uses, and a very successful line of specialty products for swimwear and intimate apparel fabrics. Through close cooperation with the marketing, sales, and manufacturing groups, all products found excellent customer acceptance. BASF is known for its emphasis on science and technology, and the research group at Enka alone has several hundred patents to its credit over the last 10 years. Current projects deal with several new carpet fiber products, advanced fibers for control of static electricity, and new introductions for the apparel textile market. The research center is proud of its state-of-the-art equipment in its laboratories, highly versatile facilities for spinning a multitude of fibers, and of its own library with several thousand volumes and a database of over 20,000 technical documents.

The Southeastern Corporate Engineering Group, under the direction of Charles M. Finley, provides design and engineering for the Fiber Products Division, as well as other BASF facilities in the Southeast. Working with a joint venture partner in China, the engineers are directing the construction of the first Nylon 6 carpet fiber manufacturing plant there. Also located at Enka are the southeastern technical purchasing department and the patent department that supports intellectual properties—that is, the patents, discoveries, and processes.

Environmental considerations rank high in company priorities that feature programs to keep the local community informed of what is happening at the site. The BASF Enka site is a low-risk facility that meets, and in some cases exceeds, the OSHA guidelines for safety procedures.

Active in the community, BASF employees support numerous organizations such as United Way, Habitat for Humanity, Junior Achievement, March of Dimes, American Red Cross, American Cancer Society, Asheville Symphony and Chamber Music, Asheville Art Museum, and many other charitable, cultural, and social institutions. ▲

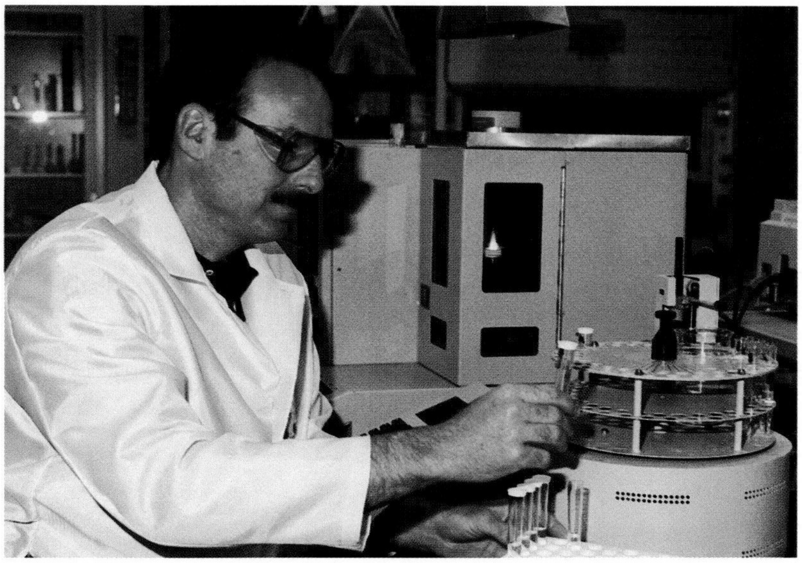

The research center is proud of its state-of-the-art equipment in its laboratories at BASF's Enka site.

Square D Company

It is easy to write a mission statement—the hard work comes in living up to it. But a combination of highly innovative designs and keenly invested employees makes the Square D Asheville mission statement read like the daily news: "...to produce electromechanical products and associated components with service which exceeds our customers' expectations and that positively contributes to our corporate objectives." That is what they do, day after day, with an impressive list of awards and certifications to prove it. Square D is a Xerox Globally Certified Supplier, and it has received the General Motors Target for Excellence Award, the Asheville Area Chamber of Commerce Manufacturer of the Year Award, and the Manufacturing Excellence Award from *Controls & Systems Magazine.* The company also earned ISO 9001 Certification four years ago, which informs—and guarantees—the world of the quality of their electrical control products.

"Every day is race day" is a motto that circulates throughout the 317,000-square-foot Square D Asheville plant. *Photo by Tim Barnwell.*

In 1991 the 88-year-old Square D Company became part of Groupe Schneider, the leading global manufacturer of electrical and electronic equipment based in Paris, France, with sales of $11 billion in 1994. Square D Asheville is part of Schneider North America, which is headquartered in Palatine, Illinois, and oversees 38 manufacturing facilities and 17,500 employees. Sales in 1994 were $1.9 billion.

"Every day is race day" is a motto that circulates throughout the 317,000-square-foot Asheville plant which began operation in 1961. This philosophy stands behind every control device manufactured by every factory associate. "We have a team of people who are giving it their best every day," states Plant Operations Manager Mike Adams. "What differentiates in manufacturing today is not quality. Fundamentally, everyone who is out there manufacturing is doing quality work. The benchmark today is customer service."

"We are a very complex operation producing 25 different product families and over 30 million configurations. Because we make so many different products, we are broken down into product work cells. Each has a manufacturing supervisor, two engineers, a materials person, and a well-trained, dedicated team of factory associates. Customers visit Asheville to see a modern, efficient, automated plant. When they get here they realize the added benefit of Asheville's natural beauty and the energy of our enthusiastic factory associates."

Environmental considerations are important to the company. A new wastewater treatment system is now in full operation. The $880,000 system was designed to process as many as 200,000 gallons of wastewater per month through a series of 27 membranes to ensure the water is safe before entering the sewer system. Employees also contribute to the recycling center—all proceeds from the drink cans, newspaper, and computer paper collected and sold make up the Helping Hands Committee Catastrophe Fund that assists employees in need. Square D associates are generous within the community, as well. Over the last 10 years they averaged nearly $100,000 per year in contributions to the United Way.

Square D is deservedly proud of its safety record. Earlier this year they attained 8 million work hours without a lost time accident. Not only is safety a good indicator of factors like efficiency, morale, and training, but also low workers' compensation premiums mean they can invest these funds in wages, training, and work environment improvement.

The company has developed an impressive series of seminars, incentives, and rewards. Consider Vision College, a training program for all Square D employees from plants across the country. Over a three-year period

The Air Switch Team received international recognition from Schneider North America as "The Team Who Made a Difference." *Photo by Tim Barnwell.*

Square D is a Xerox Globally Certified Supplier, and it has received the General Motors Target for Excellence Award, the Asheville Area Chamber of Commerce Manufacturer of the Year Award, and the Manufacturing Excellence Award from *Controls & Systems Magazine*. *Photo by Tim Barnwell.*

Square D is a very complex operation producing 25 different product families and over 30 million configurations. Because it makes so many different products, the company is broken down into product work cells. *Photo by Tim Barnwell.*

during the late 1980s, three different "campuses" hosted students for two days of classes on personal accountability, customer service, and the three Ps—power, permission, and protection. "We empower our people with the three Ps," explains Richard Hurley, Human Resources Manager. "The power to make a decision, the permission to make that decision, and the protection from any repercussions. If something goes wrong on a line, an operator can shut the line down without worrying about it." More than six years later, framed diplomas and school pennants still hang proudly in the team areas.

Awards and recognition play an important role at Square D. The Quality Certification Program, an internal Square D program started in Asheville, recognizes associates for meeting certification standards involving product quality, safety, cleanliness, and customer service. Signs with chevron-shaped emblems representing certification levels hang above each work area.

"People Who Make A Difference" is a Schneider North America reward system recognizing excellence in all 38 plant locations. This year, five factory associates who manufacture air switches used in industrial applications won North American recognition as "The Team Who Made a Difference" due to their impeccable quality record, coupled with reduced turnaround time from three weeks to three days, and dramatically increased customer service numbers. Their pride, loyalty, and enthusiasm typify the positive attitudes of self-directed teams of Square D Asheville.

Quote 2 Cash is a unique company system that can track the order from the salesperson's quote to the final payment. "Cycle time reduction is a big deal these days," Adams states. "Getting it to your customers quicker is key. Yesteryear it was, 'We'll have it for you in a couple of weeks.' Today it's more like, 'Why don't you try to get it to me tomorrow?' "

How do these innovations in management affect the finished product? "In a very positive way," Adams answers quickly. "We have seen all our measurements over the past 10 years get much better. In addition to our reputation with external customers, Square D Asheville is also becoming a fabrication hub for Schneider North America." Why? "Our people do it better. We are leading edge in many arenas because continuous improvement is a way of life." ▲

Rockwell Truck Axle Business

Rockwell Truck Axle Business has a history of doing things right—right from the beginning in 1983 when they began producing the best truck axles on the market at the best cost. What has made them so successful? "Our people," states Steve Wells, general manager of the plant, "all 750 of them."

Employee involvement is the cornerstone of what makes Rockwell work. Rather than operating under a traditional management-oriented structure, this 491,000-square-foot plant functions with 50 self-directed work teams. Not only do they work together, but they also consult on hiring and promoting, resolve disputes, and serve on various committees, and together they produce hundreds of thousands of axles for heavy- and medium-duty trucks every year. Of the three primary suppliers in the truck axle business, Rockwell enjoys the largest share of market with customers such as Freightliner, Ford, Volvo, Navistar, Paccar, Mack, and Western Star. Last year's sales were in excess of $435 million from this plant alone, representing its automotive division of parent company Rockwell International, which employs 82,000 at 450 locations in 26 countries.

Rather than operating under a traditional management-oriented structure, Rockwell Truck Axle Business functions with 50 self-directed work teams.

It takes a different style of plant manager to ensure the success of the self-directed work teams. No problem is dismissed, no concern too small to be discussed. "I came out of a union plant, and managing in this type of environment is much more difficult. But it is worth it," states Wells. "This is a fun company to work with. My door is always open, and people can come talk anytime they want. This type of atmosphere requires a different kind of manager, someone who cares about people."

No coats and ties distinguish managers from workers. No reserved parking places, no special perks. In the place of supervisors, coaches help facilitate the group, acting as someone employees can go to when they need resources outside the team. Coaches may have 1 or 10 teams, and each team ranges from 20 to 50 people. Teams learn to establish their own budgets, contact customers directly, and visit the customers and the suppliers. All of which just makes good sense to Wells. "They are the ones who understand what we do best, and they are experts in the process."

And the system works. In 1983 the plant was producing 350 axles a day. Today that number runs as high as 1,325 a day, the result of expanded shifts, a new product line, and automation. "We are the lowest cost manufacturer of drive axle components in the company today, and it is primarily because of our teams and a relentless effort to reduce costs. In May 1992, we brought the front steering axle business down here as a result of shutting down an unprofitable plant. We set out to understand the customers' requirements and turned our teams loose on it. It is doing great now."

The key words that drive manufacturing and service here are quality, reliability, and integrity. To maintain the quality they are known for, they often survey their customers to find out and stay on top of their requirements. Ask any of these team players, and they will tell you the customer is first. "There is a great pride in ownership with our delivery credibility. Most years we have 100 percent delivery. When we agree to ship to a customer, we achieve that within the time we promised."

Employees receive training on the job and are encouraged to continue their education after hours. Back in the early 1980s when Rockwell first came to Western North Carolina, most of the people hired were local, rounded out by more experienced staff from Midwestern facilities. There was a large, supportive effort by the state, Asheville and Hendersonville Chambers of Commerce, and the technical schools in training people for new industries. The state paid for materials and a full-time instructor, and Rockwell set up its own machinery at Asheville Buncombe Technical Community College for training classes in bevel-gear cutting. Welding training was accomplished through Blue Ridge Community College in Henderson County. Technical training is now conducted in-house, and in some cases, accredited by the local colleges. For those who want to pursue their associate degrees, Rockwell provides assistance, as well.

Rockwell is known throughout the region for offering the best benefits, and the reputation is well-deserved. All employees are salaried and guaranteed 40 hours weekly. If they have a dentist or doctor's appointment, for example, they do not lose their pay for that time. The company pays overtime, which is voluntary, and vacation time can run as high as four weeks after nine years. Ninety percent of the employees are shareholders in the company, and they all participate in the retirement plan, generous savings program, and a profit sharing plan that pays quarterly based on plant performance. Wells reports that

Employees receive training on the job and are encouraged to continue their education after hours.

The people of Rockwell Truck Axle Business are credited with producing the best truck axles on the market.

they survey the area annually to stay in the top 10 percent of wages. "We have no problem getting people, and we lose very few. A lot of families work here—sisters and brothers, husbands and wives. Everybody helps everybody, and that's the way it should be."

An excellent safety record is always a good barometer of other factors like training and morale. For 12 years in a row Rockwell has received North Carolina's Safety Award as well as the Rockwell President's Award for Safety. The company has also won awards for its environmental projects and processes.

Aside from what it takes to make an axle, Rockwell expends tremendous effort in the community. At every level employees are committed to programs such as Big Brothers/Big Sisters, YMCA, United Way, and working in and with the schools. Education obviously ranks high for this company, and they donate money, computers, and other equipment to local schools.

Wells is proud of his team. "We're the flagship. We are the best facility within automotive with the highest inventory turnover in the industry and lowest cost worldwide. We are the benchmark because we had the wisdom in the 1980s to hire the right kind of people. We expect a lot out of them, and they give us that and more." ▲

Employee involvement is the cornerstone of what makes Rockwell work.

NCI, Inc.

Step inside NCI, Inc.'s modern facility, and the sense that something special is happening here becomes immediately apparent. The feeling starts in the lobby, where a wall is filled with quality achievement supplier awards and continues into the modern 85,000-square-foot plant where state-of-the-art machine tools efficiently and exactingly produce gleaming precision products dedicated to the aerospace industry. Highly trained employees track and trace each product from the receiving of raw materials through the production and shipping of the finished products.

After materials pass receiving inspection at NCI, they head to the CNC lathe turning department, where they rotate while the massive lathes begin the metal removal process to meet the configuration specified on the blueprint.

NCI has earned a worldwide reputation for excellence. For the past 30 years, virtually all major commercial and military aircraft have contained NCI's precision jet engine components. But the company's history in Western North Carolina precedes its specialization in aerospace. Almost 50 years ago, the company, then known as Oerlikon Tool and Arms, was a modeling, preproduction shop that evolved to produce major textile equipment sold worldwide. During the 1960s and 1970s, the company began to turn toward the aerospace industry while under the name of Amcel Propulsion and later Northrop Carolina. In 1974 the machined products division of Northrop Carolina was purchased by King Fifth Wheel, headquartered in Philadelphia, Pennsylvania. The company then adopted the name of NCI, Inc. Seven years later the King Fifth Wheel Corporation was purchased by London-based TI Group, and NCI is now part of Dowty Aerospace, one of the three major international divisions of TI Group.

NCI is respected throughout the industry for its remarkably efficient turnaround time that never sacrifices quality. The coordinate measuring machine helps ensure that quality comes first.

Thirty-five years of experience in a variety of industries has provided NCI, Inc. with the knowledge, talent, and enthusiasm necessary to engineer and manufacture precision machined components and subassemblies for the jet engine, power generation, automotive, and textile industries. Over the years its reputation for producing quality products, with on-time delivery and competitive pricing, has grown. In fact, NCI is respected throughout the industry for its remarkably efficient turnaround time that never sacrifices quality. The product mix varies from fairly simple components produced by the thousands to extremely complex parts requiring hundreds of hours of machining time.

Change in our technology-based world comes faster every year, and systems installed today can be obsolete just a few years later. It takes vision and dedication to keep pace, and NCI is up to the task. It has to be, as the critical nature of commercial and military aircraft, after all, allows no second-best. As a result, NCI is continually reinvesting in its facilities, constantly upgrading to the latest, most advanced equipment available.

Without a loyal and dedicated workforce, it would take an army of inspectors to ensure the work is as perfect as it must be. But that is no problem at NCI. All 140 employees, many of whom have been with the company for 30 or more years, stand behind every job with unwavering integrity and initiative. Drawing on the unparalleled work ethic for which the region is known, the people at NCI can be depended upon to meet the requirements of their numerous customers. The management team, machine operators, engineers, quality control, and other support people strive for continuous improvement.

NCI relies on area technical schools such as Asheville/Buncombe Community College, Blue Ridge Community College, and Haywood Community College to

Cellular manufacturing has increased NCI's efficiency by cutting production time and better utilizing its employees.

provide the highly qualified staff required. The company also enhances the learning environment with regularly scheduled in-house training programs.

Virtually every part manufactured at NCI is accompanied by a multipage routing document—its individual road map through the plant. Every blueprint characteristic, which at times totals in the hundreds, is checked and stamped by certified operators, indication that customer specifications are met. Traceability is paramount to ensure the critical quality demanded and promised is delivered. Records are kept on each part for decades for traceability by serial number, even back to the source of raw materials.

The plant's two main operations revolve around turning and milling. After materials pass receiving inspection, they head to the CNC lathe turning department, where they rotate while the massive lathes begin the metal removal process to meet the configuration specified on the blueprint. Then on to the milling section, where materials remain stationary while a series of computerized-controlled rotating cutters continue the machining process. Grinding, gear shaping, welding, and balancing are other production steps performed at the plant.

Along the way gauges and other tools are used to check and test the process. An on-site gauge laboratory ensures the gauges are current and accurate. Nearby, the engineering department uses the latest CAD/CAM equipment to produce process designs and manufacturing operation sheets for every stage of the operation. Even more detailed than the routing document, process sheets assist employees in certifying specific details and dimensions.

Next stop is finishing, where any burrs and sharp edges are removed and polished like a piece of jewelry. Virtually every part is then powder-treated and black-light inspected to assure no imperfections. Additional testing provides readouts within a millionth of an inch.

By now it is apparent that quality control reigns supreme here—not just at the end of the line, but all along the way. NCI's quality assurance program, based on established methods and procedures that comply with the highest industry requirements, monitors the manufacturing to permit fluorescent penetrant inspection, alloy type testing, and metal hardness testing before the product is deemed worthy of shipping to the customer.

To achieve this degree of sophistication, the company adopted a number of modern work practices, including, most notably, the introduction of cellular manufacturing. A growing trend in American industry, cellular manufacturing has increased profitability by increasing efficiency in performing the operations, cutting production time, and better utilization of employees. These features, in turn, keep the company keenly competitive. The in-house cutter grinding department, which makes parts for and supports the equipment on the floor, also contributes to the plant's efficiency.

NCI, Inc. never has and never will come in second best. That is no promise—it is a guarantee backed up by the talent and integrity of the entire staff. After all, they live with the knowledge that thousands of lives depend on them every day. ▲

NCI is continually reinvesting in its facilities, constantly upgrading to the latest, most advanced equipment available, such as this five axis machining center with robotics.

Akzo Nobel

To report that Akzo Nobel was founded in 1994 makes it sound like a newcomer to Western North Carolina. But Akzo Nobel's roots here can be traced back to the early part of the century. Times change, companies merge and divest, and today Enka-based Akzo Nobel Nonwovens, Inc. is the newest North American presence of the international giant headquartered in Arnhem, The Netherlands.

Akzo Nobel is one of the world's leading companies in selected areas of chemicals, coatings, health care products, and fibers specifically for industrial and textile membranes, nonwoven geosynthetics, and other industrial products.

Worldwide, Akzo Nobel comprises many industries, each with a rich history of its own. Several are prestigious European companies dating to the early twentieth century, while others are companies founded by Alfred Nobel, the famous Swedish scientist. Together, Akzo Nobel is one of the world's leading companies in selected areas of chemicals, coatings, health care products, and fibers specifically for industrial and textile membranes, nonwoven geosynthetics, and other industrial products. More than 70,000 people in at least 50 countries make up the Akzo Nobel workforce. Akzo Nobel North America, Inc.'s sales were approximately $3 billion in 1994 and currently involves more than 15 locations and 11,000 employees.

The Enka operation specializes in nonwovens for carpet backings and roof coverings, as well as geosynthetics for erosion control, drainage, and sound control. In early 1995, Akzo Nobel acquired BASF's Colback nonwovens business in the United States. The acquisition was part of a plan that will permit Akzo Nobel to further globalize its industrial nonwovens activities and operate successfully in the growing United States market.

According to Dan Costant, executive vice president of Akzo Nobel Nonwovens, Inc., "Akzo clearly acquired the Colback business in Asheville to extend its presence into North America. Our geosynthetics business also mirrors a business in our European operations. We're the North American arm of their worldwide marketing effort with responsibility for North and Central America."

Colback's primary product applications include backings for automotive carpets and carpet tile and reinforcements for industrial roofing products. In the carpet industry, Colback enjoys the unique distinction that it is the only bicomponent product using both polyester and nylon in that market today. In addition to its superior technological properties, Colback provides aesthetic advantages, as well. When a nylon-tufted carpet backed by Colback is dyed, the backing receives color which reduces its visibility in the carpet.

Akzo Nobel anticipates that the North American acquisition, coupled with the application of the company's successful European marketing concept of tailor-making products, will generate strong growth. Plans to increase capacity are already underway with the objective of improving the company's market position and cost competitiveness. This is all part of Akzo Nobel's global strategy to enhance productivity and strengthen its position in North America, Japan, and Asia.

Both the Colback and Geosynthetics Divisions manufacture roofing products, but Dan Costant is quick to point out the differences. "Roll Vent, our geosynthetic product, is used at the top of the eave of a typical roof for a single-family dwelling. It creates a vent so that the house breathes—as heat rises, it goes out the vent. Colback makes a product that is used to reinforce modified bitumen roll roofing which is rolled out on a flat roof." Geosynthetics also manufactures nylon for subsurface drainage, erosion control, and to create sound-rated floors in hotels, office buildings, and multifamily dwellings, among others.

"Our geosynthetic products are always buried in the ground," explains Dan Costant. "For erosion control, we try to do with natural vegetation what you might otherwise do with concrete, which alters the visual and natural ecology. Take the mundane example of a highway ditch. You can pave them, but when you ride down the highway, all you see are the paved ditches. If you line it with our Enkamat, all you see is the grass. It looks beautiful yet will carry the same high velocity of water as the concrete because we have reinforced the vegetation." Enkamat is also used in many landfill operations to enhance

The people of Akzo Nobel are key to the success of this innovative and flexible organization. Akzo Nobel recognizes their importance in many ways, especially by encouraging their initiative and creative thinking, which, in turn, contributes to the company's high quality standards.

drainage, gas venting, and to avoid surface erosion.

Another geosynthetic product, Enkavent, is used to mitigate radon from under a house. The market for this product is growing as public awareness of radon hazards rises. In certain markets—real estate, for example—brokers are insisting on pre-closing radon testing and treatment.

Akzo Nobel maximizes the available technological expertise. Implementing state-of-the-art computerized process information systems is one of the key elements in producing top quality products.

The people of Akzo Nobel are key to the success of this innovative and flexible organization. Akzo Nobel recognizes their importance in many ways, especially by encouraging their initiative and creative thinking, which, in turn, contributes to the company's high quality standards. In addition, the company maximizes available technological expertise. Research and development figure prominently in the company's strategies to meet the industry's continuing requirement for technological innovation.

The concern for health, safety, and environmental issues forms an integral part of Akzo Nobel's business policy. The company actively supports the guiding principles of the Business Charter for Sustainable Development of the International Chamber of Commerce and the Responsible Care program of the chemical industry. Akzo Nobel protects the environment by preventing or reducing the environmental impact of its activities and its products through appropriate design, manufacturing, distribution, use, and disposal practices.

Being a new company, Akzo Novel Nonwovens, Inc., with the strong involvement of its employees, has introduced its new mission statement: *"We provide unique products in the durable nonwoven and geosynthetic markets and strive to be the 'best partner' for our customers, employees, and suppliers. With the personal commitment of our employees and a process of continuous improvement, it is our goal to supply our customers with products and services which meet or exceed expectations, ensuring the growth and long-term success of our companies."*

"It is our strong desire to be continuously identified with our mission statement," added Dan Costant. "In everything we do, our slogan 'Your Best Partner' has to guide our every action in order to solidify the trust in our company and its policy."

Both divisions are expanding in order to secure a strong presence in North America. In the process, Akzo Nobel's recent acquisitions, renovations, and plant expansions strengthen its long-term commitment to Western North Carolina. ▲

The Enka operation specializes in nonwovens for carpet backings and roof coverings, as well as geosynthetics for erosion control, drainage, and sound control.

Volvo Construction Equipment

To say Volvo Construction Equipment is on the move refers to much more than its world-class products—loaders, haulers, and excavators—for the earthmoving and construction industries. It speaks to an underlying philosophy as progressive as its products, combining teamwork and modern technology to produce continuous quality improvements and levels of service well beyond conventional standards.

Since 1926, the brand name Volvo has been synonymous with quality and safety around the world. The 300,000-square-foot facility in Skyland, just south of Asheville, now proudly bears that name. The facility began production in June of 1977 producing small wheel loaders as a part of Clark Equipment Company. In April of 1995, AB Volvo, a Swedish company perhaps best known in the United States as a manufacturer of quality automobiles and heavy-duty trucks, purchased Clark Equipment's interest in the business, and the Asheville facility underwent a name change to Volvo Construction Equipment.

Long recognized as a progressive company, Volvo continues the tradition in its Asheville plant with modern innovations such as advanced steel plate cutting that delivers exacting precision and robotic welders that reduce manual welding time at the same time they produce consistently superior welds. The company invests a large segment of its resources in ongoing research and development in an effort to continually improve both manufacturing equipment and techniques, as well as product design.

But the focus at Volvo Construction Equipment is on quality, safety, and environmental care—that is, technologically superior products that are safe and friendly to users and the environment. Consider the fact that the company's products typically produce the lowest emissions, least noise, and best fuel economy of any machines in the industry. Low-emission engines recently introduced by Volvo surpass current environmental standards in North America and already meet those required in the year 2000. Also, this equipment is designed with the user in mind, providing drivers more comfort and less fatigue, which, in turn, increases safety and productivity.

Much can be said about the technology, but it is, after all, the people behind the machines that make the real difference. Volvo Construction Equipment employs approximately 350 area residents at its manufacturing facility in Skyland and an additional 110 at its sales and marketing offices in Asheville. Volvo feels strongly about its people. The self-directed teams in place since 1991 are a symbol of the unity between the company and its people. Every employee from manufacturing to engineering to office and administration is part of a team with the overall objective of improving quality and customer service, setting their own goals, and measuring their progress. Since implementing teams, employees now have the confidence to stand before groups to lead meetings, make presentations, and talk to customers and visitors. Volvo employees also contribute to local charities through the annual United Way campaign, March of Dimes WalkAmerica, and through a committee of manufacturing employees who recommend and distribute the plant's contributions to area agencies.

Volvo Construction Equipment teams work together to get the job done.

Asheville plant employees and visitors enjoy the natural setting on Lake Julian.

Asheville's hardworking teams produce most models of Volvo BM wheel loaders, articulated haulers, and excavators. In 1963 Volvo BM introduced the concept of articulated haulers and today leads the world in their production. The models produced at Asheville range up to 40 tons of payload capacity. Volvo BM articulated haulers have become the standard of comparison in the industry for productivity, ease of operation, reliability, and the capacity to handle any material on the toughest terrain. They perform on the most demanding job sites where other equipment cannot work, navigating difficult terrain, driving through conditions most vehicles would find impassable. It is the only articulated hauler on the market with a fully automatic power shift transmission and true all-wheel drive. Because of all its features, more Volvo BM articulated haulers have been sold worldwide than all other brands combined.

Volvo BM wheel loaders feature a quick coupler attachment that allows an operator to quickly and easily change attachments without ever leaving the cab. Thanks to this innovative quick coupler attachment bracket and a selection of quality attachments for virtually every need, a single Volvo BM wheel loader can do the work of several separate machines.

Volvo Construction Equipment is proud of its employees and the role they have played in the successful transition to self-directed teams. These new methods of management, however, coupled with ever-changing technology, require ongoing training and development, and Volvo delivers. Employees can utilize an employee development assistance program to pay for job-related courses at local colleges and universities. In the company's own well-equipped classrooms, employees can conveniently attend college credit classes taught by faculty from Asheville-Buncombe Technical Community College and other technical colleges in the region. The manufacturing facility is also home to the NAFTA region technical training center, where NAFTA dealers and customers learn the proper servicing of Volvo Construction Equipment products. The Product Demonstration Center, located just north of Asheville, is very popular with its customers and dealers, who get the opportunity to operate equipment after product demonstrations of the machines in action.

In the future, the plant anticipates increasing the number of models manufactured at the facility. This expansion will create additional career opportunities for area residents and assist in further stabilization of the area economy through the growth of manufacturing jobs. As the company expands, however, quality and service remain a constant. Customers can count on the company's guarantee—the Volvo identity won't go on until the vehicle passes the rigorous testing and high standards that built its reputation. ▲

The two biggest models manufactured at the Asheville plant literally move mountains.

The Product Demonstration Center, located just north of Asheville, is very popular with its customers and dealers, who get the opportunity to operate equipment after product demonstrations of the machines in action.

Communications Instruments, Inc.

Past the duck pond and under the canopy of trees, the pastoral drive leading up to the CII facility belies the critically important work taking place inside. It is no exaggeration to say the quality of the products made here is of life-or-death precision. Inside the modern facility, well-trained employees are producing high-performance relays for commercial and military aircraft, satellites, and other applications dependent upon as close to perfection as human hands and high technology can produce.

Past the duck pond and under the canopy of trees, the pastoral drive leading up to the CII facility belies the critically important work taking place inside. *Photo by Tim Barnwell.*

The company started in 1979 and has grown steadily over the last 15 years by developing products internally and also through 14 acquisitions. Many of the acquired businesses were moved to the Fairview and Asheville facilities, boosting employment opportunities in the region.

There is a good reason for relocating the acquired businesses here—the people. "The work ethic here is excellent," states Ramzi Dabbagh, CEO of CII Technologies. "All our people want to do a good job. They know that the products we make are used in some very important applications. And our employees are very loyal—some have been here more than 40 years." The two plants in Buncombe County utilize almost 100,000 square feet and employ over 400 workers.

It takes an unrelenting commitment to excellence to maintain the consistent quality for which CII is known. Their entire line of relays is manufactured in accordance with the military's toughest standards—even those not destined for military applications. Raw materials are carefully selected to meet strict specifications, and detailed lot control documents accompany every part and relay through manufacturing, testing, and inspecting processes as employees check and recheck every relay.

Inside the spacious and surprisingly quiet CII plant, employees are busy producing and testing the relays. While some are using microscopes to inspect and calibrate the smallest relays, others are removing relays from giant vacuum ovens that evacuate impurities. Once cool, the relays are hermetically sealed by a precision laser beam that exactingly welds the metal enclosures without damaging the relay's intricate components. At this point the relay is virtually impenetrable to contaminants and is guaranteed to last for a very long time. Proud as they are, staff are reluctant to say "forever," but that doesn't stop one from quipping, "Our renewal part business is virtually zero."

Relays are used in a wide variety of applications from making toys operate to guidance and satellite systems. Sizes vary from minute to those weighing up to several pounds. CII makes relays for only the most exacting applications where performance and reliability must meet precise specifications. Most aircraft in the free world rely on a variety of CII relays for controlling electrical current and electronic signals in their auto pilots, guidance systems, and navigation systems. In fact, a recent inventory of the number of CII relays in each new Boeing 777 was 200 and counting.

As the company continues to diversify and expand its expertise, the future looks bright. The production of solenoids, for example, has increased over the past five years, and company leaders anticipate a tremendous growth curve over the next five years. Solenoids are devices that convert electrical energy into mechanical motion through a technology very similar to relays. They make our lives easier and safer in products ranging from remote door locks and vending machines to sophisticated airplane deicing devices.

While some employees use microscopes to inspect and calibrate the smallest relays, others remove relays from giant vacuum ovens that evacuate impurities. *Photo by Tim Barnwell.*

Communications Instruments, Inc. is a division of CII Technologies with the corporate headquarters also at the Fairview location. Three recent acquisitions by CII Technologies has resulted in the Kilovac, Midtex, and

CII Technologies is the worldwide leader in high-performance switching technology. High-performance relays and solenoids provide the advantage of small size, are lightweight, have a long life, consume little energy, and have environmentally sealed contacts. *Photo by Tim Barnwell.*

Hartman subsidiaries with plants in Santa Barbara, California, Juarez, Mexico, and Mansfield, Ohio. Collectively, the corporation employs over 1,000 workers at seven locations producing the kinds of high performance relays that have made CII a worldwide leader in high performance switching technology.

CII Technologies sells its products through an extensive network of 72 independent sales representatives and 27 distributors in North America, Europe, and Asia. The company seeks to provide customized solutions to its customers and has formed strategic partnerships with them to develop new products, improve existing products, and reduce product cost in use. The company offers a high level of services and engineering support to its customers. A key element in the services provided is assistance in the proper application of its products, thereby reducing field failures and overall product cost in use. AT&T, Boeing, McDonnell-Douglas, Hewlett-Packard, ITT Aerospace, and Lockheed-Martin, as well as many smaller companies, are just a few of the corporation's 2,100 customers worldwide.

CII Technologies started with $3.5 million in sales in 1979 and is on target in 1996 to ship over $75 million in sales, 14 percent of which are international. A breakdown of sales reflects how diversified the company has become. Fifteen years ago 80 percent of their manufacturing catered to the military. Today, defense and aerospace is 20 percent of sales, commercial aircraft and communications systems more than 50 percent, with medical, automotive, and automatic test equipment rounding out the mix.

Medical advances such as the latest heart defibrillator provide new markets for CII Technologies' relays. This lifesaving machine, designed to start hearts that have failed, is currently used by EMTs and in hospital emergency rooms. New, relatively low-cost models are being developed that will allow people with limited medical training to use them at manufacturing plants, football stadiums, shopping malls, and other public places.

New modes of transportation are also providing additional markets. General Motors' electric vehicle is already in production with CII Technologies' relays in place. Ford, Volvo, and BMW have developed their prototype electric vehicles which also include CII Technologies' relays. Ever-expanding satellite communications needs also mean new markets. Products for this industry are classified as requiring ultra-high reliability because of their use in outer space, qualifications that are standard here.

The potential uses for CII Technologies' relays are ever growing. As the world becomes increasingly sophisticated, the parts that make it function must keep pace. CII Technologies is accustomed to delivering the best, and their highly trained team of designers, engineers, production workers, and inspectors are prepared to maintain that hard earned reputation. ▲

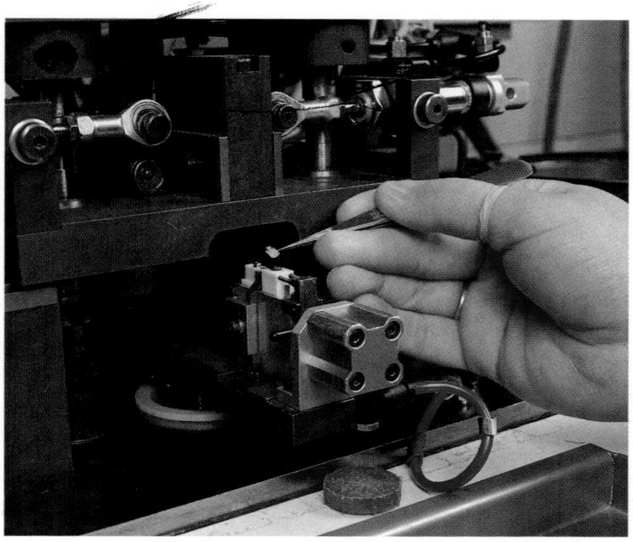

Inside the modern facility of CII, well-trained employees produce high-performance relays for commercial and military aircraft, and satellites. *Photo by Tim Barnwell.*

Day International, Inc.

There's no mystery to how the development team at Day International, Inc. finds out what customers need. They simply ask. Years ago, the company invested in a sales and technical force that visits customers around the globe in order to learn exactly how Day International's products work for them and how they could work better. This investment has yielded fruitful returns. Through innovation that stays a step ahead of customers' expectations, Day International remains a world leader in the manufacture of polymer products for the printing and textile industries—a position it's held for more than 50 years.

Trust, equitable treatment, safety, communications, and quality are the basis of Day International's management style. *Photo by Tim Barnwell.*

The story of Day International begins at the turn of the century with Dayton Rubber Manufacturing Company, a manufacturer of fruit jar rings and garden hoses. In 1910 the company added a new product line and a new name, Dayton Tire & Rubber Company. It went on to become a major developer and supplier of different types of automotive belts. The tire business was eventually sold to Firestone in 1960, and the company, now known as Dayco Corporation, narrowed its focus to the hose and belt industry.

By piloting new materials for its products, the company moved to the forefront of polymers compounding, which blends natural and synthetic rubbers for specific physical and chemical properties. Wide applications for these materials were found. When incorporated into textile machines, for example, the rubber could guide yarn from spindle to spindle without snagging or catching. Another polymer material could be used in printing to transfer the inked image of the press onto paper. Even after the hose and belt business was sold, along with the Dayco name, to Armstrong Rubber Company in 1986, the company retained several product lines that fully utilized its research in this constantly evolving field.

After the sale the company took the name of Day International. Soon thereafter it was acquired by M. A. Hanna Company and organized into business units, two of which are Day International Printing Products Company and Day International Textile Products Company. In 1995 the company was purchased by American Industrial Partners, an investment group with a strong track record of growth behind it. With the support of American Industrial Partners, Day International is ready to expand into new products that complement its existing lines, a strategy that has served the company well from the turn of one century to the turn of the next.

When the transaction with Armstrong was completed in 1986, the company began to search for a place to relocate its printing and textile operations, then based in Waynesville. The ideal spot proved to be close by. In early 1988, after hiring a new work force, Day International opened a facility in Arden, just 10 miles south of Asheville. The facility, situated on 28 acres of land, has 240,000 square feet of office and manufacturing space and houses research laboratories for product development and improvement.

As locations from Asheville to Australia attest, the company's operations are truly international in scope. In addition to the Asheville facility, Day International Textile Products, headquartered in Greenville, South Carolina, has a sales and manufacturing facility in Dundee, Scotland, as well as a sales office in Reutlingen, Germany. The company's Printing Products Division shares the use of these facilities and has two more manufacturing sites, one in Three Rivers, Michigan, and another in Lerma, Mexico. Headquartered in Dayton, Ohio,

Through innovation that stays a step ahead of customers' expectations, Day International remains a world leader in the manufacture of polymer products for the printing and textile industries—a position it's held for more than 50 years. *Photo by Tim Barnwell.*

Printing Products also has sales offices in Sydney, Australia, Villers Saint Frederic, France, and Hong Kong.

It was shortly after World War II that Day International began to produce the printing blankets used in offset presses to transfer ink from the plate to the paper. Since that time, much about the printing industry has changed—from higher-speed presses to lighter-weight papers and faster-drying inks. And with each change, Day International Printing Products has kept pace by increasing the durability of its blankets while improving the blanket's ability to release images that are solid and sharp.

The rubber compounds that make the blankets are developed for specialized properties. For example, they allow the blanket to conform to the movement of the press. In addition, these compounds create surfaces smooth enough to carry ink, but resilient to the pinholes and abrasions that would blotch an otherwise clean image transfer.

Day International's research team in Asheville continues to develop materials that improve the already strong performance of the company's products. The team has also developed new products for its printing line, such as rollers for credit card imprinters and business machines.

The company has manufactured polymer accessories for the textile industry since 1938. These accessories, which include both standard and tailor-made products, fit into the machines and help to guide the yarn through the entire fabric-making process, from carding and drawing to weaving and finishing. All of these products are certified to be at an ISO 9000 level of quality.

The Asheville facility is the largest of Day International's manufacturing sites. It's operated under an all-salaried concept that bases compensation on contributions and service, not position. Trust, equitable treatment, safety, communications, and quality are the basis of Day International's management style. Associates are carefully selected and, through process-focused teams, participate in the running of the company's manufacturing operations. Due to the contributions of these teams, Day International is streamlined to manufacture quality products more efficiently and with less scrap waste than ever before.

The input of its customers and the ideas of the men and women who work there are what have led Day International, Inc. to success in the past and, the company believes, have readied it for an even more successful future. ▲

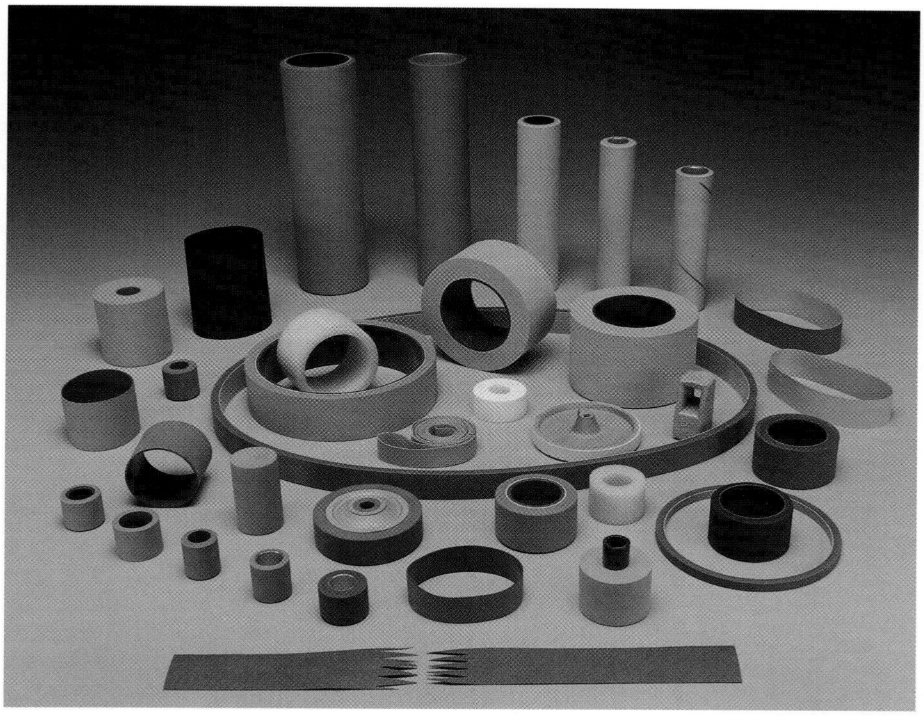

Day International is ready to expand into new products that complement its existing lines, a strategy that has served the company well from the turn of one century to the turn of the next. *Photo by Tim Barnwell.*

Day International's research team in Asheville develops materials that improve the already strong performance of the company's products. *Photo by Tim Barnwell.*

Union Butterfield

Union Butterfield's dedicated associates make the company successful.

Every day of the week, metal-cutting tools by Union Butterfield are used in the manufacture of products as diverse as lawn mowers and motorboats, trucks and airplanes. And while these tools perform different jobs—from drilling holes to shaping metal—they were all developed with one goal in mind: to help manufacturers produce their goods at less cost and with greater efficiency.

Asheville is home to Union Butterfield's headquarters and its centers for customer service and distribution. From its facility on Sweeten Creek Road, the company dispatches its line of high-speed steel tools to industrial distributors throughout the United States and Canada as well as into parts of Central and South America.

"Our mission has always been to exceed our customers' expectations," states President Adrian Waple. This mission begins on the manufacturing floor of plants in Gaffney, South Carolina, and Derby Line, Vermont, where products are engineered and crafted for consistent, durable performance. Both plants are ISO 9002 certified, a designation which attests that their processes meet internationally-recognized standards for high quality.

Union Butterfield's product line consists of more than 10,000 metal-cutting tools. The line includes drills for cutting holes, end mills to shape and profile metal, and taps, which are used to produce the internal threads in holes so that parts may be fastened together. Each type of tool is designed in a range of sizes and styles to match hundreds of different industrial applications. For example, depending on the size of the hole needed, there are drills almost too small to see and, on the other side of the spectrum, some so large they are difficult to lift. Or one type of tap may be used on stainless steel, another on aluminum, and yet another on cast iron: the tools are as varied as the products which they help to produce.

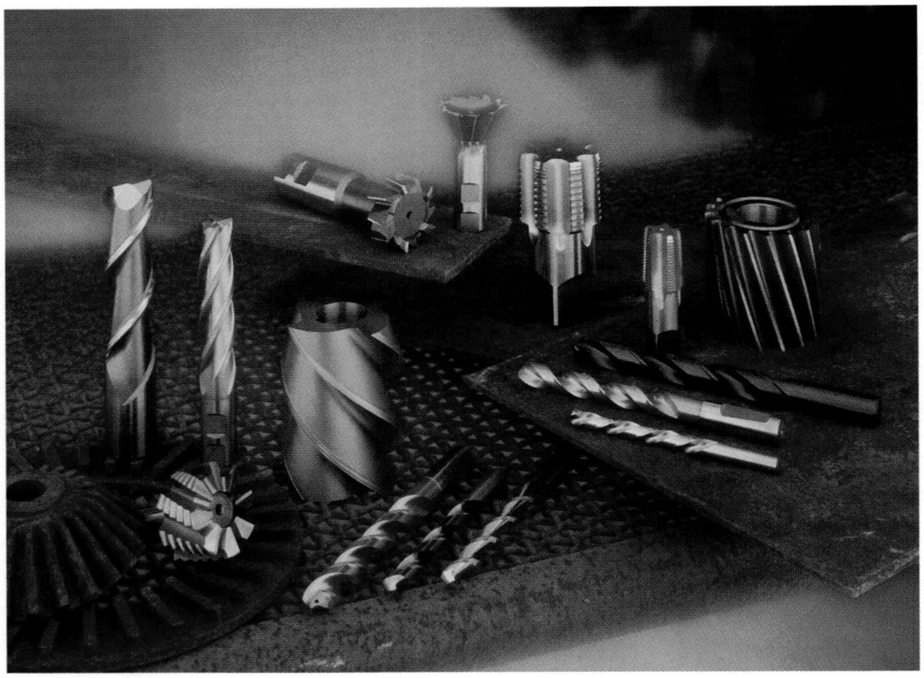

Union Butterfield's product line consists of more than 10,000 metal-cutting tools. Shown here are some typical products manufactured by Union Butterfield.

Many of these tools have only been introduced by Union Butterfield in the last few years. "We are looking for continuous improvement in our manufacturing," explains Waple. "So, in addition to improving the overall performance of our products, we've developed new products to give the customer more choice when selecting a tool for a particular job." The company has also recently expanded its ability to custom manufacture products to a customer's exact specifications. By offering tools that are precisely engineered for the task they will perform, Union Butterfield believes it can reduce the manufacturing costs of its customers.

The quality mission that begins at the factories in South Carolina and Vermont continues once the products arrive in Asheville for distribution. Union Butterfield has invested in a number of technologies at the Asheville facility that enhance its service capabilities.

The customer service center emphasizes turning orders around swiftly. Although the Asheville facility can already boast of speedy customer response—orders received by four in the afternoon are shipped that same day—it is further streamlining its operations by moving toward full integration of Electronic Data Interchange (EDI). The system is expected to eliminate much of the paperwork associated with processing orders as well as to allow shipments to be more easily logged and tracked.

From its facility on Sweeten Creek Road, the company dispatches its line of high-speed steel tools to industrial distributors throughout the United States and Canada as well as into parts of Central and South America. Over 400 orders per day are shipped from the Union Butterfield warehouse.

Bar coding is another method being utilized by the facility to increase the efficiency of both Union Butterfield and the industrial distributors that sell its products. Not only do product bar codes make it possible for distributors to quickly and accurately select products from their warehouse shelves (no small boon when one product's name may vary from its neighbor's by only a fraction), the codes can also be scanned to electronically adjust inventory levels for instantaneous record keeping.

Technical support is an important focal area for Union Butterfield. Sales associates and product specialists travel throughout the country to work closely with the company's industrial customers. "All of our salespeople are technically competent and have strong backgrounds in manufacturing," notes Waple. "They can help customers find solutions for problems they are having in their manufacturing processes."

Even Union Butterfield's sales literature aims to inform manufacturers about how the right tool for the right job can make all the difference. After listing what products are available, the company catalog explains how to pick a tool for a specific application as well as how to use it properly. Lately these communications have had a distinct twenty-first-century edge: customers are now supplied with electronic price lists and the address for the company's site on Industry Net, the Internet of the manufacturing world.

Union Butterfield is a company already familiar with such benchmark changes as the turn of a century. Its roots go back to 1880, when an enterprising resident of Rock Island, Quebec, named Lewis Young designed an axle cutter to "turn back" the worn axles of horse-drawn buggies and carts. With partner F. D. Butterfield, he set himself up in business and sold that and other products to blacksmith shops across New England. In 1913 the company was bought by Union Twist Drill, a manufacturer of drills and milling cutters, which had already been in business for more than two decades.

The company has come a long way from its picturesque beginnings, but it still enjoys the kind of reputation for quality that it takes a century to earn. Today, Union Butterfield is part of the Sandvik Group, an international manufacturing conglomerate based in Sweden. Composed of 200 companies in 60 countries, Sandvik is one of the world's largest engineering enterprises for materials technology. As a member of its CTT Tools division, Union Butterfield has access to pioneering innovations in the tooling industry.

When Sandvik acquired Union Butterfield in 1993, it consolidated a number of its operations. One of those consolidations created the company's headquarters in Asheville, a move with which Waple is pleased. "We've built a good thing here," he states. "We've been able to gather a good team of employees, and I think we're ready to move forward." It seems likely that tools manufactured by Union Butterfield will be cutting and shaping metal for many years to come—even when cars and trucks rolling off the assembly line have given way to Jetson-style spaceships. ▲

The customer service center and the customer service team, emphasize turning orders around swiftly, ensuring satisfied customers.

Steelcase

The Steelcase story is really about its partnership with nature and people. In its plant in Fletcher, on the outskirts of Asheville, Steelcase—the world's largest manufacturer of office furniture—converts the natural beauty of fine hardwoods into the best quality wood office furniture available anywhere. Each carefully crafted piece is unique, whose beautiful yet functional design and finely matched veneers denote sophistication and status. At the same time, thanks to Steelcase's strong commitment to environmentally responsible manufacturing and finishing technologies, the company helps ensure that our trees and forests will flourish for generations to come.

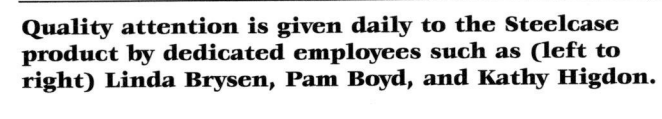

Quality attention is given daily to the Steelcase product by dedicated employees such as (left to right) Linda Brysen, Pam Boyd, and Kathy Higdon.

Steelcase has been in the Asheville area since 1973, and it's been a success story right from the start. By 1978, the plant had doubled in size. By 1982, it had doubled again, to keep pace with the steadily increasing demand. Key players in the company's continuing success are the Fletcher plant's more than 600 highly skilled employees, the ones who actually match the veneers, hand-rub the stain, and apply the varnish. Steelcase is a people-focused company, which rewards dedicated service with an outstanding benefits package. And should grievances arise, the company's "open door" policy helps ensure fair treatment for all employees. The success of this partnership is reflected in the plant's extremely low turnover (less than a dozen employees per year). Many workers have been with the company for more than 10 years. It's an efficient and innovative team, united by a shared commitment to top-quality products and service. All Steelcase furniture is built using only the finest hardwood veneers, solids, and finishes and carries a lifetime warranty. At the same time, a company-wide dedication to customer service helps ensure that customers get the quality they want when they want it.

Steelcase's Fletcher facility is among the most sophisticated furniture plants in the United States, combining state-of-the-art, computerized woodworking equipment with the most exacting design and production standards. The Cane Creek collection offers outstanding value for the company's executive-level, corporate customers. Combining equal parts of good design, craftsmanship, and people, Cane Creek delivers top-quality office furniture in a wide range of styles.

Perhaps not surprisingly, the quality of Steelcase's products and service is reflected in the company's client list. A large percentage of sales are to *Fortune Magazine's* 500 companies, including many in the financial community. Steelcase customers appreciate the best, and they understand that an investment in fine office environments can yield dividends in the form of enhanced productivity and employee satisfaction. To the twin goals of quality and service, Steelcase adds a deep commitment to preserving the environment. Some companies seem to view environmental concern as an obstacle to profit. The company's commitment to environmental excellence starts with strict adherence to all government regulations (current emissions of VOCs—volatile organic compounds—are just half of what its permit allows). But that's only the beginning. All products are made from renewable resources, carefully harvested from ecologically managed, North American hardwood forests. Steelcase leads the industry in the use of safe finishing materials, and is now experimenting with water-based solvents.

In addition, state-of-the-art emissions-control strategies and a broad-based, company-wide recycling program help keep the company moving in pursuit of its ambitious environmental goals. One exciting prospect is Steelcase Fletcher's groundbreaking partnership with North Carolina State University. The company is funding research at North Carolina State to develop a special strain of microorganism that will actually eat VOCs. The Fletcher plant will also serve as a pilot project site.

In a sense, it's all part of the company's broad-based "good neighbor" policy. At every level, Steelcase strives to be a positive presence in the community, and a good corporate neighbor. The Steelcase Foundation, headquartered in Grand Rapids, Michigan, makes significant financial contributions wherever the company. Locally, the foundation is very active in United Way, and supports a range of other local charitable organizations and efforts, including Meals on Wheels, as well as capital campaigns for Warren Wilson College, Outward Bound, Mission Hospital, and the Sheltered Workshop in Hendersonville. In addition, the plant itself has a budget for smaller charitable donations. Those gifts are determined by the plant's donations committee, which includes both salaried and hourly staff, to ensure that all levels of plant personnel have a say in where the money goes. The company also makes frequent gifts of furniture to help local organizations carry out their worthy work. Some recent recipients of furniture

State-of-the-art computerized woodworking machinery is used in the Fletcher Steelcase facility.

Churchill, one of the new product lines in the Cane Creek Collection, was introduced in 1996 by Steelcase—Fletcher wood facility.

donations include the Rape Crisis Center, the Battered Women's Shelter, Outward Bound, and the Sheltered Workshop.

But at Steelcase, community involvement means a lot more than simply signing checks and making in-kind donations. Company employees are encouraged to get involved, too, and Steelcase participates actively in the United Way's Executive on Loan program, through which company executives work for local charities for a full year, at no cost to the organization. Many Steelcase employees also volunteer for Meals on Wheels, leaving the plant around midday to deliver food to homebound and elderly people in the community.

Steelcase believes in leading by example. That means many things, including serving as a trailblazer site for the local United Way campaign, showing other companies what Steelcase has done in the community, and helping them to set their own sights higher for charitable giving. Last year, for example, Steelcase employees exceeded their United Way fund-raising goal; nevertheless, the company, through the Steelcase Foundation, made an additional contribution to United Way.

Despite its success, however, Steelcase isn't resting on its laurels. Over the last two years, the company has introduced 57 new products. Last year alone, the Fletcher facility rolled out two major new product lines, which are expected to substantially increase plant volume. Whether considering product quality, environmental concern, employee relations, or community involvement, Steelcase leads the pack. ▲

Steelcase employees show their pride in front of a Steelcase "Big Blue."

MILKCO, Inc.

"Drink your milk; it's good for you." That is true, but it takes a strong partnership between Mother Nature, regional farmers, and a company like MILKCO to produce and protect that goodness. Through an elaborate system of regulations, testing, and technology, MILKCO has been delivering the freshest milk from local dairy farms since 1982.

Milk is subject to a rigorous set of inspections and testing on the farm and in the plant from county, state, and federal agencies. MILKCO, which is a wholly owned subsidiary of Ingles Markets, not only exceeds these test standards but adds a number of their own. "Our own test standards are more stringent than the federal government requires," explains Ralph Gardner, president of MILKCO. "We cycle our raw milk every 24 hours, and that's not standard either." Other extras include shipping in insulated corrugated boxes that keep milk colder and the containers cleaner than in open milk crates.

Through an elaborate system of regulations, testing, and technology, MILKCO has been delivering the freshest milk from local dairy farms since 1982.

Each day dozens of 5,000-gallon tankers unload their creamy cargo into gleaming stainless steel holding tanks, beginning the sophisticated system that processes more than 125,000 gallons a day. First stop is a modern, fully equipped laboratory where each delivery is tested. After processing, the milk is sped along a roller coaster of conveyors and tracks to packaging and shipping. Across the way, machines mold and trim containers made from plastic pellets and shipping boxes from giant stacks of corrugated paper. Down the hall a manager figures how much whole milk, two percent milk, and skim milk to produce that day, while the distribution department process the orders. The plant is open 7 days a week, 24 hours a day, and employs over 200 workers.

Once the day's milk is processed and shipped, there is plenty yet to do. Crews sanitize and maintain equipment, and the container-making machinery runs throughout the night to get a head start on tomorrow's production.

MILKCO is a fluid product plant, which means only liquid products are produced (no cottage cheese, yogurt, etc.). Although milk constitutes 80 percent of the business, MILKCO is also a processing center for bottled water, fruit juices, and other drinks. They maintain contracts with four springs licensed by the North Carolina Department of Agriculture from which they bottle their own spring water as well as those labels of entertainment facilities, hotels, and resorts.

Forty years ago there were 22 milk processing centers west of Hickory. Today MILKCO is the only milk processing center west of Charlotte. Their market currently stretches across eight southeastern states, providing larger and more stable markets for regional farmers. Sales, which in 1982 reached 100,000 gallons a week, have skyrocketed to nearly one million gallons a week. MILKCO is also a leader in recycling efforts, converting to totally recyclable packaging over five years ago. In addition to its distribution to warehouses that supply retail supermarkets, MILKCO expanded four years ago into the food service business in order to tap the 40 plus percent of the food dollar spent outside the home. These are just a few of the innovations this dynamic company is willing to make to ensure the quality and goodness of their products throughout the region. ▲

Each day dozens of 5,000-gallon tankers unload their creamy cargo into gleaming stainless steel holding tanks, beginning a sophisticated process. First stop is a modern, fully equipped laboratory where each delivery is tested.

At MILKCO, milk constitutes 80 percent of the business, but the company also processes bottled water, fruit juices, and other drinks.

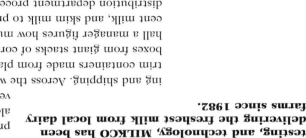

Trinity Industries

A handsomely framed article in the lobby reads, "Trinity Industries: In For The Long Haul." Since 1981, Trinity Industries Parts Division has been designing and manufacturing specialty products and replacement parts for the long-hauling railroad industry. The Asheville plant features a complete range of fabrication capabilities, including stamping, punching, forming, machining, welding, mechanical assembling, plus a comprehensive line of inventory items to serve its replacement-parts customers. Boxcar flooring, hitches to secure tractor trailers on a railroad car, rapid discharge doors under coal cars, discharge gates, and hatch cover rings for covered hopper cars are some of its most popular products. Its parent company, Dallas-based Trinity Industries, is the largest builder of railcars in the country and also deals in barge building, marine products, construction products, pressurized and nonpressurized containers, and metal components.

Trinity Industries offers its customers remarkable flexibility with the capability of making as few as one or as many as thousands of any one part. Plant Manager Duane Wilson explains why it can be more economical to rebuild a railroad car than to buy a new one. "Let's say the truck assemblies and the under frame are still good. Those are the expensive parts, so if only the side sheets and discharge doors on the bottom need replacing, it's worthwhile to have us make those parts for them."

With sales, marketing, research and development, accounting, and engineering under one roof, Trinity Industries is a complete profit center. And with research and development on-site, Trinity can manufacture products so specialized they may be used by only 50 cars in the world. "We make parts that no one else makes," Wilson states. "There are a few products we make repeatedly, but there are many things we do just one time. We have customers who say, 'I have a dream.' We look at the car and say, 'We can do that' and design a product to fit their dreams." In 1993 Trinity celebrated introducing 18 new products and 130 new jobs in one year's time.

With research and development on-site, Trinity can manufacture products so specialized they may be used by only 50 cars in the world.

Since 1981, Trinity Industries Parts Division has been designing and manufacturing specialty products and replacement parts for the long-hauling railroad industry.

A tour of the 94,298-square-foot plant reveals an interesting mix of state-of-the-art computer controlled equipment side by side with a more traditional machine shop. Of the 150 employees, more than half are welders, with machine operators, fabricators, and production helpers rounding out the roster. General Manager Orson Smith and Wilson head up Trinity's management team. "We are like a small town with a team environment. We have a lot of interaction." Employees receive full benefit packages and work in a safe environment with a low OSHA rating.

Trinity was named the Asheville Area Chamber of Commerce Manufacturer of the Year in 1993. Sales Manager Russ Long reports that the plant was rated an excellent supplier by TTX, just one of its railroad industry customers. Other customers include Norfolk Southern, CSX, Gunderson, Progress Rail, and internal sales to Trinity Industries.

According to Wilson, the years ahead look good: business is steady, the plant is functioning at top production, and employment doubled in the past three years. With indicators like that there seems little doubt Trinity is, indeed, in for the long haul. ▲

ITT Automotive

"Satisfy your customer; love your people." That is the credo that has earned ITT Automotive's Asheville facility a world-class reputation for the highest quality antilock braking systems with the best on-time delivery at a low cost. The credo also inspires the plant community of more than 900 to always do their best, treating others as they would like to be treated. Employees here are appreciated for their all-important contribution—and they know it. In a recent survey by a local newspaper, ITT Automotive Asheville took top honors as the best company to work for in Western North Carolina.

ITT Automotive (ITTA) has been an industry leader in the development and application of automotive braking technology for 90 years, pioneering such milestone products as hydraulic drum brakes, disc brakes, and, of course, antilock braking systems (ABS). ITTA is now the world leader in the production of four-wheel antilock braking systems with worldwide total sales in 1995 reaching $5.7 billion.

The ITTA Asheville facility was the first one built anywhere in the world dedicated exclusively to the assembly and testing of antilock brake systems.

The history of ITTA dates back to 1906, when a 29-year-old German engineer named Alfred Teves founded a brake company in Frankfurt, Germany. The Alfred Teves Company was acquired and became part of the Brake Systems Group of ITTA in 1967. ITTA is the world's largest independent brake manufacturer, and the ITTA Teves brand is the world's most recognizable in foundation brakes, tracking control, and antilock braking systems.

After almost two decades of ABS research, development, and testing, ITTA Systems Group branched out into Asheville in 1988. The ITTA Asheville facility was the first one built anywhere in the world dedicated exclusively to the assembly and testing of antilock brake systems. This 250,000-square-foot plant is one of only three facilities to produce the latest generation MK 20 ABS, one of the lightest, most compact, and cost-effective antilock brake systems available. Based on a modular concept for maximum component standardization, it is applicable to all brake circuit and drive configurations, including front-, rear-, and four-wheel drive cars and trucks. In addition to ABS products, the Asheville plant produces calipers and corner assemblies. The assembly technologies are all computer integrated, blending automation with manual labor. The plant's inventory and shipping identification and control functions are also highly automated.

Today, ITTA enjoys more than one quarter of the market share. Their customers are the world's top automakers, such as Ford Motor Company, Chrysler, BMW, General Motors, and Mazda, all of which have recognized the Asheville facility for its quality and service. These auto assembly plants, which run on just-in-time schedules for inventory, require on-time delivery of parts with zero defect rates, and ITTA Asheville delivers.

ITTA Asheville actively participates in the surrounding community not because that is where it sells its products but because that is where its families live. The company and its people give generously of both time and money—all part of the ethical and caring environment that has earned ITTA Asheville its world-class reputation. ▲

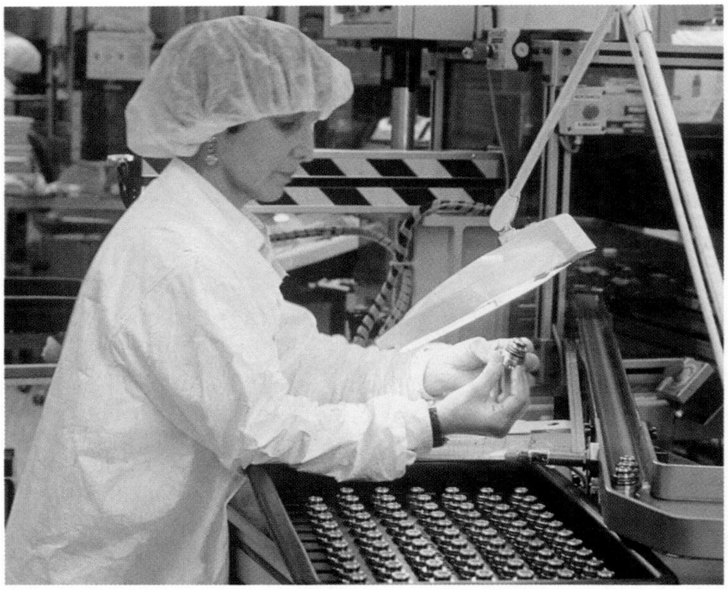

ITT Automotive's Asheville facility has a world-class reputation for manufacturing the highest quality antilock braking systems with the best on-time delivery at a low cost.

Nypro Asheville

Nypro Asheville epitomizes constancy amid change. Originally founded as an independent company known as Asheville Plastics in 1960, the company was sold in 1976 to the conglomerate GTE, who sold it in 1988 to Nypro, Inc. Since its acquisition by Nypro, the leading global precision injection molder, Nypro Asheville has been operating as a state-of-the-art automated Nypro plant. The oldest account at Nypro Asheville is Duracell batteries, for whom Nypro Asheville has made battery parts since its founding as Asheville Plastics.

The oldest account at Nypro Asheville is Duracell batteries, for whom Nypro Asheville has made battery parts since its founding as Asheville Plastics. *Photo by J. Weiland.*

With changing ownership, the constancy of the operation has been anchored in the company's loyal team members. Nypro Asheville has more 15- and 20-year veterans than any of the other 20 Nypro facilities in 9 countries except the original 40-year-old headquarters plant in Clinton, Massachusetts.

Karen Fowler, a 22-year veteran of Asheville, celebrates the development of a "family" of employees. "We've become close, and we've helped one another to find opportunity. There's more room to grow than in the old days, more promotional opportunities for everybody, including women and minorities." The result is a team approach to production and quality issues.

After only seven years under Nypro ownership, the company moved into a new building in Arden. In addition to having almost twice the room of the former facility, the new building makes a statement to customers that Nypro continues to improve in providing them the best products and service.

Nypro Asheville currently has 40 injection molding machines, and a new wing under construction that will accommodate an additional 20 machines. Unlike the old days when large molding machines needed two or three operators, robots handle repetitive tasks, allowing people to concentrate on inspection, packing, and other nonautomatic functions.

"The modernization began when Nypro took over in 1988," states Al Gass, Nypro Asheville's controller, who has been with the firm for 27 years. "That's when the new injection molding machines, the automation, and robots showed up. Nypro does nothing but plastics, and that's been nothing but good for us."

One thing that has changed considerably is the plant's relationship with its customers. Karen Fowler recalls how years ago customers rarely ventured into injection molding plants. Today, customers are everywhere. Most major customer teams include one or two people who are very familiar with injection molding processes. "The world is better educated," says Fowler, "and that shows up as partnerships as equals with our customers."

Education has also impacted the people who work at Nypro Asheville. The company offers several formal training programs, and new employees are cross-trained through exposure to specialties other than their own. Outside education is also encouraged to enable employees at all levels to advance.

Controller Al Gass sums up the plant's status by recalling what a friend told him when he joined the Asheville facility in 1968, long before Nypro came along. "You've just joined one of the finest molding plants in the Southeast," he told Gass. Today, Gass is quick to add, "And we've come a long way since then." ▲

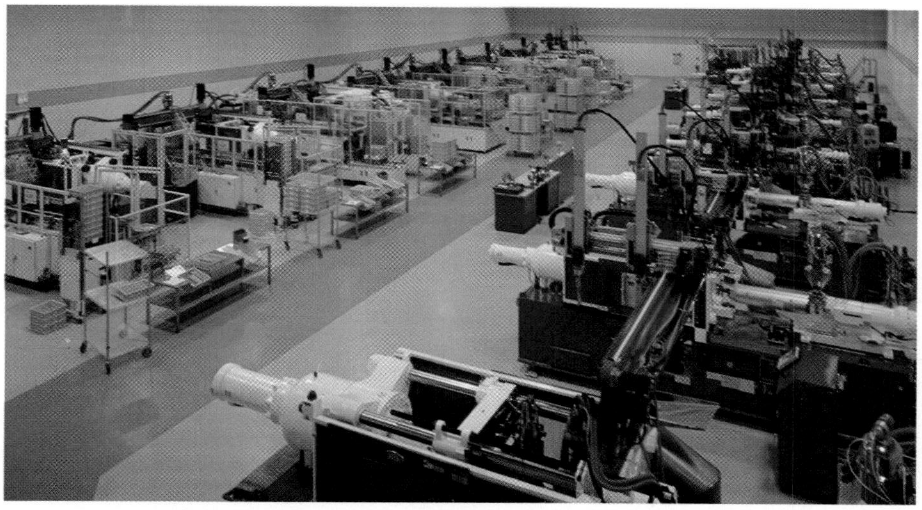

Nypro Asheville currently has 40 injection molding machines, and a new wing under construction that will accommodate an additional 20 machines. *Photo by J. Weiland.*

J. Crew Group

J. Crew Group handles all distribution to Clifford & Wills and J. Crew Factory Stores, as well as J. Crew Retail Stores.

J. Crew associates are well trained, informed, and creative—a requirement considering more than 20,000 telephone calls come in each week (a figure that soars to 200,000 calls during the holiday season).

State-of-the-art technology. Flashing red and yellow lights. Electronic messages and countdowns. Mission Control in Houston? No, J. Crew Group in Asheville, where they take their customers every bit as seriously as NASA takes a satellite launch. The company serves as a national clothing catalog operation for both Clifford & Wills and J. Crew catalogs, specializing in telemarketing catalog orders and distribution for factory and retail stores.

The success of J. Crew Group stems from two basics—excellent merchandise and quality service. Their superior merchandise is selected for its lasting quality, style, and comfort. All clothing is designed and manufactured exclusively for the two catalogs. Associates are well trained, informed, and creative—a requirement considering more than 20,000 telephone calls come in each week (a figure that soars to 200,000 calls during the holiday season). Efficient distribution of incoming calls is handled by a sophisticated computer-guided telecommunications network. Flashing lights and electronic messages help associates respond to calls as quickly as possible. And that's important; they have only 25 seconds to answer before losing a sale.

Even during the busiest times, however, J. Crew Group associates are no mere order takers. They are trained to answer inquiries about fashion, fit, construction, color, and availability. Information is at their fingertips in the computer and throughout the spacious 300-station sales area. Attractive displays of clothing showcase colors and styles alongside important tips and facts. Samples of every item carried in both catalogs hang nearby, and color swatch books are within easy reach when a customer calls to see if two separates match or clash. If they ask about seam finishes or waist measurements, associates can easily find out. Even requests for lost button replacements are no problem.

Associates are kept current on product changes that occurred after the catalog was printed through computerized "item alerts" that provide customers with up-to-the-minute information. Computer technology also helps speed up delivery—in some cases orders are shipped the same day they are taken.

The staff works under an open-door policy—literally. Manager's offices are open and accessible to the associates, and everyone is dressed casually in the comfortable offices and warehouse. Hundreds of little shifts throughout the 19-hour daily operation (7 A.M. to 2 A.M.) accommodate associates' schedules as well as peak shopping times during a typical day.

In addition to the telemarketing operation, J. Crew Group handles all distribution to Clifford & Wills and J. Crew Factory Stores, as well as J. Crew Retail Stores. Asheville's modern warehouse operation serves the stores with a network of conveyors and a sophisticated quality control department. J. Crew Group in Lynchburg, Virginia, handles distribution for catalog sales generated in Asheville and Lynchburg. And all together, the operations create a seamless and efficient shopping experience for a busy society. ▲

Quaker Oats Company

A gamble on a new snack called rice cakes yielded strong returns for the Quaker Oats Company, both on the bottom line and in the community. Already synonymous with hot cereal, Quaker branched into other healthy, grain-based foods, such as granola, in the mid-1980s. As a part of this diversification, the company bought Arden Organics, which was located on Pond Road, south of Asheville. The small but thriving business was owned by a local family credited with having pioneered the rice cake market.

Since then, the financial statistics have shot off the charts. Arden Organics averaged $7 million in annual sales at the time of the purchase. Today, sales are well over $150 million. Despite competition, Quaker has remained the leading producer of the crunchy cakes, with a firm hold on 75 percent of the market share.

This flurry of growth resulted in three expansions of the company's Pond Road plant. Finally, with no room left on the site, the time had come to move. In September 1994, ground was broken on a new 115,000-square-foot facility in the Vista Industrial Center, also south of Asheville. The $13-million project was completed in August 1995 and features an additional production line for mini-rice cakes.

Before investing in the Vista location, the company considered moving its operations out of the state. Other Quaker rice cake plants were already up and running in California, Missouri, and Vermont. And with close to $6 billion in yearly sales and 58 plants around the globe, Quaker could afford to pinpoint the location of its choice. But several factors combined to convince the company that the choice site was right here in Western North Carolina.

When word got out that Quaker might relocate, a united effort was made at both the state and local level to secure its presence in the area. In planning the new site, Quaker worked with the North Carolina Department of Commerce, the Buncombe County Commissioners, and the Asheville Area Chamber of Commerce. Also important to Quaker was the solid workforce in Asheville. Thanks in large part to its employees, the plant had a distinguished record of exceptionally efficient, low-cost production which regularly exceeded industry standards on safety, reliability, and quality.

Community ties promise to become even stronger in the future. With added production space came added employees; Quaker now employs 175 people with competitive wages and a good benefits package. And the company takes seriously its role as corporate citizen well beyond the walls of its facility. Plant Manager Jim Kloman serves on the United Way's board of directors, and the company participates in the organization's fundraisers. Quaker was also a two-year gold sponsor of the Tour DuPont bicycle race. Most recently, the plant formed an employee outreach committee to review ways in which it could become further involved in the community. This wealth of ties and commitments, activity and support are strong indicators that the success story begun at one location will thrive in the next.

Quaker Oats Company employs 175 people and takes seriously its role as corporate citizen well beyond the walls of its facility. *Photo by J. Weiland.*

Medical Action Industries Inc.

In the midst of a health care revolution, Medical Action Industries Inc. has found a prescription for success. To ensure that its line of surgery-related products remains a staple in operating rooms across the country, the company has developed three strategies that center on what Medical Action has always done well: swift turnaround on quality products delivered at a low price.

For more than a decade, Medical Action's manufacturing facility has churned out a leading market share of cotton lap sponges and operating room towels. After manufacture, these products are packaged, sterilized, and delivered to hospitals through major industry distributors. Being the market leader in both sterile lap sponges and sterile operating room towels, the Medical Action facility ships more than 8 million of these combined products each month.

To be successful in today's cost-conscious health care market, Medical Action knew that it would have to sell its products at a cost lower than ever before. In order to meet this goal, its manufacturing process has gone through many innovations. For example, lap sponges—square pieces of four-layer gauze—originally were bundled in envelope-like packages, which Medical Action found that it could wrap in the same form-filled seal machines used to package many different products for significantly less cost. Through such innovations, the company has been able to cut the price of its lap sponges in half in the last 15 years while enhancing quality.

Electronic Data Interchange (EDI) has allowed Medical Action to further cut overhead while it meets a second goal of improved service. The company receives 62 percent of its orders through its network with medical distributors, such as Baxter, Owens & Minor and General Medical. With EDI, it can ship orders within a few days of receiving them, while reducing errors and paperwork. Because of factors like these, Medical Action was named, out of a field of 2,500, as one of Baxter's 72 bronze suppliers, and expects to be a gold supplier in the future.

Medical Action, entering its 20th year, is headquartered in Hauppauge, New York, where Chief Executive Officer Joseph Meringola and President Paul D. Meringola have fostered the company's growth. An Asheville facility was first opened in 1981 near Coxe Avenue but moved to its current location on Sweeten Creek Road in 1985. The new facility, almost triple the size of the first, consists of a 54,600-square-foot plant and a 70,000-square-foot warehouse. Today, the publicly traded company employs a total of 150 people, 120 of whom live in Asheville.

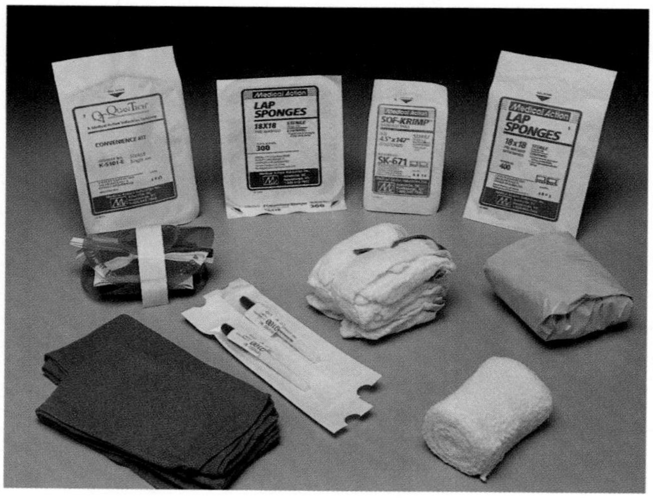

Known as the market leader in both sterile lap sponges and sterile operating room towels, Medical Action ships more than 8 million of these combined products each month.

In the beginning, lap sponges and operating room towels were the company's only products. This list has steadily grown over the years to include such products as specialty sponges and burn dressings. Medical Action's third goal for the future is to diversify further by in-house development and acquisitions similar to its August 1994 purchase of QuanTech and January 1996 purchase of Lawson Mardon. With these steps, Medical Action Industries Inc. plans to not only survive the health care revolution but also to thrive as a result of it. ▲

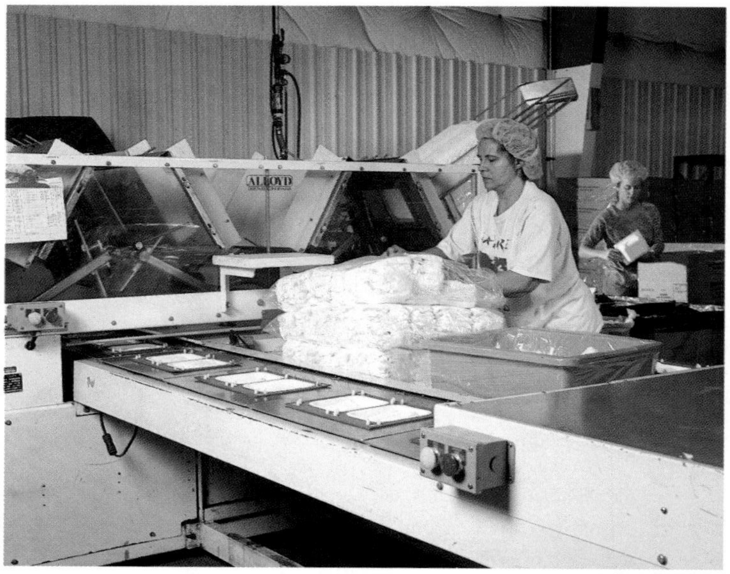

Medical Action Industries Inc. produces quality surgery-related products with a swift turnaround at a low price.

Beacon Manufacturing Company

Sold exclusively to the nation's finest department and specialty stores, Beacon's best-selling, triple-woven cotton jacquard throw featured Simba, the popular hero of *The Lion King,* the 1994 box-office hit by ©Disney.

When the 300 or so members of the Quarter Century Club at Beacon Manufacturing Company's Swannanoa plant get together for dinner, they mull over all the exciting changes that the years have brought to the facility where they work. For these employees, some of whose long service to the company puts them well past the 25-year mark necessary to join the club, steady growth has allowed Beacon to weave its way to a number one ranking as the country's largest blanket manufacturer.

The company, founded in 1904 in New Bedford, Massachusetts, moved its operations to North Carolina during the 1920s, building a facility in Swannanoa and later acquiring another in Oconee County at Westminster, South Carolina. As Beacon grew, so did the size of its manufacturing plants; presently, the huge Swannanoa facility stretches across 1.4 million square feet and employs approximately 900 people in the production of blankets and throws.

In 1994 Beacon was acquired by Pillowtex Corporation, a leading manufacturer and marketer of such home textile products as bed pillows, down comforters, and mattress pads. After the purchase, Pillowtex folded the company into its own smaller blanket operations to form the Beacon Division, now comprised of five manufacturing plants in North and South Carolina and Tennessee, with over 2,000 employees.

The acquisition proved extremely beneficial for both companies. Beacon had traditionally focused a significant part of its sales effort on the mass merchant and institutional (health care and hospitality) markets. Pillowtex, on the other hand, had developed strong distribution channels at all major department stores, national chains, specialty stores, and catalog retailers, as well as mass merchants. By combining the sales, marketing, and distribution expertise in both companies, the Beacon Division furthered its lead as the foremost provider of cotton, acrylic, and wool blankets in the United States and Canada.

The purchase by Pillowtex also allowed the Swannanoa facility to expand its operations, including the increased production of jacquard throws. Jacquards are double- and triple-woven blankets for adults and children that utilize a variety of designs and licensed characters. Steady growth in sales of these and other throws has taken the company from a nonrated status in the throw market in 1994 to a fifth-rated position by 1995.

In order to be sure that its products meet the high quality standards set by its customers, a checkpoint system inspects the product as it moves through the manufacturing process—before it's shipped, a Beacon product will have been checked 39 times for quality. The recent purchase of a yarn spinning facility in Newton, North Carolina, has further assured Beacon of hands-on control over the quality of its products, as it now manages the entire spinning and weaving process.

As vouched for by the Quarter Century Club, Beacon Manufacturing Company has deep roots in the Swannanoa community. And with the facility's production higher than ever, its members will surely have much to look forward to in the next quarter century and beyond. ▲

The Beacon Division manufactures blankets in a wide variety of constructions and fibers, including cotton, acrylic, polyester, and wool. The blanket lines feature a broad solid-color palette, as well as dyed patterns and prints. *Photo by Jamie Williams.*

Isolyser Company, Inc.

An innovator and a leader in the manufacture of disposable goods for the medical industry, Isolyser Company, Inc.'s involvement in Asheville is composed of both long traditions and new beginnings. One of the company's subsidiaries, Isolyser/White Knight, traces its association with the city back to 1947. In 1994 another connection between the Georgia-based company and the city was forged when the Isolyser Roll Goods Division was established in Asheville.

While the predecessors of Isolyser/White Knight began to do business in Asheville in 1947, it wasn't until 1968 that the manufacture of disposable medical products started. This facility produces a complete line of disposable surgical products, consisting of gowns, drapes, masks, headwear, scrub apparel, shoecovers, lab coats, and packs. These products are sold worldwide under the trade names of Orex, Isolyser/White Knight, and Precept.

Many of the company's surgical products are supplied to both domestic and international customers, which uses them as components of their own products. These assembled kits are then marketed around the globe under top brand names.

But Isolyser/White Knight is itself becoming well-known overseas as a result of its aggressive expansion into international markets where disposable products are still used less extensively than in the United States. In recognition of its contribution to export expansion, the President's "E" award from the Secretary of Commerce was given to the company.

Through its Industrial Division, Isolyser/White Knight also manufactures a respected line of safety and clean-room products. These products are utilized by the safety, automotive, and high-tech industries in their own manufacturing processes.

Isolyser Roll Goods Division represents the other half of Isolyser's operations in Asheville. This manufacturing facility is responsible for the production of Orex, the most innovative material being used in the medical industry today. Orex is a hot water-soluble fabric that can be dissolved after use, in a processing unit similar to a commercial washing machine, for safe disposal through the municipal sewer system. Surgical and industrial products made of Orex are being hailed as revolutionary because they combine safety for a hospital's staff and patients with cost-effective solutions to waste reduction and disposal.

In addition to the Asheville area, Isolyser has manufacturing facilities in New Jersey, Alabama, Georgia, Virginia, South Carolina, Texas, Arizona, and Mexico. Based on its success to date, the popularity of Orex should create growth and expansion in all of these facilities.

But a thriving business is not all that Isolyser has brought to Asheville. The company has underscored its belief in community involvement with generous support to local activities and events. These activities have included sponsorships of local youth athletic teams, Walk America, United Way, Adventure Place, and Eliada Home for Children. The company has also received the Asheville Mayor's Committee Award for Employment of Persons With Disabilities. It is through these activities that the employees of Isolyser/White Knight and the Isolyser Roll Goods Division show how much they enjoy calling Asheville home. ▲

The Isolyser Company produces a complete line of disposable surgical products, consisting of gowns, drapes, masks, headwear, scrub apparel, shoecovers, lab coats, and packs. These products are sold worldwide under the trade names of Orex, Isolyser/White Knight, and Precept. ***Photo Tim Barnwell.***

Biltmore Iron & Metal Company, Inc.

If it weren't for Biltmore Iron & Metal Company, Inc., so much scrap metal would accumulate in a year's time that the streets of downtown Asheville would be piled higher than the BB&T Building. Extend that concept over the company's 47-year history, and Buncombe County would be buried by a mountain of metal. Thanks to this third-generation, family-run business in the Biltmore Village district, 21 million aluminum cans (700,000 pounds' worth), 30 million pounds of steel, and 4 million pounds of other metals are recycled each year.

Where does it all go? To regional steel mills. In fact, Biltmore Iron is the last step in the process leading up to the mills, its team of employees preparing the scrap with huge shears, flaming torches, and baling presses.

Biltmore Iron is the largest scrap metal processor in Western North Carolina, and the staff is proud of their industry's slogan—"original recyclers." They are staunch environmentalists, and, as one staff person puts it, they have to be. "We're not only in the recycling business, but our property is also within a historic district in the Asheville city limits, and the Swannanoa River runs through our yard." In addition, family members have helped write nationally significant environmental laws and served on a number of local and national boards of environmental organizations. Biltmore Iron is also a member of the national organization Institute of Scrap Recycling Industries, Inc.

Biltmore Iron is a hot spot for artists. Artists can be found prospecting for scrap to turn into masterpieces ranging from tiny pins to huge freestanding sculptures. *Photo by Tim Barnwell.*

Biltmore Iron & Metal Company is a third-generation, family-run business, which recycles 21 million aluminum cans (700,000 pounds' worth), 30 million pounds of steel, and 4 million pounds of other metals each year. *Photo by Tim Barnwell.*

It is easier to state what Biltmore Iron does not accept—cars and appliances—than to list all the forms of ferrous and nonferrous metals that pass through the yard. The company serves 95 percent of the region's manufacturing plants, offering complete industrial service with fast, efficient pick-up on a routine or scheduled basis, within 24 hours, Monday through Friday. They supply the plants with equipment ranging from small, one-cubic-yard containers to 60 cubic yard roll-off trailers and flatbed, open-top, or van-type trailers, at no charge. Another important source of scrap is what they call "peddler trade"—people bringing in pickup truckloads and carloads of scrap all day long. Whatever the source, Biltmore Iron is recognized for paying up-to-the-minute prices based on the latest information faxed directly to their offices four times daily from the London Metal Exchange and Comex.

Biltmore Iron is a hot spot for artists. The expression "one person's junk is another's treasure" rings particularly true here, where artists can be found prospecting for scrap to turn into masterpieces ranging from tiny pins to huge freestanding sculptures. Biltmore Iron offers a scholarship fund through the University of North Carolina at Asheville which is awarded by the art department faculty each semester.

As times change, Biltmore Iron & Metal is keeping pace. Its commitment to the environment will only get stronger—serving Western North Carolina with a vital need in the years ahead. ▲

TOURISM
FILM PRODUCTION
CRAFT INDUSTRY
AGRIBUSINESS
WESTERN NC
STATE
BUSINESS DEVELOPMENT
COMMUNITIES
EXIT
ADVANTAGEWEST
CUSTOM
SONY

CHAPTER TWELVE

BUSINESS AND FINANCE

Asheville's business, insurance, and financial communities offer a strong base for the area's growing economy.

Asheville Area Chamber of Commerce

Without private initiative and free enterprise, there can be no such thing as a Chamber of Commerce. In partnership with the people of the Asheville area, the Asheville Area Chamber of Commerce, for the past 100 years, has been creating win-win opportunities for this diverse and vital community.

The Chamber works on many fronts to bolster the local business climate. Through its Economic Development Department, the organization helps bring new businesses to the area, both via targeted business recruitment and by promoting the region's strengths and assets (including its exceptional quality of life) to potential investors. Each year, the Chamber responds to hundreds of requests for relocation and start-up information from companies outside the region.

At the same time, the Chamber also assists existing industries, helping them solve problems that may limit their expansion possibilities. Providing economic statistics and research materials helps both local companies and potential investors identify market niches and site facilities.

Members are the heart of the Chamber, and member benefits and volunteer opportunities keep the organization strong. Although Asheville is the ninth-largest city in North Carolina, it boasts the state's third-largest Chamber membership. And the United States Chamber of Commerce has awarded the Asheville Chamber its 30th-year accreditation, a distinction held by only 10 percent of the nation's Chambers of Commerce.

No community, however, no matter how successful, can afford to stand still. To this end, the Asheville Chamber plays an active role in tapping into fresh ideas and developing new strategies for the future, seeking to improve economic conditions for local businesses while enhancing the quality of life for all Asheville/Buncombe residents.

Before goals can be achieved, however, they have to be identified. Accordingly, one of the Chamber's most inspiring efforts has been its participation in the Vision process. Working together over many months, this partnership involving A-B Tech, the local business community, city and county governments, many community organizations—and extensive input from the area's diverse citizenry—has produced a concrete plan for improving the area's economic vitality and quality of life as it moves into the twenty-first century.

To provide an orderly procedure for fulfilling its own vision, the Chamber has developed a five-year strategic plan. This working document developed by the Chamber staff and business leadership provides a guide for producing yearly departmental plans and a means to hold the organization accountable to the members and customers it serves.

Advantage Asheville! is the Chamber's most ambitious initiative to date. This economic program is helping the community become an economic force to be reckoned with as it begins the new millennium. Focusing on workforce preparedness, business development, and other services to businesses, Advantage Asheville! aims to create 8,000 new jobs, generate $225 million in new capital investment, recruit 10 targeted employers, and realize a total economic impact of $45 million per year, over a five-year period.

Another forward-looking program is the Chamber's Intercity Visit program, a "learning laboratory" that enables business, community, and governmental leaders to travel to other cities to learn from their successes.

Inevitably, many of these initiatives spill over into the public sector, and the Chamber's Public Affairs Department works hand in hand with local, state, and federal officials to ensure that government regulations foster a good business climate and growth opportunities. The Local and Governmental Affairs Task Forces examine issues of concern to local business and maintain contacts with key officials. Receptions, candidate forums, quarterly meetings with the Asheville City Council and the Buncombe County Board of Commissioners, regular dialogue with state legislators, and an annual meeting with area representatives in Washington, D.C. all help keep these relationships remain strong. In addition, Public Affairs works with government and business leaders to address key infrastructure needs, such as airline expansion and highway and water-source improvements.

Another exciting venture is the Buncombe County Economic Development Commission, a public-private partnership between the Chamber and the Buncombe County Board of Commissioners. This program is creating jobs, stimulating private-sector investment, and providing crucial infrastructure improvements.

Education, of course, is a key aspect of many facets of the Asheville Chamber's work. The comprehensive School-to-Work program helps ensure that both businesses and schools are "job ready" by developing clearly defined pathways from the classroom to today's high-tech workplace. Partners in Education enlists businesses to help provide schools with key resources, and Summer Shadows is just one of several programs promoting career awareness through extended on-the-job mentoring.

Tourism continues to play a major role in the local economy, and the Chamber's Convention & Visitors Bureau (CVB) actively promotes the area's multimillion-dollar tourism industry. The Visitors Center serves more than 130,000 people annually, providing valuable information about the region. In addition, the CVB's staff recruits conventions and motorcoach tours throughout the year. Together, these initiatives bring millions of tourists and conventioneers to the area each year, producing a total economic impact in the hundreds of millions of dollars.

International awareness of Asheville is also growing, due in large part to the CVB's efforts. Participation in trade shows and sales missions to Germany, the United Kingdom, and France is paying off, as area attractions report an increased number of visitors from those countries. The CVB also conducts a multimillion-dollar media campaign, marketing Asheville's tourist attractions and scenic beauty to national and international media.

Besides attending to the needs of large employers, the Asheville Chamber also maintains a broad array of programs aimed at helping small businesses flourish. Monthly "Donuts and Dialogue" meetings address the special problems of new businesses. The affordable Executive Seminar Series workshops introduce new ideas and strategies to help ensure continuing business success. And small business counseling helps entrepreneurs launch and nurture their businesses.

Finally, a variety of awards—such as Small Business of the Month, Small Business Leader of the Year, and the Athena Award (which highlights the accomplishments of women-owned businesses)—gives successful small businesses a well-deserved pat on the back.

Through all of these programs, as well as through its homepage on the Internet, the Asheville Area Chamber of Commerce is helping this distinctive community position itself for the future, preserving and enhancing its remarkable quality of life while promoting business growth and development. ▲

Pictured is a reproduction of an original watercolor painting of downtown Asheville, as seen from South Charlotte Street, by local artist Ann Vasilik. The painting is an official watercolor of the Asheville Area Chamber of Commerce, emphasizing the Chamber's role in Asheville/Buncombe's commitment to a renewed vision.

Asheville Savings Bank

It was early 1936. Later that year, the citizens of Asheville were to help FDR win a landslide re-election. They would attend, in record numbers, the Imperial Theater on Patton Avenue to view the movie *The Great Ziegfeld.* They would also help Dale Carnegie's new book *How to Win Friends and Influence People* become a best-seller across the country and at Brown's Book Company on College Street (then called Government Street).

And in February they viewed with curiosity and anticipation the formation of a new financial institution called Asheville Federal Savings and Loan Association. It was headquartered initially at 12 Church Street—a fine location, situated between a funeral home and a former speakeasy.

FDR is, presumably, resting peacefully. The Imperial Theater is now a parking lot, and Brown's Book Company closed years ago. But the financial institution, now known as Asheville Savings Bank, remains as a State Savings Bank, stronger, more viable, and more committed to the community than ever before. It has moved its corporate offices from the single room at 12 Church Street across the street to 11 Church Street and built eight branches located throughout Asheville and surrounding areas. Asheville Savings Bank is, incidentally, the largest locally owned and managed independent community mutual financial institution remaining in Asheville.

"One participant took me aside to comment on the range of products we offer and their remarkable affordability. She was amazed," states Brady Blackburn, mortgage loan originator.
Photo by Tim Barnwell.

The bank has prospered, in large measure because of its profound and genuine commitment to the people of the communities it serves, to provide competitive products at a level of service above the norm.

"I had just finished a presentation about our bank to a group of visitors, mostly from outside our area who were attending a retirement forum here in Asheville. One participant took me aside to comment on the range of products we offer and their remarkable affordability. She was amazed," states Brady Blackburn, mortgage loan originator.

Asheville Savings Bank is a retail bank—focused on people—with a full range of banking products. All savings and checking accounts are insured by the Federal Deposit Insurance Corporation (FDIC). Opportunities for savings run the gamut from the traditional passbook (the children's passbook accounts require a minimum opening deposit of only $10), to certificates of deposit with terms from 90 days to 5 years, some with a "bump rate" provision, others with a "blended rate," which allows additions to the certificate without affecting the maturity date.

"I recently received a call from a checking customer thanking us for calling her when she inadvertently forgot to make a deposit, causing a check she had written to be in jeopardy of being returned. She said the big banks don't do that. I accepted the compliment but confessed that was standard practice for us," said Becky Girard, branch manager.

"...of course we will process the application and close the loan before we leave. How else should a customer be treated?" says Susan Pike, manager of consumer loan origination.
Photo by Tim Barnwell.

Asheville Savings Bank offers seven different checking accounts designed for customer groups ranging from student accounts to retirement checking. A checking account can be opened for $50 or less. All can earn interest, be free of monthly service charges, and have a wealth of features. For example, all accounts can be supported by overdraft protection as well as ATMs, enabling customers to access their accounts around the world.

"It is not unusual for a customer to come in on Friday, 15 minutes before closing, with a request for a loan to purchase a dream car. Of course we will process the application and close the loan before we leave. How else should a customer be treated?" says Susan Pike, manager of consumer loan origination.

Asheville Savings Bank, while making its name as a mortgage lender, has an extensive consumer loan department. Requests for all types of installment loans are considered. As a community bank should, the bank works hard to keep its rates among the lowest around. For example, it offers one of the few fixed rate, no annual fee credit cards in the country, as well as "no closing costs" home equity loans. It has an aggressive automobile financing operation and has become one the area's primary personal lenders.

"Customers are amazed that we process transactions the day we receive them no matter what time they are placed in our hands. That applies to a loan payment or a deposit to a checking account. None of that 2:00 P.M. cut-off business for us. Our customers love it," states Olivia Gash, retail banking officer.

Asheville Savings Bank strives to do everything well. But one area of real expertise is that of mortgage lending. The bank has traditionally been the area's predominant mortgage lender, making more loans to more people than any other financial institution. Mortgage loans are made regardless of size. In fact, the bank has been cited by area housing groups for its activism in working with low and moderate income groups. The bank offers conventional mortgage loans, government insured loans, construction/permanent loans, fixed, or variable rates with varied terms. Incidentally, mortgage customers receive no-fee checking privileges with the bank. More information about the bank's mortgage lending activities can be obtained on the Internet.

"Asheville Savings Bank is in business to help people. We believe our customers demand innovative, affordable products as well as exceptional and caring service. We are committed to providing nothing less," states President John B. Dickson.

"The fact that we have been in business for 60 years is something in which we take a great deal of pride. Our longevity is the result of prudent, conservative management—very typical of a small community bank. We boast a healthy net worth. Our ratios [those indices examiners use to gauge our soundness] are well above regulatory requirements."

"At the end of June 1996, the bank held more than $323 million in assets. In these days of 'bigness' in the banking industry, we revel in our uniqueness—in our 'smallness' and, therefore, in our ability to provide the communities we serve excellence in financial services," concludes Dickson.

Asheville Savings Bank is rooted in the past—poised for the future. ▲

"Customers are amazed that we process transactions the day we receive them no matter what time they are placed in our hands," states Olivia Gash, retail banking officer. *Photo by Tim Barnwell.*

There are eight Asheville Savings Bank branches located throughout Asheville and surrounding areas, such as this Skyland location. *Photo by John Dickson.*

BB&T

(Left to right) BB&T City Executive Doug Roth, and David Hughes, Chief Financial Officer of McKibbon Brothers, Inc., discuss the final construction phase and grand opening of the Courtyard by Marriott Hotel, financed by BB&T, which was completed in August of 1996. *Photo by Tim Barnwell.*

In 1995 BB&T enhanced its relationship with Western North Carolina when it established a regional headquarters in Asheville. For a financial institution that has made a hallmark of its personal approach to banking, this move reinforced its commitment to provide a high level of service in the area.

As a result of the regionalization, BB&T added a full cadre of bank officials and specialists to its downtown Asheville office. For their clients, these in-house resources translate into quick, flexible decision-making, be it on a loan or a service question. "We like to be in touch with our clients," said Fred Groce Jr., president of BB&T's western region. "Our aim is to operate like a community bank with the resources of a larger bank."

But how many hometown banks can boast $21 billion in assets? BB&T's recent merger with Southern National Corporation gave it the second largest market share in North Carolina and the third largest in South Carolina. Through the 1995 merger, the bank also maintains a strong presence along the east coast of Virginia.

This tristate territory was divided into 16 regions after the merger, each with its own center of operations. "It's really the best of both worlds for our clients," noted Groce of the BB&T network. The responsiveness of a local headquarters is combined with a full range of large bank products, such as leasing, cash management, investment, and trust services. Call centers field customer inquiries 24 hours a day. And PC-based banking will soon be available.

The bank's commercial services and lending programs cater to small and middle-market businesses (defined as having anywhere from $1 to $50 million in sales). BB&T prides itself on having more long-term partnerships of this kind than any other bank in the Carolinas.

BB&T's presence in Western North Carolina involves work with a number of community organizations. The bank plays an active role in the Asheville Area Chamber of Commerce. It also provides support to many nonprofit agencies, such as the United Way and the Arts Alliance.

The institution's beginnings can be traced back to Branch Banking and Trust Company, founded in Wilson in 1872; it remains North Carolina's oldest bank. The company survived the Depression and even managed to open new branches at a time when many banks were closing their doors. Gradually BB&T worked its way west, earning as it went a reputation as one of the country's safest and soundest financial institutions. In its western region alone, BB&T now operates 25 branches in 9 counties and employs approximately 260 people. And Groce foresees more branch openings over the next few years.

As a relative newcomer to this market, BB&T has a simple plan to gain recognition: provide unmatched client service. According to Groce, employees have responded to the challenge of breaking new ground. "I think that in their desire to grow, our people are just much more willing to go the extra mile for their clients." ▲

(Left to right) Becky Hughes, regional mortgage manager, and Emily Lineberger, mortgage loan officer, review mortgage financing options with developer D. Brent Nappier, owner of Nappier & Gunnels Construction Co., Inc. at Biltmore Commons in Asheville. *Photo by Tim Barnwell.*

Colton Groome & Company

The firm of Colton Groome & Company understands that many people feel immobilized by the increasingly complex world of finance—where each day a new crop of products and programs seems to spring forth with uncertain promises. That is why this Asheville financial services firm has developed its own unique method to guide both its individual and corporate clients through the steps of financial and benefit planning, an approach it terms as "sophisticated simplicity."

The "sophisticated" half of the phrase comes from Colton Groome & Company's ability to offer a full spectrum of products and strategies that protects and maximizes clients' assets. Through strategic partnerships and proprietary alliances with many of the leading institutions and analytical minds involved in finance today, the firm can sift and search through various markets to find the services which best suit the particular needs of each client.

Colton Groome & Company brings "simplicity" to the table when presenting its recommendations to clients. Sophisticated and complex analyses are reduced to their essential elements that make the concepts easy to follow. Armed with a clear understanding of the choices in front of them, clients are motivated to make their financial decisions.

George Groome brings "sophisticated simplicity" to the table when presenting recommendations to clients. Analyses are laid out in terms that make complex concepts meaningful. *Photo by Tim Barnwell.*

Founded by (left) Henry Colton, the company's list of clients has grown to include area physicians, dentists, lawyers, accountants, company presidents, and business owners—in short, a who's who of Asheville's most successful individuals. *Photo by Tim Barnwell.*

The firm was founded in 1953 by Henry E. Colton, a lawyer from Morganton, North Carolina, as a life insurance planning organization that specialized in retirement and estate planning. In the late 1960s, the firm began its expansion into a broader range of financial services. George Groome joined the company in 1974 and continued establishing the firm as a leader in the areas of comprehensive financial planning, corporate benefit planning, group benefit programs, and insurance and investment services.

Over its 45 years of business, Colton Groome & Company's list of clients has grown to include area physicians, dentists, lawyers, accountants, company presidents, and business owners—in short, a who's who of Asheville's most successful individuals. The firm also works with more than 100 corporations, coordinating multiple benefit programs for some 10,000 participants in the region.

Many of the firm's relationships with clients stretch back 10, 25, and, in some cases, even 45 years. Of its new clients, the vast majority are referred to the firm by their attorneys, accountants, and associates who are already clients of Colton Groome & Company. Obviously, this retention rate and chain of referral depends on a proven track record of success. That success stems from the firm's close attention to the goals and priorities of its clients, a knowledge which is continuously updated and fine-tuned as the relationship develops over time. Most importantly, Colton Groome & Company gives its clients the tools to measure that success because benchmarks and timetables have been clearly articulated at the outset.

The firm's reputation for quality, value, and integrity has been earned over four decades of business. For the future, the firm of Colton Groome & Company is committed to remaining on the leading edge of financial services that are unsurpassed in their sophistication, and which are based on the simple belief that the client always comes first. ▲

First Union Corporation

Under the direction of Don Harrison, Asheville market president, First Union offers a line of investment and trust services as well as annuities.

Go back far enough in the family tree of First Union Corporation, the nation's sixth largest banking company with 2,000 branches from Newark, New Jersey, to Miami, Florida, and you'll find roots which begin in Asheville. In fact, as a result of a 1958 merger between First National of Asheville and Charlotte's Union National, Asheville put the "First" in First Union. First Union-Asheville is noted as one of the company's top performers with a leading market share in the area. The strength of that bond is evident today in First Union's choice of Asheville to test its latest banking solutions.

In 1996 First Union began a pilot program in its Asheville branches that transformed them into banks of the future—complete with advanced ATMs and interactive video kiosks. Asheville's banks will test new methods of delivering financial services before they are implemented throughout First Union's branches. While these innovations take many forms, they share an old-fashioned principle: always exceed the customer's expectations.

First Union National Bank offers its customers 24-hour banking at eight convenient locations across Asheville.

And that means convenient banking anytime, anywhere. So in the future, First Union customers can check their account balance over the phone when they get off work, even if that's at midnight. They can pay bills over the Internet while seated in front of their home computer or check the latest mortgage rates from a kiosk in their local branch.

"I think it's a real compliment to Asheville and our employees here that we were chosen to pilot these new systems," said Don Harrison, Asheville market president. From the pilot bank project, First Union will learn which systems customers prefer. "Our challenge is to make sure that we stay in tune with our customers and what their needs are," said Harrison. "The pilots are our way of meeting them on their terms."

First Union's penchant for technology extends into their product line as well. The bank now offers Smart Cards which can be used in place of cash. The small plastic cards have an embedded microchip that stores the cash value remaining after transactions.

But many of the bank's products do not rely on microchips for their sophistication. A popular new financial tool called a CAP Account combines everyday banking with investment banking. In addition, First Union offers a line of investment and trust services as well as annuities. And First Union's Evergreen Funds are a highly rated family of mutual funds managed by the institution.

"On the one hand, we're an old, established bank here in Asheville," said Harrison. "On the other, we're an institution with $132 billion in assets that's been a part of some fast-paced changes." And First Union-Asheville branches are a perfect illustration of the company's commitment to the city where it got its start. ▲

Insurance Service of Asheville, Inc.

When James W. Stickney III founded Insurance Service of Asheville, Inc. (ISA) in 1958, he knew that its success would depend on the company's ability to match clients with the policies that best fit their needs. To do so, the independent agency built a diverse portfolio of carriers from among the most prominent in the industry. But more importantly, ISA began a tradition of personal service to make certain it was always in touch with clients' needs—a commitment that continues today.

As an independent agency representing many top-rated carriers, ISA offers customers competitive markets and individualized services for virtually all lines of coverage. In addition to personal insurance such as home, auto, and life, ISA carries a complete commercial line that can accommodate small firms to large, complex accounts. Many area businesses and institutions are insured through the agency, including a large segment of the medical community. In fact, ISA is one of the largest and oldest agencies in the state to specialize in insurance for health care providers.

After careful analysis of an account, ISA moves quickly to sort through these options for the right coverage, carriers, and prices. "Because of our knowledge of various insurance markets, we can find the best terms and rates for our customers," explained James W. Stickney IV, who recently replaced his father as president of the agency. ISA also uses its leverage with carriers to negotiate favorable terms and to act as an advocate for clients should a claim problem arise.

ISA insureds ordinarily deal with only one familiar agent or assigned technician for all services, from orders and claims to account questions. "It is important to us that we handle each client on a one-on-one basis so that they can be assured that whoever meets with them has extensive knowledge of their particular account," said Jim IV.

With an average of 14 years of experience, the staff has the skills necessary to manage and interpret insurance needs and available policies. Low turnover—recent retirements came after 25 and 30 years of service—means that the agent a customer works with today will more than likely be there tomorrow.

This sense of continuity runs through all aspects of ISA. "We've been in business for almost 40 years now and as a family- owned business, we plan to be around for 40 more," said Jim IV. His father maintains a strong advisory role in the company, and his brother, Sam Stickney, acts as the agency's senior vice president. Together, ISA's principals and staff have kept the company's founding philosophy of personal service a vital component of daily operations.

The Stickneys are lifelong residents of Asheville, so it is not surprising that ISA is active with many organizations dedicated to improving the area's quality of life, such as United Way, the YMCA, and the American Red Cross. It is just another way in which Insurance Service of Asheville serves the community by insuring its future. ▲

ISA principals (left to right) James W. Stickney IV, president; James W. Stickney III, founder and chairman; and Samuel M. Stickney, senior vice president, have a combined 68 years of insurance experience and service to Asheville area families and businesses. *Photos by Sandra Stambaugh.*

The ISA staff makes certain they are always in touch with their clients' needs.

Benchmark Business Products

When a dedicated local business teams up with an innovative world-class corporation, something exciting happens for their customers. Case in point: Benchmark Business Products, the authorized Xerox sales agency for 11 Western North Carolina counties, founded by Mark Lindsay in 1990. So successful was this partnership that within two years Benchmark expanded from serving Buncombe and Henderson Counties to include Transylvania, Haywood, Jackson, Macon, Clay, Cherokee, Graham, Swain, and Madison. Since then, staffing has risen from one to seven, office space has quadrupled, and sales have increased a remarkable 300 percent.

Lindsay is quick to credit his company's success to Xerox's innovative way of doing business. Its leadership through quality strategy utilizes quality processes in everything from service, supplies, and manufacturing to marketing and administration. Xerox also employs a sales system known as the agent channel in which independent business people represent Xerox in their communities.

"Sales agent channels are so successful," Lindsay explains, "because they give local business people the opportunity to sell a full array of world-class products and solutions backed by Xerox. This channel is unique to our industry, which means we can do things for our customers that no one else can." Benchmark and Xerox are able to offer a total document solution with a complete product line that includes fax machines, laser printers, digital products, scanners, color copiers and printers, software, and, of course, copiers—ranging in size from tabletop models to publishing systems almost 30 feet long.

Benchmark shares Xerox's priorities—customer satisfaction is number one, employee satisfaction runs a close second, with return on assets third. "We figure if you take care of the first two," Lindsay adds, "the third one will take care of itself."

Their approach to sales is also threefold. First, agents determine needs and make recommendations. Next, they provide quality equipment at competitive prices, and, finally, they deliver after-sales support backed by Xerox's total satisfaction guarantee. "We want to be partners with our customers," Lindsay states. "If we can provide these services reliably, customers will call on us again when other needs arise."

The team at Benchmark is able to provide a total document solution for their customers by utilizing the latest technology from Xerox Corporation.

Today, rapid change has become a way of life, and Benchmark deals with technological advancements almost daily. Digital and color equipment, for example, are changing the workplace, and Benchmark and Xerox are well-positioned to take the lead. Color copying costs continue to come down while the quality goes up, and digital equipment cuts time and improves the quality of the finished product. To keep pace, agents receive extensive training which positions them as valuable consultants to their customers.

Owner Mark Lindsay feels Benchmark and Xerox are well positioned to help customers transition to the new generation of color and digital products like the Majestik Color Series shown here.

The company also contributes to the community through active participation in the United Way, WNC Child Abuse Center, KidCare ID Programs, and the Asheville Area Chamber of Commerce. Lindsay served for two years as vice chair for the Chamber's Community Development Committee and chair of its Education Council.

Lindsay sees his company as a partner with its customers, the community, and, of course, Xerox. "This allows us to work with our customers to analyze their document needs. Then we can recommend a total document solution that will have a positive impact on the customer's entire organization." ▲

S. LEXINGTON
WALK

CHAPTER THIRTEEN

PROFESSIONS

From law to architecture, accounting to graphic design, Asheville's professional firms are recognized as leaders in their field.

Roberts & Stevens, P.A.

From the upper floors of downtown Asheville's tallest building, the law offices of Roberts & Stevens, P.A. look out upon a panoramic view: the bustle of city streets gives way to the trees and distant rooftops of the surrounding countryside. A blue perimeter of mountains stretches across the horizon. The view underscores the law firm's own regional outlook, serving clients, as Landon Roberts puts it, "from the Tennessee line to the Catawba River."

Under the direction of (standing) Landon Roberts and (seated) John S. Stevens, the law firm of Roberts & Stevens was formed when two Asheville firms combined in 1986. *Photo by Tim Barnwell.*

Roberts & Stevens was formed when two Asheville firms combined in 1986. Both firms had long histories in Western North Carolina but contributed different areas of expertise. Roberts Cogburn McClure & Williams, P.A. was an active trial firm, while Redmond Stevens Loftin & Currie, P.A. had earned an excellent reputation for its work in the corporate sector. "We found that the two complemented each other," said James Williams, now a senior partner at Roberts & Stevens. "It just made sense for us to join forces to better serve our clients."

The goal of the firm, which remains one of the largest in Western North Carolina, is to provide its clients with a full range of legal services. To ensure the quality of those services, attorneys concentrate on individual areas of practice and have an in-depth knowledge of their respective fields. These areas of practice include litigation, corporate, business and banking law, real property, estate planning and administration, tax, work with public sector organizations, health law, environmental law, employment law, education law, and bankruptcy.

A substantial portion of the firm's practice is in the area of health law. "We represent a large number of hospitals, physicians, and other health care providers," noted Williams. "Our lawyers keep abreast of the significant changes occurring in the delivery of health care today."

Members of the firm take a responsive approach to their relationships with clients. Emphasis is placed on personal attention and open communication. Roberts & Stevens' long list of clients vouches for the popularity of its methods as well as the diversity of its practice. The list includes some of the region's best-known businesses and organizations, such as the Biltmore House and Gardens, Champion International Corporation, Memorial Mission Medical Center, and Asheville-Buncombe Technical College. The firm also stands high in the eyes of its peers in the legal community. This respect was shown when John S. Stevens, a former state legislator, was asked to serve as president of the North Carolina Bar Association in 1995-1996.

Asked the reasons for the firm's success, Stevens says, "I just received a letter from a client of ours that I think says it best." He retrieves the letter and reads it aloud with obvious pride. (Although, ever the attorney, he does not reveal the client's identity.)

A story unfolds in which the client wished to acquire some property, but the purchase had become mired in a series of complications. The deal seemed hopelessly bogged down for months until Roberts & Stevens was called in. Within days, an "aggressive game plan" was in place, wrote the client. An attorney from Roberts & Stevens who works principally in environmental law oversaw the project. He coordinated efforts with two other attorneys from the firm who specialize in corporate law and real property. Together, the lawyers tackled all aspects of the transaction in order to move it toward a swift resolution. The letter went on to praise the team's initiative, rapid follow-up, frank opinions, and full disclosure of costs.

From the upper floors of downtown Asheville's tallest building, the law offices of Roberts & Stevens, P.A. look out upon a panoramic view: the bustle of city streets gives way to the trees and distant rooftops of the surrounding countryside. *Photo by Tim Barnwell.*

The firm draws on many resources to solve clients' legal problems. "It's always been our desire to deliver services promptly, efficiently, and accurately," said Williams. "In order to do that, we've really pushed ahead in the area of technology." Roberts & Stevens uses state-of-the-art systems to network its computers. In fact, their network was sophisticated enough to warrant a visit from

To ensure quality services, attorneys concentrate on individual areas of practice and have an in-depth knowledge of their respective fields. *Photo by Tim Barnwell.*

the North Carolina Bar Association, which later adopted a similar system for its new center near Raleigh.

Members of the firm can use the network to access the firm's documents from their desktops. Specific documents can be recalled and searches done by key words and subject matter. Because materials and data are easily shared, duplication of effort is avoided. On-line services and CD-ROM libraries contain recently released legal, medical, and scientific information from around the world. The firm's laptop computers are networked, too—lawyers away on business have complete research capabilities through communication lines.

Roberts & Stevens strives to be a pleasant, friendly place for clients to visit. It also strives to be a nice place to come to work. "We try to be people-oriented, and provide our staff and firm members with a positive environment," Williams explains. The firm is made up of more than 50 people who work as attorneys, legal assistants, and administrative staff. They work together to create the ideal atmosphere at Roberts & Stevens—one that blends professionalism and integrity with warmth and camaraderie.

By its client list alone, Roberts & Stevens' claim to a regional outlook would be well-founded. But the firm's interest in Western North Carolina extends to support numerous charitable and non-profit organizations as well as the region's arts through a generous program of giving back to the community. The firm has sponsored the Asheville Symphony and The Acting Company at Pack Place. It is also an underwriter for WCQS public radio. According to Stevens, the reason is a simple one: "The arts make a community liveable." Through its sponsorship of the arts in Asheville, Roberts & Stevens shows its appreciation for a remarkable city that is big enough to support theater and ballet, yet small enough to require only a ten-minute commute to work.

Efforts to improve the area's quality of life carry over to many other local organizations. Roberts & Stevens contributes to Big Brothers/Big Sisters, Pisgah Legal Services, Mountain Area Hospice, Manna Food Bank, and United Way, as well as local schools and hospitals and numerous other organizations. Firm members are encouraged to actively participate in these groups. For example, members of the firm serve or have served as board members and officers of such organizations as Memorial Mission and St. Joseph's Hospitals and their foundations; Daniel Boone Boy Scout Council; Pisgah Girl Scout Council; Mountain Area Hospice; The Red Cross; Greater Asheville Chamber of Commerce; Community Foundation of Western North Carolina; and the Airport Authority, among others. "It's our attempt to be a good citizen," said Roberts. All of these activities might be another way to say that when the members of Roberts & Stevens look out their windows, they don't simply see a map of clients—they see a region to which they are committed. ▲

The lawyers of Roberts & Stevens work to blend professionalism and integrity with warmth and camaraderie. *Photo by Tim Barnwell.*

Van Winkle, Buck, Wall, Starnes & Davis

Van Winkle, Buck, Wall, Starnes and Davis is one of the oldest law firms in North Carolina with a long, distinguished history. At the turn of the century, Kingsland Van Winkle came to Asheville to assist George W. Vanderbilt with real estate titles for the vast mountain acreage which would become the Biltmore Estate. In 1907 Thomas J. Harkins, national head of the Masonic Order, joined Van Winkle, and their practice prospered. A merger in 1931 with Kester Walton, a consummate litigator, and Charles Buck, a real estate specialist, created what has become the region's largest law firm. Van Winkle and later Buck each served many years as chair of the State Board of Law Examiners.

Over the years, the firm of Van Winkle, Buck, Wall, Starnes and Davis has expanded its areas of practice to provide a wide variety of services for its clients' changing needs. *Photo by Tim Barnwell.*

These early partners established the Firm's consistently high standards of practice and commitment to client relations and public service. Consider the impressive list of accomplishments of its principals. O. E. Starnes, its senior practicing member, is one of the few attorneys in North Carolina inducted into the North Carolina Bar Association General Practice Hall of Fame; Roy Davis is past president of the North Carolina State Bar; Larry McDevitt is past president of the North Carolina Bar Association; and Brian Lavelle was the first Board Certified Specialist in Estate Planning and Probate Law in Western North Carolina. In addition, three attorneys are Fellows of the American College of Trial Lawyers; three are Fellows of the American College of Trust and Estate Counsel; six are listed in the publication *Best Lawyers in America;* four have served as members of the Board of Governors of the North Carolina Bar Association; four have served as President of the Buncombe County Bar; two have served on the North Carolina Board of Specialization; and five have advanced degrees of master of laws or have received specialty certification. More than plaques on the wall, these distinctions represent peer recognition for the quality and commitment of Van Winkle attorneys.

Over the years, the Firm has expanded its areas of practice, building upon the real estate expertise of Van Winkle and Buck and the trial skills of Harkins and Walton to provide a wide variety of services for their clients' changing needs. Clients include individuals from all walks of life, as well as partnerships, public and closely held corporations, small- and medium-sized businesses, banks, insurance companies, realty agents, doctors and professionals of all disciplines, municipal and county governments, regional planning bodies, charitable and religious organizations, and various health care providers, among others.

While the Firm maintains an active general civil practice, it has taken the lead in an age of specialization to serve its diverse client base. Specialists in litigation, business, real estate, taxation, estate planning and probate, bankruptcy, employee benefits and executive compensation, health care, banking and commercial law, administrative and regulatory law, and bond financing have earned the Firm an outstanding reputation throughout the region and the state.

Additionally, all attorneys in the Firm are encouraged to provide pro bono representation of those unable to pay for services and to serve the community. An impressive list of community service work includes board membership, counsel, and leadership for the Asheville Area Chamber of Commerce, American Red Cross, Habitat for Humanity, American Cancer Society, Land of Sky Regional Council, Rotary Club, Zeb Vance Debating Society, Western North Carolina Community Foundation, Carolina Day School, Buncombe County Women's Involvement Council, Friendship Force, North Carolina Center for International Understanding, Mainstay, Asheville Tax Study Group, Pack Place, Memorial Mission Hospital, Handi-Skills, Asheville VISION, YMCA, YWCA, ABCCM, Community Arts Council, UNCA, and the United Way, to name a few.

The Van Winkle firm continues to grow, maintaining offices in Asheville and Hendersonville with 26 attorneys and 40 support staff serving both offices. In 1986 the Firm purchased and renovated a four-story, historic building on North Market Street for its Asheville offices and in 1995 acquired and restored quarters on Main Street for its Hendersonville offices. ▲

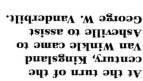

At the turn of the century, Kingsland Van Winkle came to Asheville to assist George W. Vanderbilt.

Killian, Cole & Marshall, P.A.

From inception as a one-man firm in 1966, Killian, Cole & Marshall, P.A. has grown to include four principals, eight other professional personnel, six support staff, and various seasonal and part-time staff. As the economy and the community around it change, this 30-year-old firm is evolving to better serve its clients with a continuing emphasis on personalized professional services. In addition to traditional services dealing with annual financial reporting and tax returns, the firm has emphasized related small business consulting and tax planning services, periodic business accounting services, and specialized areas such as business valuations and estate tax planning.

Active principals in the firm include Chuck Killian, president; Harold Cole, treasurer; Wayne Marshall, secretary; and Jim Hunter. Their commitment to Western North Carolina is evident in their contributions to civic and professional communities. Each has taken an active role in organizations like the North Carolina Association of CPAs and the Asheville Chamber of Commerce, and numerous civic and religious organizations. In addition to membership of the firm's individual CPAs in the American Institute of CPAs, the firm is a member of the Private Companies Practice Section of the AICPA.

This dynamic firm is committed to maintaining the highest professional standards through continuing education and specialization. "The public accounting profession has traditionally avoided specialty designations," Chuck Killian states. "But this has changed in recent years. The American Institute of CPAs has developed several specialized educational programs which include a specific group of courses, each with its own examination. Upon successful completion of the program, the AICPA awards a Certificate of Educational Achievement (CEA) in the subject area." At this time, Wayne Marshall and Harvey Jenkins have earned CEAs in taxation of small, closely held businesses and their shareholders, which is a major point of emphasis for this firm; David Cabe has earned the CEA in government and not-for-profit accounting; and Chuck Killian has earned the CEA in business valuation. Killian also recently received the designation of Certified Valuation Analyst (CVA) from the National Association of CVAs after completion of a competitive examination.

Under the direction of partners (left to right) Wayne Marshall, Chuck Killian, Harold Cole, and Jim Hunter, the 30-year-old firm has evolved to better serve its clients with a continuing emphasis on personalized professional services. *Photo by Tim Barnwell.*

As a major firm in the region with many years of cumulative professional experience and expertise, Killian, Cole & Marshall provides financial statement audit, review, and compilation services, and tax preparation services to a wide variety of established and new businesses in Western North Carolina.

Monthly accounting services also figure prominently in the firm's offered services. Experienced accountants assist small businesses, providing a full range of periodic accounting and tax reporting services under the direction of a principal or manager in the firm. "Our clients provide basic information, and we take it from there. This service has proven to be very cost-effective. Our clients receive sophisticated periodic reporting which many could not generate internally, while benefitting from the expertise and counsel of our experienced professionals. Our business clients have a minimum of two principals or managers who understand their business, so they are not reliant on only one individual. Our clients are not just a number with us. As a firm, we take pride in working together to meet a client's needs," Killian concludes.

Killian, Cole & Marshall strives to maintain this close bond with its clients. Emphasis and specialization in personalized services like consulting, tax planning, business valuation, and litigation support are some of the reasons customer loyalty figures prominently in their success. ▲

The dynamic firm of Killian, Cole & Marshall is committed to maintaining the highest professional standards through continuing education and specialization. Pictured are (left to right) Evon Morse, Harvey Jenkins, and David Cabe. *Photo by Tim Barnwell.*

Daniels Graphics

The initial inventory of Daniels Graphics was a stenopad and a handful of pens; its headquarters a park bench. Today, it is a prosperous company with three locations and a breadth of services almost too wide to fit under its "commercial printer" label. What brought it from then to now? Lots of ink, a little more elbow grease, and a willingness to not just go with the times, but to grow with them.

When he first came to Asheville in 1948, Ernest Daniels called on the businesses clustered around downtown's Pritchard Park to peddle his secretarial skills honed with a Florida company during World War II. If needed, Daniels could be found at his bench in the park—the second from the left, in front of what is now Wachovia Bank. A few years later, he got his first office, and, with a $50 loan, bought a mimeograph machine and a used Royal typewriter.

His son James Daniels, now president of the company, grew up with the clatter of the equipment and the whirlwind rush to get orders out. He and his sister worked after school, chipping in to crank the mimeograph machine, proofread, and collate.

With the purchase of a duplicator, the business quickly evolved from secretarial work to printing. James and his father puzzled for some time over the duplicator before they learned, by trial and error, how to run it. And that is how the company flourished. "People would ask us if we could do something new, and we'd say yes, as long as we could figure out how," James recalls.

While the "can-do" attitude remains, Daniels Graphics has come a long way from its mimeograph past. Files are now shipped through digitized computer networks, not in manila folders. "We work primarily with industrial marketing departments who have exceptional needs where time and quality are concerned," James states. Through technology, the company stays synchronized with those needs.

Daniels Graphics can take a printed piece from design to fulfillment, from idea to mailbox. A 24-hour call center can even track to which mailboxes the piece should be sent. "When an ad in the back of a magazine offers an 800 number, you might get us," James explains. "We send you the literature that you're asking for." Market support services like these are a new area of concentration for Daniels Graphics, one that James expects will grow over the coming years.

Daniels Graphics can take a printed piece from design to fulfillment, from idea to mailbox. *Photo by Tim Barnwell.*

The park bench has been transformed to a 60,000-square-foot facility on Sweeten Creek Road with additional offices on Rankin Avenue. The company further extended its territory in 1993, when it acquired Clay Printing Company's facility in Hickory. Between its locations, the 110 employees of Daniels Graphics provide printed materials as far east as Winston-Salem, west into Tennessee, and south into upstate South Carolina.

And just as the company expanded from a downtown Asheville park bench years ago, Daniels Graphics continues to establish benchmarks for service, quality, and an approach that says "we'll figure out a way to get it done." ▲

Daniels Graphics is a prosperous company with three locations and a breadth of services almost too wide to fit under its "commercial printer" label. *Photo by Tim Barnwell.*

McGuire, Wood & Bissette, P.A.

McGuire, Wood & Bissette, P.A. is the oldest law firm in Asheville, continuously engaged in the practice of law since 1894. That was the year Haywood Parker gave up teaching and became an attorney. The following year he joined Louis M. Bourne, a native of Tarboro, to establish the firm of Bourne and Parker in an office at 12 South Court Square, in close proximity to the Buncombe County Courthouse. That building vanished long ago, but the firm endures. Today, McGuire, Wood & Bissette, P.A. has continued to maintain its downtown presence and recently relocated to the restored Drhumor Building at 48 Patton Avenue on the corner of Church Street.

The firm engages in a general civil practice, with a focus on the business, financial, and litigation needs of its clients. The firm's practice, although tailored to the needs of Western North Carolina, enjoys client relationships throughout the United States. Providing the full complement of services, the firm offers its clients consistently high standards in the practice areas of corporations, bankruptcy and securities; health care; labor and employment relations; litigation; media; probate and estate planning; real estate and construction; and taxation.

McGuire, Wood & Bissette, P.A. draws upon the varying expertise and experience of its members, most of whom are native to North Carolina. Attorneys include Richard A. Wood Jr., W. Louis Bissette Jr., Douglas O. Thigpen, Joseph P. McGuire, Doris Phillips Loomis, M. Charles Cloninger, Thomas C. Grella, Grant B. Osborne, T. Douglas Wilson Jr., John N. Fleming, Richard A. Kort, and Walter R. McGuire (of counsel). A well-qualified and dedicated staff of secretaries, paralegals, and other support personnel complete the Asheville office.

McGuire, Wood & Bissette, P.A. recently relocated to the restored Drhumor Building at 48 Patton Avenue on the corner of Church Street.

McGuire, Wood & Bissette, P.A. is the oldest law firm in Asheville, continuously engaged in the practice of law since 1894.

Throughout the years, McGuire, Wood & Bissette, P.A. has displayed a strong commitment to public service and the welfare of the community. Members of the firm have been active in community life, lending vision and leadership to ensure the quality of the region's development. Most notably, Mr. Wood (1971-1975) and Mr. Bissette (1985-1989) have served as mayors of Asheville. Currently, Mr. Cloninger is serving on the Asheville City Council.

The firm's commitment to Asheville includes the purchase and extensive restoration of the Drhumor Building, one of the finest buildings and the oldest standing commercial building in downtown Asheville. The firm's new headquarters was constructed in 1895 by the W. D. Johnston family and was named for its ancestral Irish homeplace. The brick building trimmed with rock-faced limestone is of Romanesque Revival design and is highlighted by its curved corner windows overlooking Patton Avenue and extensive high-relief limestone frieze work on the first floor depicting mythological figures. It was built on the site of W. D. Johnston's farmhouse, which became home to Asheville Female Academy in 1835. The location can also boast the fact that America's first woman doctor, Elizabeth Blackwell, taught music there. The firm's offices occupy the first two floors of the four-story building. The acquisition of the Drhumor Building reemphasizes the firm's long-standing confidence in and commitment to the economy of the region and the vitality of downtown Asheville.

ENG/6A

The largest architectural-engineering firm in Western North Carolina, ENG/6A is as accustomed to looking at the whole picture as it is to blueprints. Whether it means selecting a building's site, selecting its furniture, or taking an active and ongoing role in the construction process, the firm is dedicated to delivering a building exactly as the client envisioned it—right down to the color of the carpet.

The company develops long-term relationships with its clients. For example, after designing a distribution center for PYA/Monarch, Inc. in Charlotte, the company went on to design another center in Raleigh as well as an addition to a PYA/Monarch, Inc. facility in Columbia, South Carolina.

Originally founded in 1942, ENG/6A has developed into a dominant force in commercial and industrial projects throughout the Southeast. Its team of architects and engineers provides a full breadth of integrated design services under one roof. These services include not only the design of the building and all of its systems—such as lighting, HVAC, plumbing, and communications—but also interior design and landscaping. "We are prepared to assist clients on whatever level they desire, from a set of basic design drawings to acting as a single source provider for their entire project," states Douglas R. Campbell, AIA, president of ENG/6A.

To take advantage of the best features of both the traditional approach to building, where design and construction are handled by separate firms, and the newer approach to building, where one project team often handles both design and construction, ENG/6A pioneered the position of the administrative architect in Western North Carolina. The administrative architect provides technical support for the building's owner throughout the construction process, from establishing the scope of the project through preliminary plans to performing inspections at the job site.

The firm resulted when a group of Asheville architects and engineers came together during World War II to create a firm large enough to manage military contracts. Since then the firm has prospered by adhering to its founders' original vision of innovative, high-quality design and efficient professional services—and by an attention to detail that meshes the expertise of ENG/6A point by point with its clients' expectations.

Repeat clients make up more than 80 percent of the firm's workload and include such organizations as the United States Postal Service, BellSouth, and Sara Lee Knit Products. "We try to develop a long-term relationship with clients so that we can then handle all of their project needs for them," Campbell explains. After designing a distribution center for PYA/Monarch, Inc. in Charlotte, for instance, the company went on to design another center in Raleigh as well as an addition to a PYA/Monarch, Inc. facility in Columbia, South Carolina.

The firm's list of recent credits also includes a number of projects in the Asheville area, such as the Black Mountain Elementary School, the Vocational Education Building at Asheville-Buncombe Technical College, and renovations to the new district headquarters for Public Service Company of North Carolina. Although ENG/6A's work has historically been based in the Southeast, the past several years have brought projects which extended that geographic radius into Florida, Puerto Rico, Oklahoma, and New Jersey—proving that the firm is truly willing to go the distance to meet its clients' needs. ▲

The firm's list of recent credits includes renovations to the new district headquarters for Public Service Company of North Carolina. *Photo by J. Weiland.*

CHAPTER FOURTEEN

BUILDING GREATER ASHEVILLE

*From concept to completion,
Asheville's building and real estate industries shape
tomorrow's skyline and neighborhoods.*

Sunrise from the clubhouse at Mountain Air finds clouds blanketing the surrounding mountain peaks. *Photo by Warren Grant.*

Mountain Air Country Club

It is not the unsurpassed natural beauty, the championship-caliber golf and tennis, or the other world-class amenities that make the private Mountain Air Country Club community the utterly incomparable place it is. It's not even the private, mountaintop airstrip featuring the highest runway east of the Rockies, enabling residents to tee off within minutes after landing.

No, when all is said and done, it's the people—the Banks and Young families, their skilled staff, and long-time friends and neighbors—whose fundamental love of place and unswerving dedication to providing the ultimate in service and amenities who make the crucial difference.

Other mountain communities may boast of views and facilities, but none can offer the security, commitment, and overwhelming sense of place that are so lovingly provided by Mountain Air's owners and managers. Built on family-owned land by the family's own heavy-construction company using family funds, the Mountain Air Country Club is truly a labor of love, a pooling of the diverse talents and interests of various family members in pursuit of a common dream: to build the most magnificent private country club and year-round residential community in all of Western North Carolina.

It is a vision that makes the impossible possible. Fourth-generation area residents are hard at work developing precisely the kind of community they want to live in themselves. Family members are actively involved in the day-to-day operation of Mountain Air. And, unlike communities owned by large corporations with widely scattered interests, Mountain Air is this development company's only project. That ensures residents a level of accessibility to management, and accountability and responsibility on the part of management, that is simply unmatched.

Perched atop gorgeous Slickrock Mountain at 4,700 feet, Mountain Air unquestionably delivers the finest views to be found in the vista-rich North Carolina mountains. The adjacent Black Mountains include Mount Mitchell, at 6,684 feet the highest point east of the Mississippi.

And that elevation means summer temperatures are wonderfully cool—usually 10 or more degrees lower than the surrounding valley communities. The mercury rarely reaches 80 degrees, the spring and fall are glorious, and even winters are generally mild. It's a moderate four-season climate that's ideal for year-round living, including winter golf.

Speaking of golf, the 6,425 yard, 18-hole, par 71 championship course, designed by longtime Pete Dye associate Scott Pool, is the third highest golf course east of the Mississippi. Almost every hole offers 25- to 100-mile views, with range upon range of the Blue Ridge Mountains rippling away in the distance.

It's only 35 minutes from a workday in Asheville to a home at the top of Slickrock Mountain. *Photo by Warren Grant.*

Miles of underground irrigation lines blasted out of solid rock keep the tees and greens carpet-lush, and the dramatically placed boulders, waterfalls, and ponds may even pry your eyes away from the mountains now and then. It's not all show, either: it is a challenging but fair course, with level landing areas that reward a centered drive, and multiple sets of tees to accommodate different skill levels.

Jim McQueen, Mountain Air's director of golf, grew up in the business in Florida. His dad, Jim Sr., is well known to golfers for his beautiful illustrations of the Jack Nicklaus lesson series in *Golf Digest*. And Jim Jr. picked up key expertise via stints at Myers Park Country Club in Charlotte and Biltmore Forest Country Club in Asheville, en route to Mountain Air. His wife, Julena—the cousin of Mountain Air President and General Manager Randy Banks—brings her expertise as a fashion merchandiser to her role as manager of the pro shop.

Sports-minded residents also enjoy the two fast-dry, clay championship tennis courts (one lighted for night play) and a swim club featuring a heated pool with two 75-foot exercise lanes, plus a kiddie pool. Both of these facilities offer equally stunning views.

It's almost as if it were all meant to be. With more than 40 years' experience in the lumber and construction businesses, respectively, and a history of successful cooperation on other shared business enterprises, Mountain Air's two "founding families" seemed perfectly positioned to realize the long-standing dream of developing their pristine land on Slickrock Mountain.

But that was only the beginning, because even those children and grandchildren who had moved away came back to pitch in and help build an enduring vision—bringing with them the precise blend of skills and experience they would need. Julena's brother, Sam, grew up in the construction business, alongside his dad, Earl Young. The two of them, plus Jim McQueen, have been the driving force behind one of the most incredible construction challenges ever seen hereabouts.

The Mountain Air clubhouse is an embracing blend of rustic good looks and mountain elegance.

The historic charm of Burnsville's town square is just minutes from the entrance to Mountain Air. *Photo by Warren Grant.*

One spectacular fruit of their labors is the splendid, 12,000-square-foot rustic mountaintop clubhouse, handsomely crafted out of native stone and timber, the perfect setting for unwinding and fine dining. Longtime timberman Bill Banks, whose family has owned this land for decades, spent four months hunting up the perfect, massive 1,200-pound logs for the mantels—and the logs themselves spent upwards of a century getting ready for the assignment.

Other fine touches come from craft artists in the community, such as the wrought-iron railing handcrafted by a local blacksmith, or the fine appointments created by master artisans from nearby world-renowned Penland School of Crafts.

Residents of the 500-acre community enjoy an inviting mix of single- and multifamily homes. *Photo by Warren Grant.*

In this stylish yet casual atmosphere, members enjoy feasting in the dining room, or lounging on the balcony admiring those ubiquitous, picture-postcard sunset views. The clubhouse also boasts a grill, pro shop, Mountain Market, indoor driving range, exercise room, game room, pilot room, and sales office.

It's an alluring place, and the challenge of helping manage it drew Mountain Air President and General Manager Randy Banks back to the area in 1990, after nearly a 20-year absence. During that time, he worked with such well-known resort and residential real estate companies as Wintergreen in Virginia, Hilton Head Company in South Carolina, and Gulfstream Development in Florida. Randy's wife, Jeani, who is now his assistant at Mountain Air, spent many years working at Amelia Island Plantation in Florida.

That's good news for Mountain Air residents, who can count on the most attentive service as they discover the difference between living in the mountains and living on a mountain.

The Mountain Air golf course drops through 1,140 feet of elevation in 11 holes. Shown is the par 3 tenth hole. *Photo by Warren Grant.*

Residential alternatives cover a broad spectrum, everything from one-bedroom lodges to five-bedroom, mountaintop homes. They all, of course, offer outstanding views plus convenient access to the club's many amenities. In fact, the hardest thing about living at Mountain Air may be finding a reason good enough to come down off the mountain.

But if rural splendor, small-town charm, or more urban enticements sound appealing, they're all readily accessible from Mountain Air. And far from being an isolated enclave, the country club is proud of its place within the greater community, and works hard to be a good neighbor.

The lovely little mountain town of Burnsville, nestled in a valley just three miles away (and 2,000 feet below the country club), is really a latter-day Mayberry, where friendliness comes easy and good neighborliness is a way of life. Little has changed, in fact, since General Manager Randy Banks was growing up here.

The century-old NuWray Inn serves up authentic mountain cooking, and the Parkway Playhouse and Toe River Arts Council offer a full schedule of summer

The highest airstrip east of the Mississippi is perched near the 4,700-foot peak of Slickrock Mountain. *Photo by Warren Grant.*

The seventh green at Mountain Air looks across to the 6,500 foot peaks of the Black Mountains. *Photo by Warren Grant.*

theater and concerts. Burnsville's retail merchants are equipped to meet most residents' daily needs, and treasure hunters will delight in the wares of local artisans and antique shops.

Yancey County is also home to some of the finest trout fishing in the mountains, as well as white-water rafting and kayaking, hundreds of miles of spectacular hiking trails, the world-famed Blue Ridge Parkway, and (when the weather permits) winter sports such as snow skiing and ice skating.

The unique mountain city of Asheville, a mere half-hour away, offers a broad range of fine dining, shopping, cultural events, and other urban amenities. The unparalleled luxury of Biltmore Estate (America's largest private residence) is a must-see. And baseball fans can enjoy the Asheville Tourists, a Colorado Rockies minor league affiliate, at beautifully renovated, historic McCormick Field, where Babe Ruth himself once swung for the seats.

Ranging farther afield, the pro basketball, football, and hockey of Charlotte and Atlanta are only two-and-a-half and four hours away, respectively—and a fraction of that, if you're flying.

Oh, and about that runway. It's 4,400 feet high, 2,875 feet long, and carved right out of the mountainside. Aviation guru Richard L. Collins visited Mountain Air recently, and wrote this rave in *Flying* magazine: "What I found was the most spectacular and unique mountain hideaway that I have ever seen. Whether you're a golf, tennis, aviation, mountain or loafing junkie, the place is indeed a paradise."

It all comes together here, high atop Slickrock Mountain—the incomparable beauty, the outstanding amenities, the blended contributions of a large and loving family, and the sincere support of the surrounding community—to make the Mountain Air Country Club a dream come true. And, best of all, it's a dream that residents can share with their loved ones...and pass on to their grandchildren. ▲

Beverly-Grant, Inc.

Like the level of quality it delivers, Beverly-Grant service also exceeds the standard. They often help clients on the front end of the project, work on feasibility studies, or assist with locating property. *Photo by J. Weiland.*

Just inside the new headquarters of Beverly-Grant, Inc. is a large window etched with the company logo emerging from a range of misty mountains. More than an attractive centerpiece, it symbolizes Beverly-Grant's reputation for quality that grew from the mountains of Western North Carolina.

According to Jerry Grant, president of Beverly-Grant, Inc., commitment to quality is what built this company. "The most important thing to any company is the way you are perceived by your clients. It comes from the jobs you do for them, the load of work you can take off of them, the ways you make them comfortable. We do exactly what we tell our clients we will do, use exactly the materials we tell them we will use, and do it in the time frame we tell them."

For more than 40 years Beverly-Grant has been living up to those promises. As a result, repeat business is so consistent the company does not have—or need—a marketing department. There is a corporate brochure, but even that is in a binder so that constantly improving services and steadily increasing projects can be kept current. The first client listed in the brochure already has completed 13 projects with Beverly-Grant, a 14th is about to be finished, and they were just awarded the 15th. "These are major projects—new plants or major expansions of existing plants. With another client we have completed 9 projects and are working on 10 and 11. The job we do for our next client must sell the jobs we are going to do four and five years from now. Our clients are our marketing department."

The company works in a five-state area, although Grant says they will follow a good client wherever they want them to go. They are currently discussing a project as far away as Nevada.

For more than 40 years Beverly-Grant has been living up to its promises of quality. As a result, repeat business is so consistent the company does not have—or need—a marketing department. Sonopress is an example of this successful relationship between contractor and client. *Photo by J. Weiland.*

Many of the staff have been with the company a long time—new employees are generally a result of expansion. The first employee Grant's father hired in 1955 is still with the firm. Another was hired in 1957 and only retired recently. "One of my first jobs was to follow him around and keep track of his tools. Occasionally we will call him back to help us out on a project." Opportunity for advancement through the company is good. Two current superintendents worked their way through the ranks from laborers, and the newest project manager came up through the field.

Grant knows the business literally from the ground up. As a boy he started by picking up nails on the construction site and advanced to digging footings, carpentry, supervising, estimating, and managing. Today he sees himself more as a coach. "Our firm runs on teamwork. I'm the coach and the project managers are quarterbacks. I get involved in projects on the front end, and while I'm constantly discussing the projects with them, they run those projects themselves. I've coached our people to the point they don't need a lot of help, which allows me more freedom to pursue future work and investment properties."

He has coached them so well that it is difficult for Beverly-Grant to hire personnel who have been with other construction companies. It seems that while everyone claims to produce quality products, quality is still a relative term. "They don't understand our level of quality. Ours is 10 notches above the industry standard. Quality and consistency are the most important things we can produce. It's hard for a client to recommend you if he sees cracks and peeling wallpaper or doors that don't close."

Beverly-Grant's new headquarters is living proof of the quality that goes into their work, down to the last detail. Senior Vice President Richard Grant, Jerry's brother, works from an office in which the cherry casework and

Nypro boasts a clean room environment where the company produces plastic parts for the medical components industry. *Photo by J. Weiland.*

marble and cherry fireplace inform the client of the superior craftsmanship Beverly-Grant is known for. The exquisitely furnished conference room is another fine example, while the offices of Senior Project Managers Henry Watts and Norris Pegg, as well as the other managers, showcase a variety of materials and finishes to help clients visualize their options.

Like the level of quality it delivers, Beverly-Grant service also exceeds the standard. They often help clients on the front end of the project, or work on feasibility studies, assist with locating property, and fill in whatever services the Chamber or State cannot provide. Grant recalls how they have even found jobs for wives of employees of clients being relocated. "We try to entertain these people and introduce them to those who can give them confidence in the area."

As Grant pursues future projects, he spends time on the road, traveling to Detroit, Los Angeles, San Francisco, Chicago, Japan, Korea, and Singapore looking for people to build in Western North Carolina. He serves as an ambassador for the entire region, working closely with the Asheville Chamber of Commerce and State development agencies. Community support by all of their management over the years includes serving on boards ranging from Eliada Home to Memorial Mission Medical Center.

As for the future, the company is, of course, committed to continued growth to fill their clients' needs. But Grant is cautious. "I don't ever want to grow for growth's sake. We are a service company. We don't want to grow past the point of being able to better serve our clients. We want to become more sophisticated in our methods and equipment to better serve them. For instance, we don't buy new computers for our ego but to better serve our clients."

"There's an old adage in the construction industry," Grant adds. "You can have it quick, you can have it cheap, and you can have quality, but you can't have all three. Well, we try our best to produce something that gives the client all three of them." ▲

Beverly-Grant is responsible for the Nypro complex. *Photo by J. Weiland.*

Hayes & Lunsford

For more than 70 years, the firm of Hayes & Lunsford has provided a full spectrum of electrical services to business and industry throughout the Southeast. The contracting division engineers and installs electrical systems in myriad settings, from retail shops to factories and hospitals. And the electric motor repair division couples craftsmanship with state-of-the-art equipment to maintain and repair an extensive range of electrical apparatus. Whatever the application, expertise and a dedication to service combine to make Hayes & Lunsford a leader in Western North Carolina.

The Asheville firm became involved in electrical contracting in 1928, when Ralph Presley joined the motor repair company founded two years before by Van Hayes and Oak Lunsford. And while some things have changed since that time—for example, computer cabling is now a routine part of the firm's installations—the goal has remained the same: to provide quality workmanship on projects that are completed on time and within budget.

With over 150 employees, Hayes & Lunsford can handle electrical contracting projects of all sizes, no matter how sophisticated the systems. "A real asset to our firm is our experience on larger jobs," states Eugene Presley, president of Hayes & Lunsford Electrical Contractors, Inc. "We know how to manage large jobs quickly and efficiently because we've worked on them for years and years." He and his brother Ralph began work at their father's firm in 1960; their youngest brother, Richard, came on board in 1971 and is currently serving as vice president of the firm's electrical contracting division.

The electric motor repair division of Hayes & Lunsford couples craftsmanship with state-of-the-art equipment to maintain and repair an extensive range of electrical apparatus.

Quality workmanship is a facet of everything Hayes & Lunsford does. An example of this commitment is evidenced in the Quaker Oats Company building. *Photo by J. Weiland.*

Hayes & Lunsford's experience in a variety of markets has attuned the firm to the specific challenges each type of project brings. In recognition of the time constraints that govern many industrial and commercial projects, for example, the firm can provide their customers with custom design and installation on a fast-track basis. Likewise, Hayes & Lunsford is equipped to perform the varied electrical work necessary in schools and colleges, from large auditoriums and cafeterias to small classrooms and computer labs. The firm has also completed a number of government projects for such federal agencies as the Veterans Administration, the Department of Defense, and the Corps of Engineers.

But perhaps the firm's projects in the health care industry best demonstrate its high level of capabilities. After all, where could these capabilities be more important than in a hospital where all systems must be a go? And considering all the lighting, equipment, intercoms, and nurse call needs, where are such systems more abundant? In installations for regional hospitals and medical practices, Hayes & Lunsford strives to ensure that these electrical systems remain fully operational at all times.

Hayes & Lunsford takes a team approach to each of its projects. Through computers, technical data is shared among all personnel, from managers through estimators and engineers to field technicians. Shared data allows the firm to quickly and accurately plan, price, and track each job.

Over the years, the company has grown and diversified to meet the needs of Asheville's thriving business community. Hayes & Lunsford Security & Alarm is an example of this: with the advent of computers and other

The firm has completed a number of government projects for such federal agencies as the Veterans Affairs Department.

expensive technologies, the firm noticed that its customers had more to protect than ever before, and created its security division in response.

From the company's main facility on Hilliard Avenue in Asheville, Hayes & Lunsford tests, repairs, and improves the performance of thousands of electric motors each year. These motors range in size from tiny subfractionals to motors whose shafts stand eight feet off the ground. The firm repairs AC and DC motors and all of the electrical apparatus associated with motors too, such as generators and blowers.

Should breakdown occur, the firm responds promptly—24 hours a day, seven days a week—to perform emergency repairs, both on- site and off. Ralph Presley (also known by his middle name "Phil"), who serves as president of Hayes & Lunsford Electric Motor Repair, Inc., explains that motors are an intricate mix of materials such as wires and insulations that require the dexterity of a craftsman to successfully repair. The skill of Hayes & Lunsford's technicians is utilized to the fullest on the shop's machinery, which is the latest the industry has to offer including an eight foot VPI tank with epoxy resin. "We remanufacture the motor to the specifications of the original manufacturer, so that the repaired motor performs as when it was installed," adds Phil. After repair, customers receive a printout of test results that demonstrate the performance of the electrical equipment.

With over 150 employees, Hayes & Lunsford can handle electrical contracting projects of all sizes, no matter how sophisticated the systems.

But an important mission of the company is to prevent the need for such repairs through predictive maintenance. Together, Hayes & Lunsford's technicians and sales staff serve as industrial problem-solvers. The sales staff, which works with a large inventory of motors and electrical apparatus, can tell customers how to place the right equipment in the right place. And during a plant's regular operations, the firm's technicians use technologies such as infrared imaging and vibration analysis to check the performance of equipment. Potential areas of trouble can then be remedied before breakdown.

Quality workmanship is a facet of everything Hayes & Lunsford does. While providing an in-house apprenticeship program that lasts four years, the firm encourages all employees to attend seminars and workshops to help them remain at the top of their field of expertise.

An integral part of the firm's training program is safety precautions. After training, personnel continue to be involved in safety through formal guidelines, departmental meetings, and specific campaigns with set goals and objectives. Such measures, combined with an overall commitment to excellence, guarantee that the firm of Hayes & Lunsford will continue to provide the best in electrical services for yet another 70 years. ▲

Beverly-Hanks and Associates

When the principals behind Beverly-Hanks and Associates opened the firm in 1976, they acted upon the belief that professional services offered by professional people will always be well received. It was a belief that tested well in the marketplace. Today, Beverly-Hanks and Associates stands as the largest full-service real estate firm in Western North Carolina.

Although professionalism may have spurred the success of Beverly-Hanks and Associates, credit for the company's beginnings belongs to its founder's allergy to tobacco dust. A native of Laurinburg, North Carolina, George W. Beverly Sr. soon discovered his allergy after he arrived in Durham, where he was enrolled in an executive training program with a tobacco company. The dust being inescapable in the city, Beverly was transferred to Asheville to supervise cigarette sales in the state's western region.

Beverly-Hanks and Associates stands as the largest full-service real estate firm in Western North Carolina.

Later he met and married an Asheville woman and decided to make Asheville his home. In 1946 he left the tobacco firm and opened the Beverly Realty Company. The firm did well, and in 1961 Beverly was joined by his son, George Jr., a graduate of Duke University who had been working in sales in Atlanta.

The other half of Beverly-Hanks and Associates arrived in town in the capacity of a public official. W. Neal Hanks came to Asheville in 1967 from Mobile, Alabama, to serve as the city's planning director, in charge of planning, zoning, and the development of urban renewal projects. Five years later he resigned his position with the city and opened his first real estate office.

What began as a healthy competition developed into a strong friendship. When Beverly and Hanks met, a frequent topic of discussion was the need for a truly professional real estate company in Asheville, where only "small shop" firms had existed previously. By 1976, the two firms joined forces to become Beverly-Hanks and Associates.

The merger proved successful from the start. In its first year of business, sales totaled $16 million, the largest volume of any real estate company in Western North Carolina. And the company has grown steadily since, with total sales in 1995 of more than $209 million.

Beverly-Hanks and Associates established its presence in the community by building a large office in downtown Asheville, specifically designed for use as a real estate agency with comfortable meeting areas and conference rooms. It opened in 1976 with a sales staff of 13, and today more than 50 sales associates work from the downtown office. To accommodate that growth, as well as to refurbish and modernize its interiors, the office was renovated extensively in 1996.

A second office, located on Hendersonville Road in south Asheville, also recently underwent an expansion and modernization, tripling its size to 6,000 square feet with 36 associates. "The office now represents state-of-the-art real estate facilities with all modern technology," comments Neal Hanks. Opened in 1979, the firm's south location already enjoys a statewide reputation as one of the most productive per agent offices in North Carolina.

But Asheville is not the only Western North Carolina market that Beverly-Hanks and Associates has taken by storm. In 1985 the company opened an office in Hendersonville, staffed by a manager and four sales associates. Over the next five years the office generated enough business to give it the number one position in the city's market area. In 1989 it moved to the Beverly-Hanks Center, a professional park located north of downtown Hendersonville, which created room for 28 sales associates.

Beverly-Hanks and Associates deals in residential, commercial, and industrial properties. It also manages and rents property. Currently, Hanks oversees the residential business, and Beverly heads up the commercial and industrial division. The rest of the management team is comprised of three office managers and a marketing and training director.

In its development projects, the firm probably has made as big a mark on the community in its time as E.

W. Grove, the patent medicine king who built many memorable structures in Asheville, did in his time. Over the years the firm planned, developed, and built such top-drawer residential areas as Oak Forest, Happy Valley, and Botany Woods on the east side of Asheville. It also developed Executive Park, a five-building downtown office complex on urban-renewal land, adjacent to the firm's office.

In addition to assisting in the development of manufacturing plants for such companies as Westinghouse and Reliance Electric, Beverly-Hanks and Associates has handled the relocation of personnel for many of the corporations that have established bases in Asheville. "We visit the company to meet with the people they're sending and to tell them all about Asheville," explains Beverly. "And then we do whatever is necessary to get them settled, whether it's finding a rental or a home to purchase." As a member of PHH Home Equity, the firm has access to the largest relocation network in the world.

No one can accuse the firm of Beverly-Hanks and Associates as having rested on its successful laurels. Whether through the expansion of its existing facilities or by moving into new market areas, the firm continues to reposition itself for future growth. But the guiding code of professionalism on which the creation of Beverly-Hanks and Associates was based is still firmly in place.

"The fact remains that with each and every one of our clients, the purchase or sale of a home is probably going to represent one of the most important financial transactions of their lives," notes Hanks. "We never lose sight of that." From the days when its sales staff numbered 15 to today's staff of 115, the firm has relied on its high-caliber associates to make the name Beverly-Hanks synonymous with the best service a real estate company can provide. ▲

Beverly-Hanks and Associates established its presence in downtown Asheville in 1976. To accommodate the company's growth, the office was renovated extensively in 1996.

A second office, located on Hendersonville Road in south Asheville, enjoys a statewide reputation as one of the most productive per agent offices in North Carolina.

In 1985 the company opened an office in Hendersonville, and in 1989 it moved to the Beverly-Hanks Center, a professional park located north of downtown Hendersonville.

Coldwell Banker Harrell & Associates

A few clicks of the keyboard and it flashes onto the computer screen. Maybe it's a Dutch Colonial with four bedrooms, or perhaps one-level living with a double garage. Whatever your preference, Coldwell Banker Harrell & Associates, Realtors locates it by taking advantage of its many resources, including its state-of-the-art computer systems, top-of-the-line software programs, and a highly trained, dedicated sales and support staff.

When Asheville natives, brothers (left to right) Gerald and Michael Kasey, bought Harrell & Associates in 1988, the company was already a leader in the real estate industry. Three years later the company affiliated with Coldwell Banker Corporation, and sales have been on the rise ever since.

Sprinkled throughout its two offices, one at 1280 Hendersonville Road in south Asheville and a second office located downtown at One Tunnel Road, are computers which communicate not only with the two Multiple Listing Services of which the company is a member, but also an Internet connection where Coldwell Banker Harrell posts residential listings on its on-line site, considered by many to be the most comprehensive source of real estate information in the industry. Buyers like the ease with which they can pinpoint any of Coldwell Banker's locations and see what properties are available for sale, complete with pictures.

When Asheville natives, brothers Gerald and Michael Kasey, bought Harrell & Associates in 1988 from Charles Harrell, the company was already a leader in the real estate industry with an annual sales volume of $15 million and 15 sales associates. Three years later the company affiliated with Coldwell Banker Corporation, and sales have been on the rise ever since. In 1996 sales will exceed $75 million, and among the current sales staff of 65 and support staff of 10, several have been with the company from the beginning.

The decision to affiliate with Coldwell Banker came after the Kaseys met with the corporation's senior management team and discovered that they and the group shared a very important dedication to growth and service. The largest real estate company in the country, Coldwell Banker Corporation has doubled its size in the last 10 years to more than 2,400 offices and 55,000 sales associates nationwide. Combined, these offices handled some 492,000 transactions in 1995, with a total value of $63.3 billion. As evidence of its own contribution to these impressive statistics, Coldwell Banker Harrell & Associates, out of 362 affiliates in the Southeast and Puerto Rico, attained the highest percentage increase in closed revenue units during 1995.

Another powerful incentive for the Kaseys to join Coldwell Banker was the corporation's referral network. Because of a name that is easily recognized by potential clients from coast to coast, every day the two Asheville offices receive both telephone calls and "hits" on the Internet from all over the country inquiring about properties for sale in the Asheville area. Affiliates also are able to offer their clients the marketing tools and systems that are the fruits of the corporation's tremendous investment in research and development, as well as benefit from strong national print and telecommunication advertising campaigns.

An increasingly significant aspect of Coldwell Banker's growth is its relocation network, a result of its alliance with more than 2,400 other real estate companies around the globe. Major companies all over the world depend on Coldwell Banker to assist entire families with a smooth transition into a brand new environment. Coldwell Banker Harrell & Associates is actively involved in this service, ready to provide to newcomers all necessary information, from recreational and cultural opportunities to educational and health facilities in and around Asheville. As an affirmation of their efforts, last year the corporation received a 99 percent satisfaction rating from these major companies using the relocation services network.

Explains Michael Kasey, "In our service to home buyers and sellers, we want to use everything we can to assist them in completing their transactions as quickly as is feasible, with the least amount of inconvenience to them as possible. After all," he adds, "in essence, all we have to sell is our service."

As part of its commitment to quality service, Coldwell

Banker provides a written, step-by-step service guarantee which promises both buyers and sellers that their sales associate will be on hand for every phase of the purchasing or selling process, from the beginning to the closing table.

Upon joining the company, which has four divisions, including residential sales, commercial and industrial and investment properties, land development, and new construction, all Coldwell Banker sales associates undergo an intensive training process. This program enables associates to fine-tune their skills in evaluating and listing properties, familiarize themselves with the characteristics of the local as well as cosmopolitan markets, and see how to make use of Coldwell Banker's computer systems and software and other resources. Upon completion, sales associates are able to develop marketing plans plus live up to the service guarantee. This program, as well as state-required mandatory and elective continuing education courses, is taught by the company's certified, full-time, on-site trainer.

"Our goal remains unwavering: To develop a real estate firm that is a leader in both the community and the real estate industry," states Michael Kasey. As part of its commitment to the community, the Asheville offices support Habitat for Humanity, the official charity of Coldwell Banker Corporation, by donating both manpower and capital to the organization's building projects.

And as its commitment to the real estate industry continues, the thread of family comradery and support runs true throughout the entire company and into its extended family of satisfied clients. As its sales associates assist in transactions which run the gamut of price ranges, from million-dollar luxury homes to modest "fixer-uppers" for first-time homebuyers, the commitment of Coldwell Banker Harrell & Associates, Realtors to quality service remains consistent, with a willingness to travel every avenue necessary, whether it be down a winding country lane or by the lightning speed of the Internet. ▲

Coldwell Banker Harrell & Associates, Realtors serves its clients from a convenient Hendersonville Road location in south Asheville. *Photo by Tim Barnwell.*

A second Coldwell Banker Harrell & Associates office is located downtown at One Tunnel Road. *Photo by Tim Barnwell.*

Southern Concrete Materials, Inc.

When Southern Concrete Materials recently invested in a recycling program that cut waste and reused raw materials, it was only acting in character. After all, this is a company that has been building for Asheville's future since 1958.

In fact, Southern Concrete's resume is imprinted on downtown Asheville's skyline. The company helped to create the block-long Biltmore Building as well as the firm foundations that allow the BB&T Building to pierce the sky and the new Federal Building to shine. Materials mixed by Southern Concrete can also be found in area homes, hospitals, schools, and shopping centers, not to mention the roadways and bridges that link them together.

Southern Concrete can handle any size concrete project.

While concrete usually relies on the same ingredients—sand, gravel, crushed stone, water, cement, and special additives—the way these materials are mixed changes with each project. Southern Concrete's computer contains nearly 100 different formulations for concrete, with every one yielding special properties for the final product. The different mix designs can control structural considerations such as strength and drying time, and can also affect aesthetic properties such as coloration and texture. These "recipes" ensure that materials provided by Southern Concrete will always meet the specific engineering challenges of each project.

Based in Asheville, Southern Concrete operates 22 plants located throughout the western and Piedmont regions of North Carolina, serving a radius that extends into South Carolina and north Georgia. And, while its name has become associated with dozens of high-profile construction projects, Southern Concrete still maintains the type of equipment and trucks necessary for small projects often too difficult for other companies to reach, such as mountain-side driveways.

Southern Concrete has completely computerized and automated the process it uses to produce concrete. Not only does this system make it easier to mix larger batches of concrete—up to 1,500 cubic yards per day—but it also guarantees the concrete's quality by reducing the chance of human error.

Just as it has made strides to improve the quality of its product, Southern Concrete has also improved the quality of life in the Asheville area by implementing a recycling program that reduces waste. In 1993 the company invested in a state-of-the-art concrete recycler which, through a conveyor belt system, separates materials left over at the end of a project back into concrete's raw components of sand, stone, and water, which then can be reused to make new concrete. With the recycler, Southern Concrete reclaims more than 175,000 gallons of water each month, in addition to 600 tons of sand and stone. Even rainwater caught in the company's yard is reused.

Southern Concrete Materials' dedication to quality and service on the job is matched by its commitment to the community. The company is active in groups that touch a number of lives, such as the United Way, Habitat for Humanity, and the American Cancer Society. These contributions stem from its working principle that a community is only as strong as its foundations. ▲

Another of Southern Concrete's community activities is a company sponsored Little League team.

Grove Stone and Sand Company

Grove Stone and Sand Company is a business run on old-fashioned principles and proud of it. Since 1924, this family-owned and operated company has remained true to its three-fold mission of delivering quality products at a fair price to satisfied customers. It produces a line of construction aggregates, which are crushed stone graded from boulder-sized rocks down to gravel and sand.

As a basic materials industry, Grove Stone products are used in virtually every phase of construction. Case in point: consider the surprising fact that each person in Buncombe County uses about 12 tons of crushed stone per year. Crushed stone is literally the material of which the community is made. It is used in building homes, businesses, hospitals, landscaping, churches, airports, roadbeds, erosion controls, and schools. A new home alone uses 45 tons of aggregate in its construction.

Grove Stone takes its name from founder E. W. Grove, an important Asheville developer who is most noted for his Grove Park Inn. The company's original granite quarry in Swannanoa, first opened to supply road materials for a nearby residential development, was later purchased by Hedrick Industries, a construction material company based out of Salisbury. In 1979 a second granite quarry located near Weaverville was added to Grove Stone's operations.

Gone are the days when breaking rock was a job for men with sledgehammers. Today, controlled blasting transforms the walls of the quarry into boulders. Earthmovers scoop the boulders into immense trucks which haul the stone to the quarry's main complex. There the stone is laid out on a conveyor belt and fed through a series of crushers that grind it down to size. Afterwards, vibrating screens sort the stone into nearly 20 different grades of aggregate.

As the trucks hustle back and forth across the quarry, they are passed by a tanker truck which showers the road with a mist of water at the first sign of dust. This dust-abatement procedure is just one of the ways that Grove Stone has kept pace with the industry's growing environmental consciousness. Through landscaping projects as well as extensive reclamation programs, the company strives to keep its operations in harmony with the natural surroundings. Recently, Grove Stone was recognized by the National Stone Association with its "100 Percent Showplace Award" for outstanding beautification efforts.

The company frequently hosts field trips for area schools, in addition to donating classroom media materials for geology and earth science. At the quarries, science comes to life, as students see first-hand the geological formations that make up Western North Carolina.

As a company, Grove Stone works hard to make sure that its customers receive the right products at the right time. But hard work is not the only old-fashioned belief to which the company subscribes. Through participation in numerous charitable groups and community organizations, Grove Stone employees demonstrate that they stand firm on enriching the quality of life for Western North Carolina. Grove Stone is proud of its old fashioned values and equally proud to be a part off the Asheville community. ▲

Shown is the Grove Stone mining operation loading material for transfer to the processing plant.

A Grove Stone plant entrance blends into the surrounding community.

Perry M. Alexander Construction Company

Shown is the site work preparation for the True Temper Sports Manufacturing facility prepared by Alexander's staff.

In a hallway at Perry M. Alexander Construction Company, a long row of photographs tells the story of how four generations of the Alexander family have shaped the Asheville landscape. So long has the earth-moving firm been in business, its story travels from color prints back to the early days of black and white.

In the first photograph, a team of mules drags away a load of dirt from a site worked by Charles Alexander soon after the turn of the century. Another picture, taken shortly after Charles's son Perry founded the present company in 1920, shows a crew excavating Municipal Stadium with a steam shovel, the first used in Western North Carolina. A third is an aerial view shot in the late 1950s when Perry Jr. ran the firm. It captures the company's employees and equipment grading what is now known as Interstate-240, west of the Beaucatcher cut. Next to these pictures hangs North Carolina contracting license number 53—one of the oldest still in use—at a time when five-digit license numbers are the norm.

A 1956 advertisement reads, "Perry M. Alexander Construction Company moves the earth to make way for progress." Over the years, the company has prepared sites for industrial complexes, shopping malls, and countless grocery stores. It has created athletic fields for schools, razed ground for hospitals, and carved out lakes and reservoirs. And when its crews prepared the land for many of Asheville's hotels and apartment complexes, they also graded the stretches of highway in between. In fact, there are few kinds of building projects in which the bulldozers and steam shovels of Perry Alexander Construction have not played a part. With each project, the firm further earns its reputation as a company that customers can trust to get the job done right.

The construction firm is now headed by W. Thomas Alexander, the fourth generation, who became president after his uncle Perry Jr. died in 1981. As a child, Tom visited project sites on Saturday trips with his father Walter, then the firm's vice president. In high school, he took summer jobs with the company, learned how to run the heavy equipment, and eventually even managed a small crew. After college, Tom worked for two major contracting firms in Charlotte and Burlington before he rejoined his uncle and father in 1978. His experience in Charlotte—which took him from the mountainous terrain of Western North Carolina to the swamplands of the coast and beyond to Puerto Rico— broadened his knowledge of how to manage large jobs, from bid to construction.

Steam shovels were used by Perry M. Alexander Construction Company to construct Asheville's Municipal Football Stadium. (circa 1925)

When Tom became president, the company performed predominantly highway construction. Since then, while the firm continues to work on highways, its focus has shifted toward commercial and industrial site preparation. In addition to excavation, the firm installs water and sewer lines, installs underground storm drainage, and places stone for pavements. It also handles any demolition of existing buildings required to clear a site. More often than not, these projects demand swift turnaround, and Perry Alexander Construction has a long history of fast-track projects. As the contractor who readies the site for others, they recognize the need to work fast and smart so that the building construction can begin.

Samples of the company's work in the retail market are everywhere. Along Tunnel Road, the firm prepared sites for Wal-Mart, Innsbruck Mall, the Marriott Courtyard Hotel, the Hampton Inn, Overlook Village, and several expansions of the Asheville Mall. Other shopping centers to its credit are River Ridge Marketplace, Westgate, Home Depot, Oakley Plaza, and River Hills.

The firm's industrial projects include a Steelcase Furniture plant in Fletcher, True Temper Sports in Seneca, South Carolina, and numerous jobs around Asheville for companies such as Gerber and Square D.

Perry Alexander Construction has been grading roads since the 1920s when Perry Sr. graded the first road up Mount Mitchell. The company can also boast work on one of the country's most famous highways—the Blue Ridge Parkway. Tom Alexander is especially proud of the company's contributions to creating the roads and other infrastructure for the Billy Graham Training Center at

Alexander's crew prepares another site for Ingles Markets.

the Cove. But as the national highway system is now mostly complete, the nature of the company's projects has changed over time from the construction of new roads to the widening and safety improvements of existing facilities. Perry Alexander Construction has responded to these changes with the necessary specialized equipment and engineering.

"It's never been my desire to measure our success by the dollar volume of contracts constructed annually," said Tom. "Instead, our company looks to provide quality and service to our clients and to assist in anyway to deliver a successful product." This attitude has brought steady returns for the company in the form of repeat customers. For example, a relationship begun 25 years ago in Western North Carolina with Ingles Markets has now carried Perry Alexander Construction to Georgia, South Carolina, and Tennessee to prepare the grocery store chain's many new locations. Tom estimates that the company has participated in the construction of over 75 of Ingles shopping centers and has recently provided construction services for a new distribution center.

Oakley Plaza and River Ridge Marketplace were both constructed by Perry M. Alexander Construction Company.

The company's equipment and employees have stayed busy in the community after hours too. Perry Alexander Construction has lent a hand (and a shovel) to help clean up rivers, build church parking lots, even putting in a septic system for a local high school. In addition, the company has continued a tradition of donating funds to programs for children and young adults, as well as support of groups like the Arts Alliance.

If there's earth to be moved around town, the Alexanders will be there pitching and shoveling for a long time to come. Tom has two sons—a fifth generation waiting in the wings.

Tom has served on the board of Advantage West, a regional economic development organization that, among other projects, works to lure the film industry to the area. Asked if this work had paid off for the company in glamorous contracts, he laughs. "Well, once when they were filming *Last of the Mohicans,* they called us for a load of tree stumps." From the days of black-and-white photographs to today's technicolor film, Perry M. Alexander Construction Company has been—and will continue to be—a star performer on the Asheville landscape. ▲

M. B. Haynes Corporation

M. B. Haynes Corporation has earned a strong reputation for reliability, safety, and quality through projects such as the Jewish Community Center. ***Photo by J. Weiland.***

In 1921 Marion B. Haynes obtained the third electrical license issued in North Carolina. Today, companies holding licenses one and two are long gone, while M. B. Haynes Corporation has established itself as number one in longevity, reliability, and service to the region. "From that early start," states N. E. "Buzzy" Cannady III, president of the corporation, "we grew to meet our customers' needs, and now our corporation includes divisions for electrical, mechanical, general contracting, and telephone interconnect."

"That makes us unique," adds Brett Cannady, president of H & M Constructors, one of the corporation's divisions. "We can single source most trades from this one office, and because so much of the work is in-house, we can maintain superior quality control. For example, in our construction on the Biltmore Estate Winery expansion, we handled virtually every aspect of that project from design through construction of the process piping work. Our financial strength is another plus which removes customer risks and guarantees job completion."

H & M Constructors was founded in 1975 to specialize in commercial and industrial projects. The company currently enjoys one of the best reputations in Western North Carolina as a first quality general contractor.

H & M Constructors' mechanical division handles all aspects of industrial process related projects, including multifaceted process piping applications, equipment setting, rigging and relocation, precision millwright application, specialty steel fabrication, code welding, repair alterations to pressure vessels, and power boiler assemblies.

Haynes Technologies, another of the corporation's divisions, handles signal systems such as fire alarms, cable television, electronic equipment repairs, paging, and intercom and sound systems, with local 24-hour emergency service.

Haynes Electric Utility Corporation has been involved in electrical powerline construction for more than 50 years and is acknowledged as the regional expert in this field.

Telephone Systems of Asheville, a corporate division, offers superior telephone interconnect and service.

M. B. Haynes Corporation has earned a strong reputation for reliability, safety, and quality. As a result, the company enjoys a healthy growth curve, reflected in its annual sales of over $30 million, an unlimited bonding capacity, and a workforce of over 400, which has more than doubled since 1990. Buzzy Cannady expects this trend to continue, thanks to the highly qualified and trained staff.

Another example of M. B. Haynes Corporation's reliability and service to the region is the Mountain Area Family Health Center.

"Our employees are well trained—they have to be so we can keep pace with all the late-breaking technological advances. Nothing is as simple as it used to be. For example, Haynes Electric Construction's electricians no longer just run conduit and wire. They have to constantly upgrade and train in new technology since they are involved in wiring buildings to accommodate sensitive electronic equipment and controls or programming and designing automated industrial systems. We are confident that we have the most qualified group of electricians and technicians in this part of North Carolina." ▲

McCarroll Construction, Inc.

An interior warmed by golden woods and copper touches, smooth ceiling beams and a slate floor—these are the elements of the Bistro Restaurant, adjacent to The Winery at Biltmore Estate, completed by McCarroll Construction, Inc. in 1995. These elements also represent the marks of quality that have earned the construction firm a reputation for excellence throughout Western North Carolina. "The best compliment I ever received on that project," recalls Rick McCarroll, who founded the company in 1987, "was from a friend of mine who asked, 'What was the building before it was the Bistro?' And I had to tell him it was a parking lot." The restaurant illustrates the detailed craftsmanship that McCarroll Construction brings to each of its projects, skills so polished that they seamlessly blend into a turn-of-the-century estate famous around the world.

These skills have complemented another well-known Asheville property, the elegant Richmond Hill Inn. A few years after completing the cottages that sit on the edge of the Richmond Hill Inn croquet field, the firm began construction of a 26,000-square-foot addition which houses a restaurant, retail stores, and guest rooms overlooking the inn's gardens and grounds. Features like a two-story mahogany stairwell showcase the finely honed abilities of McCarroll Construction's carpenters.

But the firm's projects are by no means confined to inns and restaurants. As a general contractor, McCarroll Construction has worked with architects and engineers across the region to build beautiful homes, doctors' offices, apartment complexes, and multifamily dwellings. The firm has also become well-known for its work on Western North Carolina churches. Most recently, the company constructed Saint Philip Episcopal Church in Brevard, built large additions to the Presbyterian Churches of Montreat and Black Mountain, and completed a number of projects for the World Methodist Assembly at Lake Junaluska.

Rick McCarroll came to Asheville in 1987 with vast experience in construction. Previously, he had been president and cofounder of Mountain Builders, a Waynesville firm that he sold after 14 years with his partner's retirement. With the help of his wife, Lee, McCarroll grew his new company from a small general contractor into a firm with 75 employees and a satellite office in Knoxville.

But McCarroll is quick to hand over the credit for the company's success to its employees. "The real key to this operation is the people who are involved," he notes. "It's been a real pleasure for me to have a second company and see these men and women take something and build it for the future." In recognition of the high caliber of its employees, the firm has implemented a profit-sharing program to reward their efforts.

McCarroll believes that the beauty and liveability of Asheville make the city a haven for the sort of talented craftsmen that have become his employees, people who combine their skills with a steady, reliable work ethic. One glance at the firm's completed projects is all it takes to see that everyone at McCarroll Construction understands that quality work speaks louder than words.

The skills of McCarroll Construction have complemented the elegant Richmond Hill Inn. A few years ago the company completed the cottages that sit on the edge of the Richmond Hill Inn croquet field.

An interior warmed by golden woods and copper touches, smooth ceiling beams, and a slate floor—these are the elements of the Bistro Restaurant, adjacent to The Winery at Biltmore Estate, completed by McCarroll Construction, Inc.

*Carroll*Butler*Demos The Real Estate Group*

A new day is dawning in Western North Carolina, and it begins with Carroll*Butler*Demos. *Photo by Jon Riley.*

In the city of Asheville, Carroll*Butler*Demos-The Real Estate Group found its model. Although the firm is one of the four largest in the city and offers an array of distinctive services, Carroll*Butler*Demos mirrors the small-town friendliness and personal touch that has made Asheville beloved by visitors and residents alike.

The firm was formed in 1992 by a merger of John Carroll Associates and Anron, Inc. (also known formerly as ERA Butler Associates). The merger brought together a management team of John Carroll, Ron and Cathy Butler, and Mike Demos, who combined more than 50 years of experience in the local real estate industry. It also gave the newly formed company the chance to launch a line of programs not offered anywhere else in town.

First to be implemented was a computer system that takes buyers on tours of available homes while they sit in the firm's offices on 50 Orange Street. Six pictures of each listed home are shot with a special camera that downloads directly into a computer. These full-color pictures carry buyers from yards into kitchens and baths, allowing them to decide whether they like a home on more than an exterior shot. Not only can the system show more properties in less time, but it can be used by the firm's 30 associates to access loan information, compile competitive market studies, and make creative flyers.

Through an Exclusive Homes program, the firm targets properties valued at more than $200,000 for special services and marketing. The program includes large advertisements in a number of trade publications and video tours for out-of-town buyers. But the biggest draw for the homes comes from advertisements on television. Carroll*Butler*Demos is the only firm in the area to put its listings in locally aired broadcast television commercials.

Another unique choice for sellers is the Certified Homes program. Before these homes are put on the market, they receive an appraisal, home inspection, and termite report by licensed professionals. They are also put under a one-year home warranty. The program assures sellers that their home is priced properly for the market. Buyers, in turn, have all the information they need to make decisions. And both parties are guaranteed that a deal will not fall apart at the last minute because a report comes back with unexpected results.

All of these programs are enhanced by how Carroll*Butler*Demos uses its advertising dollars: 95 percent is spent on actual properties, and only 5 percent on the firm itself. Where a real estate firm may have once been content to put a sign in the yard and an ad in the newspaper, Carroll*Butler*Demos-The Real Estate Group takes an active role to guarantee that its clients' homes sell quickly. Through all of these services, the firm not only shows what it has learned from Asheville about gracious hospitality, but it confirms its commitment to give back to the city, as well. ▲

The offices of Carroll*Butler*Demos-The Real Estate Group are located at 50 Orange Street. *Photo by Jon Riley.*

Abbott Construction Company

Ever since John W. Abbott founded Abbott Construction Company in 1954, it has been turning first-time clients into long-term friends. And that keeps the general contracting firm on its toes. "Because we have so many repeat customers," explains Vice President John Eller, "we're only as good as our last job. Our emphasis has always been on fast-track quality construction, and while we may not be the largest contractor, we like to think we offer the best product in the area."

That attitude has served the company well over its five-decade history. One of the oldest continuously operated general contractors in Asheville, Abbott has scores of restaurants, banks, public housing, general commercial, and industrial work to its credit.

McDonald's is one major client for whom they have built over 100 restaurants throughout the Southeast during the past 20 years. Abbott projects span seven states, utilizing a network of loyal subcontractors who know—and deliver—what Abbott has come to stand for.

Abbott prides itself in giving the client something extra, even artistic. Consider the McDonald's in Weaverville with its handsome brick mural depicting a menagerie of animals. The mural was a joint project utilizing the skills of Boren Brick and ceramic artist Alma Johnson. "We were able to bring the artist and supplier together with McDonald's," states President Ronald Gustafson. "The result is an excellent exterior decor element which markets to the 40 percent of McDonald's customers who never see the interior of a restaurant."

The efficient, timely completion of Abbott's numerous commercial projects also requires a special quality in the construction process as well as in the finished product. Production in the confined spaces of their restaurant projects requires extremely tight coordination of trades with cooperation and singleness of purpose among craftsmen and suppliers. "If you can achieve this, then the exacting quality standards which our clients demand can be achieved cost effectively," states Gustafson. "This is a skill which we have developed and honed over years on the fast-paced McDonald's projects." The result is a reputation for integrity and quality. These are the tenets of the business established by John Abbott 40 years ago and by which Abbott continues to operate today.

To maintain this Abbott-style quality, the firm provides skilled superintendents who carry its exacting criteria to every project and subcontractor. While Abbott's official roster averages 30 full-time employees, the firm provides opportunities for a network of hundreds of vendors and subcontractors across the South.

"It's a team effort," states Eller. "We have a good relationship with architects, subcontractors, suppliers, and the development community." In turn, many of Abbott's contracts, such as the renovation of Town and Country Shopping Center, are negotiated, which means their reputation is so strong that clients choose them without sending the job out for bids. And why bother? Knowing Abbott Construction Company's reputation for efficiency and fine quality, they simply are not interested in having any other company build their projects. ▲

Most of Abbott's contracts, such as the renovation of Town and Country Shopping Center are negotiated, which means their reputation is so strong that clients choose them without sending the job out for bids. *Photo by J. Weiland.*

McDonald's is one major client of Abbott Construction for whom they have built over 100 restaurants throughout the Southeast during the past 20 years. *Photo by J. Weiland.*

Cooper Enterprises

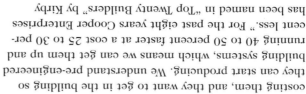

At Cooper Enterprises, Inc., "what you see is what you get" tells only half the story. In fact, their customers get a lot more than meets the eye. This 22-year-old general contracting firm is involved in all types of construction, but their specialty is pre-engineered metal buildings. Not long ago, the mention of a metal building conjured images of military-style Quonset® huts. Today, metal buildings can be finished with attractive exteriors of wood, stucco, brick—virtually any finish surrounding the durable and cost-efficient infrastructure. Cooper Enterprises projects include sleek and modern buildings for clients such as Benchmark Business Products and Kinkos Copies, and hundreds of other projects including warehouses, office buildings, shopping centers, machine shops, manufacturing, and auto dealerships.

Cooper Enterprises is involved in all types of construction, but their specialty is pre-engineered metal buildings.

Pre-engineered metal buildings save another precious commodity—time. "When people decide they want to build, they want it now," states Wade Cooper, president of the firm. "They've gotten their financing, and that's costing them, and they want to get in the building so they can start producing. We understand pre-engineered building systems, which means we can get them up and running 40 to 50 percent faster at a cost 25 to 30 percent less." For the past eight years Cooper Enterprises has been named in "Top Twenty Builders" by Kirby Building Systems, Inc., one of the country's top 10 metal building manufacturers.

Cooper Enterprises, Inc. was founded in 1974 by Wade Cooper and his partner Steve Cooper, vice president of the corporation. A few years ago, Rusty Scott joined the team as secretary. Over the years, Cooper Enterprises has grown substantially, in part due to the improvements in the metal building trade, but more because they deliver what their customers want. "It's really pretty simple," Wade adds. "We work with the philosophy that you give customers what they bargained for." The firm is known as a design/build contractor—that is, they offer customers everything from evaluation and site work to building design and construction. And the company maintains its own equipment, concrete, carpentry, and erection crews to retain greater control over projects.

Their successes grew as their reputation spread, but Wade is quick to point out there have been hard times and plenty of hard work. That's nothing new to this crew. By the soft age of eight, Wade was behind a team of horses, plowing his daddy's tobacco fields. Years later there were projects like the one in a remote part of Virginia—the local crew quit when the work turned tough, and Wade and Steve finished the job alone, determined to live up to their word, whatever it took.

Many factors go into Cooper Enterprises' success—persistence, managing people, giving customers what they want—but the way Wade sees it, hard work reaps the biggest rewards. "I never started playing golf until 1981—I didn't know what it was." He chuckles, then pauses, as though weighing the results, and adds, "But any way you look at it, we've been blessed." ▲

Cooper Enterprises projects include sleek and modern buildings for clients such as Benchmark Business Products and Kinkos Copies.

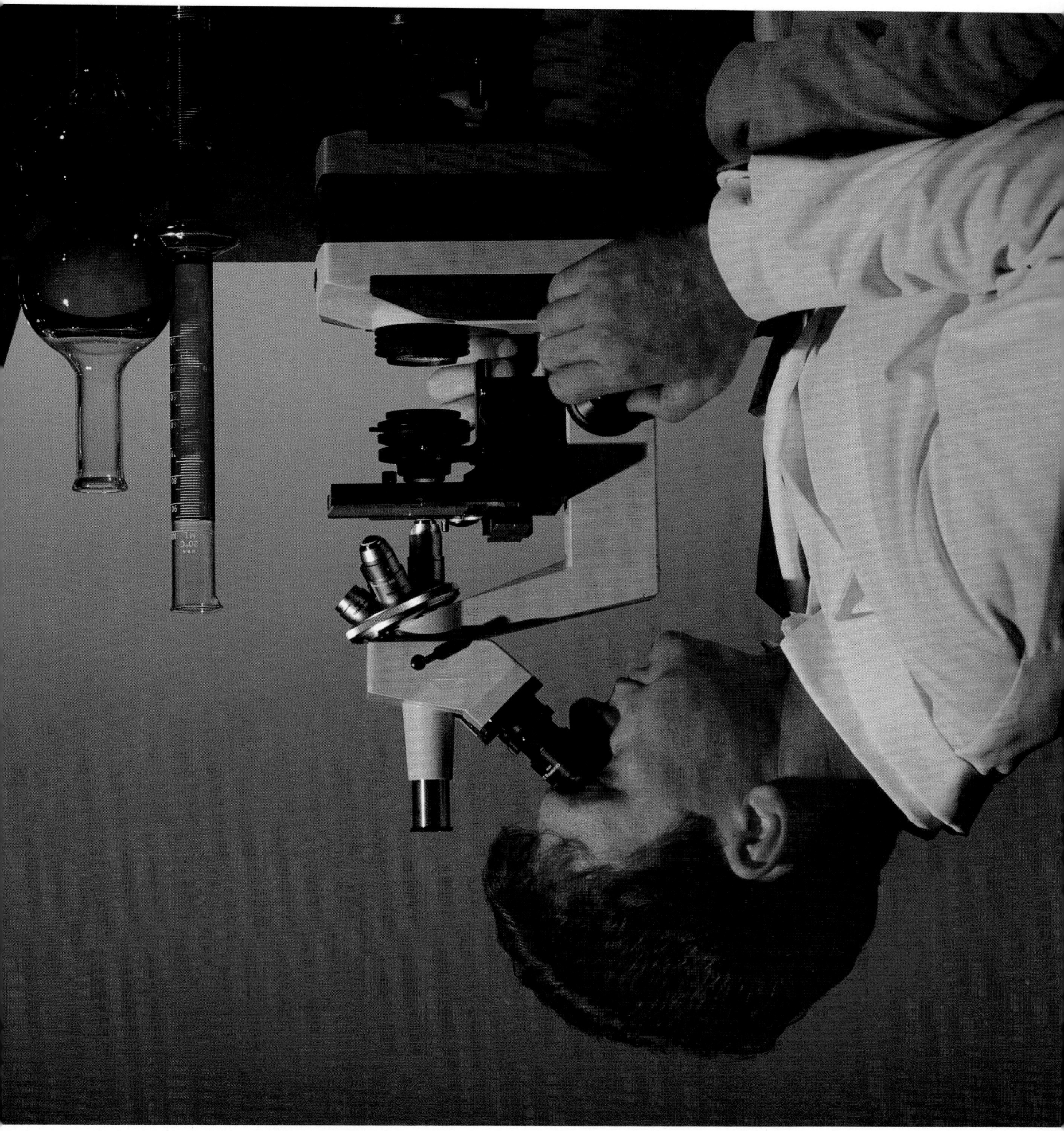

CHAPTER FIFTEEN

HEALTH CARE

The Asheville area's extensive health care system provides the best in comprehensive care.

Mission + St. Joseph's Health System

In late December of 1995, Asheville's medical community made history. While the world around them was celebrating the holidays, leaders of Memorial Mission Hospital and St. Joseph's Hospital were receiving final approval from the State of North Carolina to forge a new kind of hospital partnership. It would be the first of its kind in the state, and one of the few of its kind in the nation.

Mergers, buyouts, and takeovers among hospitals were proliferating all over the country. But this one was different. It brought together the region's two major acute care hospitals to form a third entity, the Mission + St. Joseph's Health System. Each hospital maintained separate capital assets. Each kept its proud legacy of tradition and service. But together, they formed a new organization that has synthesized the best of each into a new creation energized to meet the health care needs of the region well into the twenty-first century.

Crisis and Opportunity

A look back to the early 1990s will show how well they succeeded. Both hospitals had made vigorous efforts to contain charges, but costs of health care were still rising. Access was often limited. Between them, Asheville's hospitals offered the latest and best in technology and treatment, yet sometimes the people who needed them most could not get these services. Some lacked adequate health insurance. Some were blocked by geography, poverty, or pride from seeking medical help. And many people existed in a gray zone—not clinically sick, but far from well, and at needless risk for illness, expensive medical care, and diminished lives.

Although the partnership between Mission and St. Joseph's Hospitals is relatively new, the two institutions grew side by side for decades, and during that time developed programs and services that complemented, rather than competed with each other. This history of informal cooperation helped make their partnership successful from the beginning.

Along with needs, there were opportunities. Western North Carolina was blessed with excellent physicians and a network of strong community hospitals. St. Joseph's and Mission, as the two largest, each had excellent services and facilities. Their staffs were skilled and dedicated. By working together, the possibilities for improving care and access could be limitless. Each hospital could share its best practices and successes with the other, and in turn learn from its former rival. The tradition of excellence which each had nurtured would be continued and strengthened.

Costs could be better controlled. As partners, the two would have more purchasing clout. Overlapping functions could be eliminated. Costly building programs planned by each institution could be scaled back or even canceled. The money and resources saved could then be pooled and used to improve the health of the people of Western North Carolina.

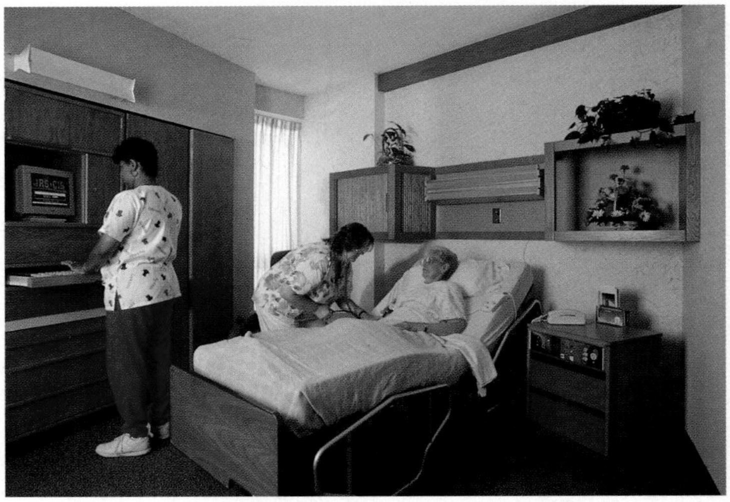

Private rooms and loving care help make a hospital stay as comfortable as possible. Computerization of patient records helps ensure that nothing is overlooked, and that care is delivered at the best time. The result: Shorter hospital stays, quicker recovery, and more satisfied patients.

And the improvements and innovations would be local, developed and driven by local talent and local leadership, rather than imposed from the outside by government or by corporations more committed to a bottom line than to caring for neighbors.

By 1993, the needs and opportunities had become so obvious that the two hospitals set aside a century of competition and started hammering out details of a partnership. Each was determined to preserve for itself and the other the best of their history, organizational culture, and excellent medical care.

There was much to honor.

Women Pioneering for Compassionate Care

Hospital care in Asheville had begun in 1885 with three determined women, $10 dollars in cash donations, a five-room cottage, and conviction that the poorest of citizens should be cared for during illness and childbirth. They called themselves the "Flower Mission," because along with loving attention, that is what the early volunteers gave their patients. It was the first hospital in the mountains, and the second in the entire state.

At the turn of the century, another group of determined women expanded health care in Asheville. They

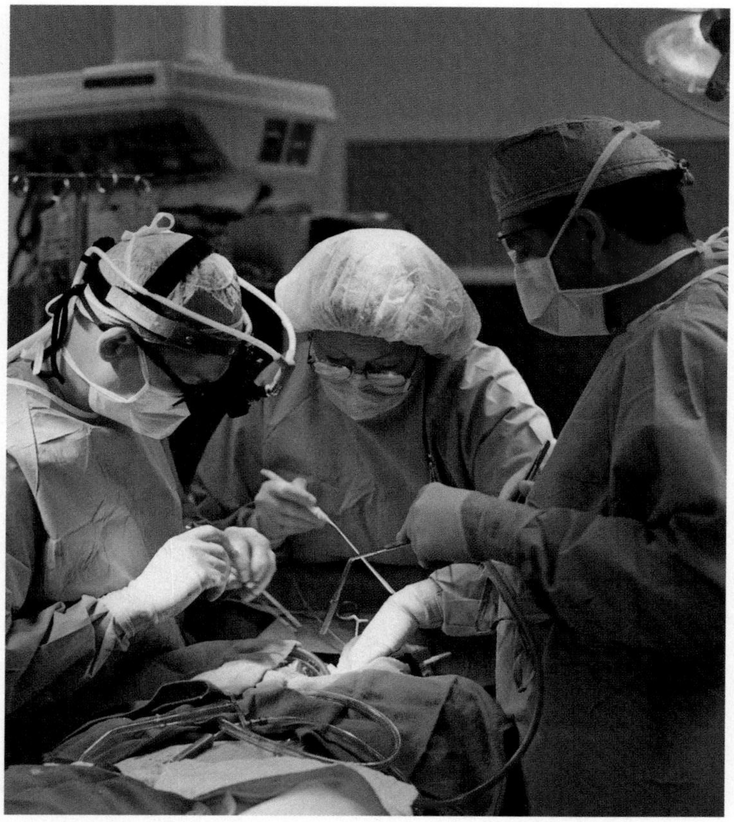

A full complement of both inpatient and outpatient surgery facilities is offered through Mission + St. Joseph's Health System, with a number of specialized operating rooms for procedures in urology, orthopaedics, neurology, and cardiology.

were the Sisters of Mercy, sent by Belmont Abbey near Charlotte to establish a sanatorium for tuberculosis patients in the healthy mountain air of Asheville.

As Asheville grew from a rough mountain town into a sophisticated resort city, so did its hospitals. In 1908 the Sisters purchased the present St. Joseph's site on Biltmore Avenue for their sanatorium. In 1974 they constructed an entirely new hospital. Meanwhile, the Flower Mission evolved into Mission Hospital, then shortly after World War II, combined with Biltmore Hospital, Asheville Colored Hospital, and the Victoria Hospital to form Memorial Mission Hospital. A modern new facility was constructed on a hill across Biltmore Avenue from St. Joseph's.

Competitors with a Common Cause

From the beginning, the two hospitals had competed. Yet even during the years of their most intense rivalry, they had much in common and managed to plan and work in ways that complemented rather than undermined each other.

Their most important bond was the fact that each was a private, not-for-profit hospital with one overriding mission: care for the sick and injured. Revenue and margins were never an end; rather, they were always a means of providing more and better service. Millions each year were spent caring for those with no means to pay.

Instead of shareholders, the hospitals were driven by volunteer community leaders who served on their boards of directors and demanded from them high standards of service and financial accountability. Largely because of these volunteer leaders—whose first loyalty was to the greater community—Asheville's rival hospitals avoided two pitfalls which undermined the health of countless other health care communities in the '80s and '90s: over bedding and the needless duplication of services.

Each board guided each hospital toward services that complemented the other's. Mission, for example, came to handle major trauma and childbirth services. St. Joseph's developed psychiatry and urology as specialty areas. In fact, when the time came for St. Joseph's to purchase an expensive lithotripter but the state balked, Mission joined the community effort to win approval for the new technology. The state relented.

A powerful component in this evolving cooperation was Asheville physicians, most of whom chose to practice at both hospitals.

Physicians: Key to Asheville's Medical Sophistication

From the beginning, Asheville's medical community had been larger and more advanced than would be expected in a small mountain city. Asheville itself was a major reason. Its beauty and liveability have for decades lured faculty physicians from major university medical centers. They brought with them the latest medical techniques and high standards of care. By the 1970s Asheville's medical community had reached a level of sophistication that was in itself attractive to other excellent physicians.

These physicians worked at both hospitals. They saw the strengths of each. They were early advocates of a partnership that would preserve the strengths of each hospital, while focusing their energies on innovation and service.

As more and more services became available on an outpatient basis, the Mission + St. Joseph's Health System added spacious and comfortable facilities for patients. Outpatient care helps control costs and is often better for the patient.

And they, like the hospital boards and administrations, were driven by a passion for excellence. By 1990, both St.

The Mission + St. Joseph's Health System has its own ground and air transport system to ensure that patients get to help as quickly as needed. The helicopter can turn a two-hour trip over winding mountain roads into a 20-minute flight.

Joseph's and Mission had established philosophies of excellence, based on the conviction that there is always a better way to provide service. Both had been recognized for their accomplishments: Mission was named one of the nation's Top 100 Hospitals by *Modern Healthcare* magazine in 1994, and months later, St. Joseph's received the North Carolina Quality Leadership Award. Both honors recognized the essential balance the hospitals were achieving between controlling costs and improving services.

With so much to bring them together, the difficulties involved in a partnership were chipped away one by one. By the time the partnership was approved, it had come to seem not only possible, but inevitable. As hospital leaders said, it was "the right thing, at the right time, for the right reason."

Immediate and Continuing Benefits

Today their vision has been fully vindicated. As soon as the partnership was approved, physicians and staff went to work to organize the Mission + St. Joseph's Health System into a powerful force for building a healthier mountain community. The benefits were obvious within months, and they continue to increase.

Community outreach programs are flourishing. A bold purple-and-white mobile dental van named ToothBus carries dental care to children in remote towns. Closer to Asheville, family resource centers take health promotion programs and basic health care to communities where needs are great and doctors scarce. The hospitals work with agencies such as the Buncombe County Medical Society, Asheville-Buncombe Community Christian Ministry, and regional health departments to find innovative, lower cost ways to get medical care to people who need it.

Inpatient hospital care is focused on excellence and achieving results. For example, "clinical paths" have been developed for the most common types of hospital stays. These clinical paths choreograph every step of patient care, so that nothing is overlooked, and every treatment is provided at the right time. The result? Hospital stays are better planned, thus shorter, and thus less expensive. Patients actually recover faster and better.

Programs to prevent illness and encourage good health are flourishing. Pneumonia, for example, once claimed the lives of thousands of older Americans, yet there is now an inoculation that can prevent most cases. Today, when an adult is hospitalized at Mission + St. Joseph's Health System, his or her medical records are checked to see if inoculations are current. If not, they are given along with other treatment. Illness is prevented, a life possibly saved, at the cost of a few minutes and a few dollars.

The centers of excellence at each hospital are stronger than ever. The term "center of excellence" describes a medical service which is outstanding for the professional caliber of its physicians, the sophistication of its technology, and the breadth of its specialty services. Within the

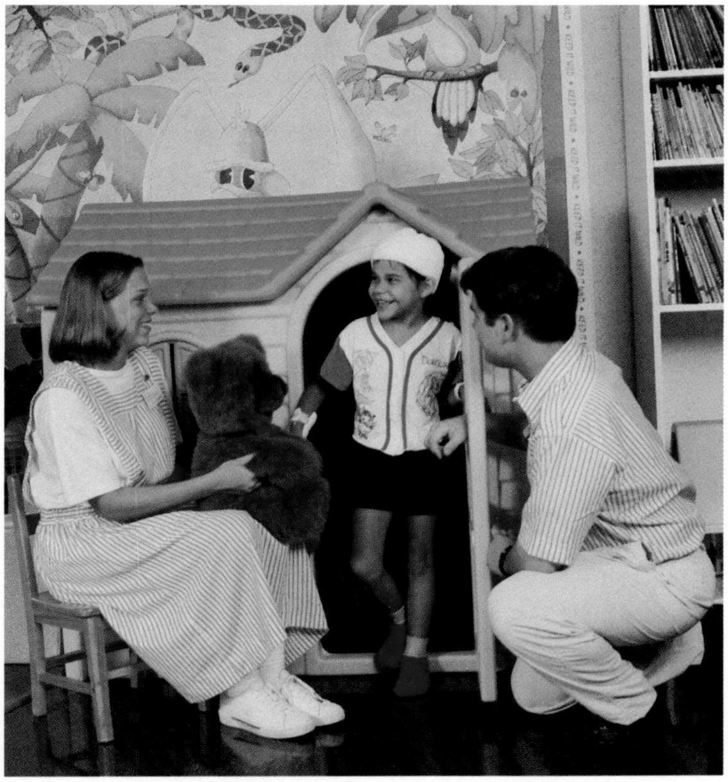

Nearly 1,000 volunteers work at the hospitals in virtually every department, bringing warmth and personal commitment to their work. Many junior volunteers go on to careers in health care. *Photo by Terry Davis.*

Mission + St. Joseph's Health System, eleven centers of excellence have been identified. They are:

• Adult medicine: Services range from intensive care to speciality units in areas including pulmonology and nephrology. Outpatient services, such as the Diabetes Center, provide education and support to patients and families.

• Cancer services: In addition to sophisticated diagnosis and state-of-the-art treatment, this center emphasizes prevention, education, and patient and family support. Participation in national research studies is available.

• Ruth and Billy Graham Children's Health Center: Almost all pediatric subspecialties, including intensive care, surgery, and oncology, are available. Family involvement, prevention, and wellness are emphasized. Many programs are offered on an outpatient and outreach basis.

• Emergency services: Care is available around the clock for all levels of illness and injury. The system is a designated Level II Trauma Center with both air and ground ambulances.

• The Owen Heart Center: Complete services in medical cardiology and heart surgery are offered, along with cardiac rehabilitation. The Owen Heart Center is housed within a new five-story tower. It includes designated intensive care units for heart and heart surgery patients.

• Neurosciences: This center provides intensive and progressive care for patients with injury or disease of the brain and central nervous system. Emphasis is placed on early rehabilitation.

• Orthopaedics: Surgical treatment and comprehensive rehabilitation are provided for people with bone and joint problems caused by trauma, degeneration, or birth defects.

• Psychiatry and behavioral medicine: Skilled intervention combines medical care and compassionate counseling. Addictions recovery services are also offered.

• Surgery: The system has inpatient and outpatient services and facilities for virtually all surgical specialties, with designated operating rooms and capabilities for laser-assisted, endoscopic, and microsurgery.

• Urology: Comprehensive medical and surgical services are available, including the region's only lithotripsy center, and programs for improving continence.

• Helen Powers Women's Health Center: This program reaches out to women of all ages with services and information. Childbirth services, including high-risk obstetrics, are provided in a family-centered atmosphere. Medical and surgical services are planned to meet the needs and preferences of women.

In addition to these Centers of Excellence, the Mission Genetics Center offers diagnosis, laboratory testing, and counseling for individuals and families who may be affected by inherited health problems.

Growing to Serve the Entire Mountain Region

From the beginning, the vision for the Mission + St. Joseph's Health System has been to lead the region in developing a broad network of health care organizations to serve Western North Carolina. This is occurring through both informal and more structured relationships among hospitals in the region. These networks have the same goals as the original Mission + St. Joseph's Health System partnership: improve access to care, control costs, and enhance quality.

Thanks to these efforts, the people of Western North Carolina have the best of two worlds. On one hand they enjoy life within the healing embrace of close communities, open sky, and sheltering mountains. But thanks to hospitals dedicated to their health and well-being, they also have big city health care delivered with hometown warmth and compassion. It is a combination that makes for good living. ▲

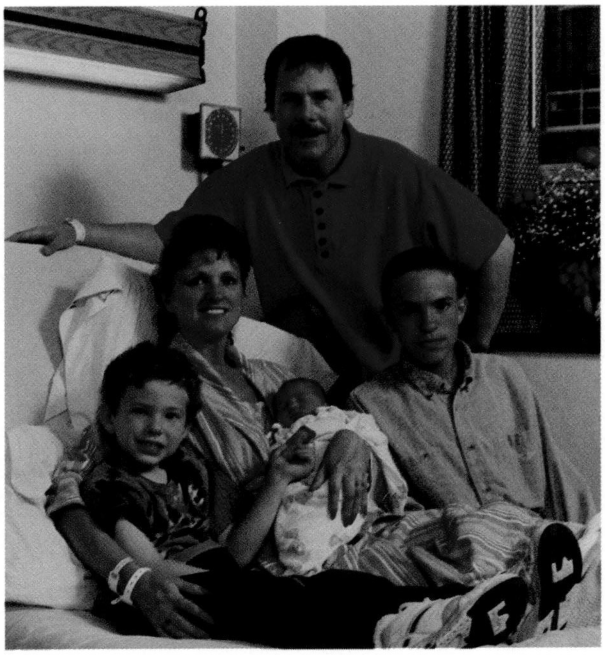

Families are involved with patient care—especially when it comes to new arrivals. Infants and their mothers stay together, and family members are always welcome. *Photo by Terry Davis.*

Partners In Community Care

It was Asheville's own Thomas Wolfe who said, "You can't go home again." But when an individual has experienced acute care hospitalization, a return to home and the community is the primary goal. Helping to make that possible is a group of area health care providers working together to ease the transition from one level of care to another.

Cooperation is nothing new to the dedicated professionals at GreenTree Ridge nursing facility, MountainCARE adult day center, Mountain Area Hospice, Thoms Rehabilitation Hospital, and Visiting Health Professionals home care agency. These nonprofit organizations have, for many years, worked closely with physicians, hospitals, and other health care providers to make a positive difference in the lives of Western North Carolinians. This partnership ethic is expanding dramatically as they reach out to one another and other local agencies, working together to provide seamless, community-based care to this area's growing population through every stage of their lives.

There are many sound reasons for promoting interorganization cooperation: increased efficiency, enhanced cost-effectiveness, and better quality services. But to Visiting Health Professionals President Rod Baird, there's another reason—one that far overshadows all of these. "What we're about," he says, "is people, and making their lives better and healthier."

No one knows that better than Dandy Dixon. After years of helping to prepare individuals for surgery at Memorial Mission Hospital, Dandy suddenly found himself a patient when he suffered a heart attack. Because of the impairments caused by a lack of oxygen to the brain,

Through the cooperative efforts of GreenTree Ridge nursing facility, MountainCARE adult day care, Mountain Area Hospice, Thoms Rehabilitation Hospital, and Visiting Health Professionals home health agency, these individuals are able to enjoy life in Western North Carolina.

Lucille Holmes and Dandy Dixon enjoy the gardens at MountainCARE, a day center for older and impaired adults. Because of MountainCARE, Lucille and Dandy are both able to remain at home rather than be institutionalized.

Dandy was then referred to Thoms Rehabilitation Hospital, an 80-bed regional referral center for the rehabilitation of traumatic brain injury, stroke, spinal cord injury, multiple trauma, and other handicapping conditions. Under the direction of a physician specializing in physical medicine, Dandy's team of therapists helped him relearn how to walk, talk, feed himself, and take care of his personal needs. "He had to learn everything all over again," says daughter Sarah.

After three months of intensive therapy at Thoms, Dandy was able to return to his daughter's home, where his therapies continued through the help of Visiting Health Professionals. One of the nation's largest home health agencies, VHP also provided nursing care to Dandy, enabling him to return to the active life he had always enjoyed.

Having Dandy at home with her was what was most important to his daughter. But as the mother of two hearing-impaired children and herself battling chronic illness, Sarah sometimes needed help caring for Dandy. And he needed contact with others his own age. That's when Sarah and Dandy learned of the services of MountainCARE, a day center for older and impaired adults, located on the campus of Thoms. At MountainCARE—Center for Adult Respite and Enrichment—Dandy enjoys daily contact with other adults, hot meals provided by the Thoms Food and Nutrition Services, monitoring of his medications by an on-site nurse, therapy when he needs it by Thoms professionals, and activities that are fun and meaningful.

The close working relationship between Thoms, VHP, and MountainCARE enabled Dandy to achieve the highest level of functional independence, a mission that is shared by the other partners in community care.

Five-year-old Mary Alexander Reidinger and her family are other beneficiaries of this partnering philosophy. Known affectionately as Alex, this brave little girl is recovering from Wilm's Tumor, a type of cancer that requires months of radiation and chemotherapy. Though

Children with life-threatening illness may require early morning lab work before going on a family outing. Circle of Care, a joint project of Mountain Area Hospice and Visiting Health Professionals, provides this among its many services.

Since 1938, Thoms Rehabilitation Hospital has provided services to help individuals of all ages enjoy the highest possible level of functional independence. Specialized programs include the Center for Work Rehabilitation & Pain Management to help those with industrial injury and chronic pain return to work.

Besides providing comfort and services to those with terminal illnesses, in their homes or in other facilities, Mountain Area Hospice helps families through the loss of a loved one with its Good Grief program. Short-term respite is also available through the Take A Break program.

Alex is returning to normal, her condition still limits some of what the Reidingers can do. "There aren't many opportunities for trips or outings," says her mother, Patti. "It always depends on her therapy, platelet counts, illnesses, and other issues."

Visiting Health Professionals, in collaboration with Mountain Area Hospice, has created a pediatric program called Circle of Care to help families like the Reidingers. This innovative program offers a full array of professional services for children needing health care at home, and empowers families to be expert providers for the special needs of their children. Thanks to Circle of Care, Alex can receive laboratory services right at home on the morning of a family outing, enabling the Reidingers to get a last-minute okay from her physician that Alex is well enough to take the trip.

Circle of Care also offers respite services for families of these fragile children, which Patti Reidinger says are a great help. "You need to talk about [your child's illness]," says Patti. "You can't understand what it's like until you're there. Friends can listen for a month or two; then they're sick of it. Someone to talk to helps a lot."

Once again the goal of being at home is shared by the cooperating organizations. VHP brings needed care and services into the home, allowing patients to remain close to family and friends and helping them make the transition from the hospital. Mountain Area Hospice offers palliative care to thousands of Western North Carolinians and their families, in their homes if possible.

The story of Loraine Olsen involves the fifth partnering organization, GreenTree Ridge nursing facility. Besides offering long-term care, GreenTree also operates a subacute rehabilitation program, a collaborative effort with Thoms Rehabilitation Hospital. The first service of its kind to be developed in a nonhospital setting in Asheville, the subacute program offers a level of care to fill the gap between hospital and home care for patients who need short-term rehabilitation.

Such was the case for Loraine, 70, who found herself in the intensive care unit of Memorial Mission Hospital battling Guillain-Barre Syndrome, a disease that causes varying degrees of paralysis but is usually reversible. After four months of round-the-clock care at Mission, much of that time fighting for her life, Loraine entered Thoms Rehabilitation Hospital for three months of intensive therapy. From there she went to the subacute program at GreenTree Ridge. "We designed our program for people just like Loraine," says Mary Ann Bosserman, GreenTree's Director of Social Services, "people who no longer need an intensive rehabilitation setting like Thoms' inpatient program but who need more therapy than is available through most skilled nursing facilities. The goal with our subacute patients is to get them to the point that they can safely return home and to an independent life."

And return home she did. With the help of Visiting Health Professionals, Loraine continued to get physical

The Olson Huff Center for Child Development at Thoms Rehabilitation Hospital offers evaluation and treatment of infants, children, and adolescents with difficulties in physical development, behavior, and/or learning. The center is named for its founder, Olson Huff, M.D., a developmental pediatrician known nationally for his work with children.

and occupational therapy and nursing care. In addition, a VHP aide helped her bathe and clean house. Today Loraine's life is back to normal.

Collectively, the broad range of health care services provided by GreenTree, VHP, Thoms, Mountain Area Hospice, and MountainCARE covers individuals at all stages of life, from newborns to the very old, from the survivors of catastrophic injury to the terminally ill. And, as partners in community care, these health care providers have recognized how each one's range of services can complement the others', avoiding useless duplication and pooling available resources to provide a full continuum of care. "In today's rapidly changing health care environment, there is a greater need than ever before for innovation and vision on the part of the health care community," says Thoms President Chat Norvell. "The partnership we have proactively sought with one another is leading to smarter, better health care for our community. It's an exciting relationship."

The words of Sarah Dixon, Patti Reidinger, and Loraine Olsen echo those thoughts. "If it weren't for them, I don't know what I'd do," says Sarah. "I can't think of anything VHP could have done better," Patti states. "I'm so grateful for everything that they've done for me," adds Loraine. "Every day I just get better and better."

Proof that—if you join hands and work together as a family—you *can* go home again.

GreenTree Ridge nursing facility resident Ella Philson meets with Margaret Noel, M.D., on the center's patio. One of the few geriatricians in the area, Dr. Noel is the medical director of both GreenTree Ridge and the Center for Older Adults, an outpatient program of Thoms Rehabilitation Hospital.

After her retirement, Irma Smathers, M.D., was able to remain in her home with the help of home care aides provided by Visiting Health Professionals home health agency. An obstetrician, Dr. Smathers delivered more than 2,000 babies during her 40 years of service.

Mountain Health Care

Mountain Health Care is one of Asheville's largest locally owned and operated Department of Insurance registered Preferred Provider Organizations providing "one-stop shopping" for employers' health care needs. The company was established in 1994 as a provider-owned preferred provider organization (PPO). Since then, Mountain Health Care has grown to represent more than 350 primary care and specialty physicians who are committed to promoting and maintaining the wellness of more than 25,000 residents in Western North Carolina. The company's tradition of innovation enables it to offer a selection of cost-effective, managed care products to meet the diverse needs of both small and large employers.

Mountain Health Care offers a PPO, utilization review, and medical management, which together allow members to maintain lower premiums and costs.

Emotional and addictive problems cost Americans approximately $129 billion in 1995, and behavioral health care expenses are increasing at twice the rate of other medical care. Mountain Behavioral Health, an affiliate of Mountain Health Care, provides a comprehensive network of behavioral health service offerings to address the challenges facing purchasers of health care services.

Established in 1996 as a private, community-owned mental health network, Mountain Behavioral Health System provides leading-edge intervention and creative and progressive program offerings that are less restrictive, community-based alternatives to inpatient hospitalization and treatment. The behavioral network provides multiple benefits to the community, including services individualized to consumer needs with the goal always to stabilize patients, return them to a safe environment, and oversee their transition to an outpatient care program for continued treatment.

Mountain Behavioral Health services are offered seven days a week, 24 hours a day. Emergency services are available for those in crisis. Services include, but are not limited to, prevention, outpatient, day treatment, substance abuse, crisis intervention, case management, and inpatient services for children and adults.

No matter what the product, Mountain Health Care strives to create a true partnership with all parties involved in the delivery of health care. Whatever an employer's specific needs may be, Mountain Health Care has a plan to meet them and effectively control escalating health care costs. ▲

Mountain Health Care, established in 1994 as a provider-owned preferred provider organization, has grown to represent more than 350 primary care and specialty physicians who are committed to promoting and maintaining the wellness of more than 25,000 residents in Western North Carolina.

Asheville Cardiology Associates, P.A.

Asheville Cardiology Associates, P.A. (ACA) was established in 1971 by Drs. John Russell and Wade Saunders as the first single medical specialty group practice in Western North Carolina. Drs. Russell and Saunders had been practicing at Duke University during a time when invasive cardiology as a subspecialty was developing along with the coronary care unit (CCU), cardiac catheterization, and open-heart surgery. The CCU became the standard of care for all hospitals, and the success of coronary bypass surgery provided a treatment for more patients than the university hospitals could manage. With a grant from the Fullerton Foundation, Memorial Mission Hospital built a cardiac and intensive care wing, starting a cardiovascular program in Asheville that included catheterization and open-heart surgery. Drs. Russell and Saunders were recruited from Duke to lead the program.

Responsibility for acute complex illness in a community hospital required a management team approach. The cardiologists trained CCU nurses to interpret EKG monitoring and respond to medical emergencies with treatment protocols and CPR training. Physician assistants were recruited to assist with cardiology procedures.

In 1974, ACA was asked to provide cardiology service for St. Joseph's Hospital. On call for the two hospitals, increasing patient responsibilities, and advancing technology required continuous recruitment of cardiologists from training programs that were advancing the subspecialty. These doctors include Kent Salisbury, John Lawrence, William Maddox, David Serfas, Charles Vasey, Eric Van Tassel, Robert Hanich, James Usedom, William Kuehl, Oscar Jenkins, Marjorie Tripp, and Todd Hansen.

Asheville Cardiology Associates is a leader in the latest procedures and innovations that track effectiveness, safeguard the patient, and foster preventive treatments to build a healthier community.

Each cardiologist brought new skills, developed new programs, and contributed to the ongoing local training and treatment guidelines for physicians, nurses, and technicians. Cardiology services were comparable to university programs with the benefit and efficiency of patient care under the direct management of the cardiologist rather than on a teaching service. For this management and recruitment strategy, ACA was recognized with an Asheville Area Chamber of Commerce award in 1992.

Asheville Cardiology Associates, P.A. was established in 1971 as the first single medical specialty group practice in Western North Carolina.

ACA led the hospitals in program development and assisted in the necessary facility expansion. This required relocation of ACA offices to McDowell and Frederick Streets. Asheville became the referral center for tertiary cardiology management. A physician network was assisted by a dedicated cardiologist available for telephone consultation. ACA affiliates were established with cardiologists based in Hendersonville and Sylva and outreach clinics in Franklin and Crossnore. Mobile echocardiograms were interpreted for regional hospitals and led to the current interhospital network.

ACA is a leader in educational programs that offer improved services to the community. ACA conducts a weekly cardiology physician education conference and biannual cardiology symposium. Patient education is directed through Heart Path and office protocols. The cardiologists have tutorial teaching programs for residents in family practice and medicine, practitioners, physician assistants, nurses, and pharmacists. The ACA practice research department participates in clinical trials of new medications providing the latest pharmaceutical developments, which can provide considerable cost savings. Asheville Cardiology Associates is a leader in the latest procedures and innovations that track effectiveness, safeguard the patient, and foster preventive treatments to build a healthier community. ▲

Charter Asheville Behavioral Health System

The history of mental health and Asheville have a long, rich tradition. For more than a century, Asheville has enjoyed a national and regional reputation for high quality mental health treatment. Many people in delicate health traveled to Asheville for its restorative mountain air and peaceful natural beauty.

During the early 1900s many grand hotels were built for vacationers and those seeking treatment. The Kenilworth Inn was built during this era and was first used by people on vacation. In 1916 the Kenilworth Inn was purchased by a physician to provide residential treatment for psychiatric disorders, alcoholism, and drug addiction. The hotel was renamed Appalachian Hall and was the perfect setting with its wide lawns, old established trees, and natural beauty.

Charter Asheville is located in historic Kenilworth, a quiet residential neighborhood of Asheville.

In 1994 Appalachian Hall, with its excellent treatment programs for children, adolescents, adults, and seniors, was purchased by Charter Medical Corporation. Charter is a fully integrated mental health system with more than 100 facilities in the country. Appalachian Hall was renamed Charter Asheville Behavioral Health System.

Charter Asheville has expanded its treatment programs to meet the changing needs of Western North Carolina and eastern Tennessee. Today one out of every three people will face emotional, behavioral, alcohol, or drug problems in their lifetime. In addition to inpatient care, Charter also offers a variety of outpatient services that allow people to keep up their responsibilities at work and home while they receive treatment. "The advantage to our patients is that they can plug into whatever level of treatment they need, whether that be as an inpatient or as someone who comes in for treatment in the evenings after work," explains Tammy Wood, Charter Asheville's CEO.

A tightness in the chest, shortness of breath, and sweating are not only symptoms of heart problems, but also of panic attacks. But where as a heart attack is likely to be diagnosed in an emergency room, a panic attack may not—unless the attending physician has been taught what signs to look for. Charter Asheville regularly hosts conferences for members of the local medical community to teach them about mental illnesses that they may encounter in their practices. "We want to do everything we can to educate people about why physical symptoms might be there and how they can be helped."

Charter Asheville regularly sponsors education programs for the community and teachers. An example is a state accredited program educating teachers about behaviors in children such as eating disorders and suicidal depression, as well as appropriate techniques for intervention. All education programs are offered by Charter at no cost. But according to Wood, "The expense is well worth it. If we can help one teacher prevent a suicide or one doctor to name an illness that might have remained a mystery otherwise, then we've done our job."

As a result of its caring professionals and innovative programs, including its Working Well employee assistance program, individuals and families are stronger and employers are improving productivity and lowering health care costs. ▲

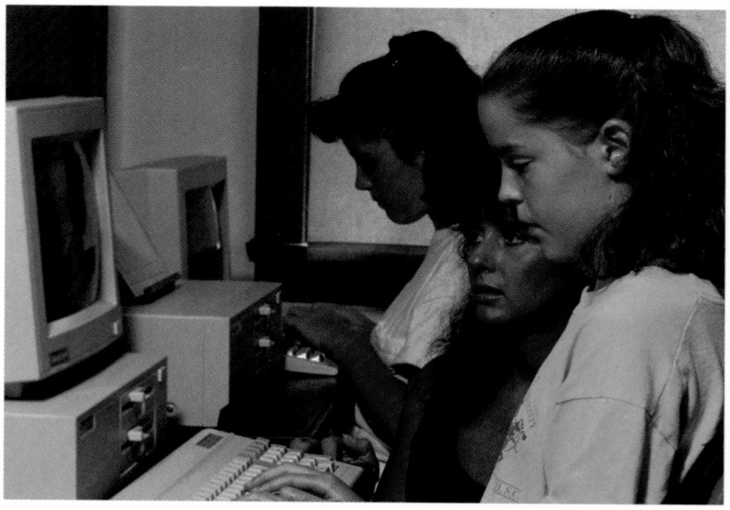

School-age patients continue their education at Charter's state accredited Griffin School.

B. Keith Black, D.D.S., M.S., P.A.

For anyone who may not think of orthodontics as fun, Dr. Keith Black says "think again." No one will deny the importance of a winning smile, and great smiles are what orthodontics is all about. Treatment can enhance self-confidence, promote self-esteem, and improve dental health. Patients gain a lifetime of reasons to smile. "That," says Dr. Black, "is fun…for both patient and practitioner."

With more than 900 patients in braces, B. Keith Black, D.D.S., M.S., P.A. is one of the outstanding orthodontic practices in Western North Carolina. Besides the usual complement of youngsters and teens, Dr. Black treats many adult patients. "Because braces today are less visible and treatment is more convenient, adults can also enjoy the benefits of orthodontic treatment," he says.

Since establishing his practice in 1986, Dr. Black and his staff have focused on confirming the phrase "caring professionals" by providing exceptional treatment in warm, friendly surroundings. From the first visit, Dr. Black strives to establish rapport. During the initial consultation, a state-of-the-art computer video imaging system takes pictures of the face, teeth, and jaws. Dr. Black uses the pictures along with x-rays and a thorough oral exam to develop a diagnosis and treatment plan on that very first visit, something traditional practices may require up to five appointments to achieve. "This shows people that I value their time," he explains.

Even the open, airy design of the facility on Yorkshire Street reflects a welcoming environment. "I encourage parents to come back to the treatment area and talk with us," he states. "They should feel that we are one big family."

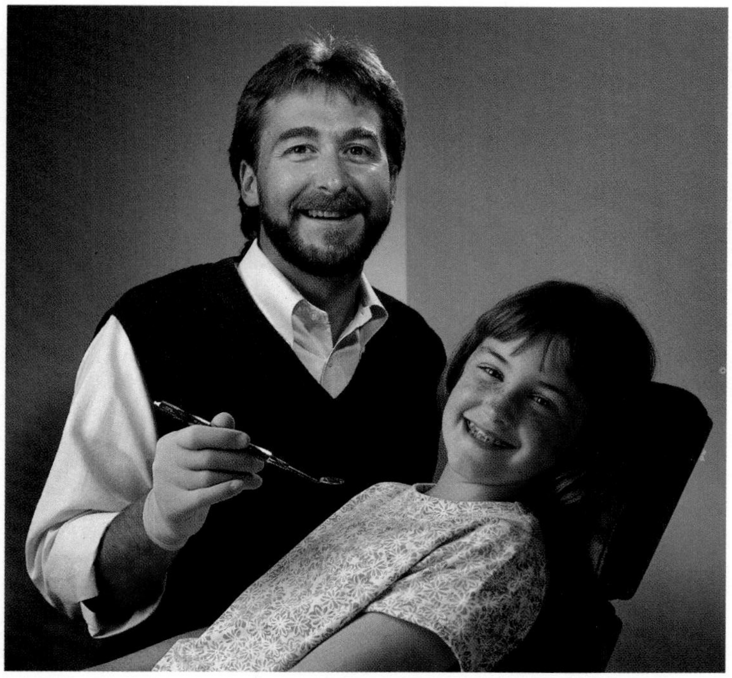

With more than 900 patients in braces, B. Keith Black, D.D.S., M.S., P.A. is one of the outstanding orthodontic practices in Western North Carolina.

The open, airy design of Dr. Black's office on Yorkshire Street reflects a welcoming environment.

Dr. Black imposes rigorous continuing education demands on himself and his staff. He wants to assure that care in his office remains on the cutting edge of treatment technology. Staff members are required to complete 30 hours of continuing education annually, more than twice the national requirement.

Dr. Black is frequently invited to lecture throughout North America on practice management and efficient clinical systems. He returns each year to his alma mater, the University of North Carolina at Chapel Hill, to lecture orthodontic residents at the UNC School of Dentistry.

Dr. Black has served as president of Big Brothers/Big Sisters, sponsors a class through the Partners in Education Program, and works with other civic organizations. In 1994 he was selected Small Business Leader of the Year by the Asheville Chamber of Commerce.

With all these activities, Dr. Black's time is in high demand. Being a devoted husband and father, Dr. Black makes certain his schedule allows time to enjoy his two daughters, Michelle and Kathryn, and his wife, Susan. Dr. Black believes finding time for work, family, and community service brings important balance to his life.

"Knowing a patient has achieved lifetime benefits from treatment in our office and seeing those great smiles is a fantastic reward for doing something I love," he says. He loves what he does…and it shows.

Under the leadership of (left to right) Doug Broome, Bill Groce, Dale Groce, and Bob Hembree, Groce Funeral Home has evolved into Asheville's largest funeral service provider. *Photo by Tim Barnwell.*

Groce Funeral Home

At a time when many funeral homes are owned by megacorporations listed on the New York Stock Exchange, Groce Funeral Home is bucking the trend by remaining a local family business. "We feel strongly that we can serve Asheville families better if we ourselves are family-owned and operated," explains Dale Groce.

Groce Funeral Home was founded in 1932 by the sons of the Reverend T. A. Groce, a circuit-riding Methodist minister who traveled the mountains of Western North Carolina by horse and buggy. After the deaths of Robert Groce, in 1985, and Willis H. "Bill" Groce Sr., in 1991, and the retirement of Fred F. Groce, the home's tenets of honesty and fairness have been carried on by Reverend Groce's grandsons, Dale and his brother Bill Groce.

Due to the family's reputation for integrity and the efforts of a dedicated staff, Groce Funeral Home has evolved into Asheville's largest funeral service provider. In addition to providing traditional funerals, Groce also handles national and international transfers, cremations, and prearrangements.

The Groce family has traditionally taken active roles in civic and church activities at both the local and state levels. Bill has followed in the footsteps of his father, Willis Sr., by being elected to the North Carolina Board of Mortuary Science (the state licensing and regulatory agency), where they both served as president. Both father and son were also president of the North Carolina Burial Association Commission, and Dale has been a district director and member of the Funeral Service Advisory Board of First Citizens Bank.

While the Groces respect their heritage, they are also progressive and innovative. Groce was the first funeral provider in the area to itemize charges and the first to provide six-door limousine service for the comfort of the families they serve. Most recently, the Groces have gone "online" with E-mail to provide information and receive messages. Responses to post-service surveys have consistently shown an approval rating of greater than 99 percent for Groce's staff and facilities, yet the Groces are constantly seeking to improve in all areas.

The funeral home on Patton Avenue is actually two separate buildings, joined by a port cochere. The business and arrangements offices are in a 1929 mansion originally built by Dr. J. B. Anderson, while the chapel and visitation rooms are in a separate building, helping to ensure privacy. A major remodeling in 1996 updated the arrangements building, making it a more comfortable and inviting area.

In addition to Bill and Dale Groce, the operation is dependent upon senior staff members Bob Hembree, Doug Broome, and Hilda Jones, as well as John Prock, Mike Hembree, Mike Neubert, Neil Meadows, Eddie Ray, Jerry Bradley, Hugh Groce, Keith Stoffels, Wilton "Pug" Moore, Terrell Ballard, and Tommy Sellers.

"People come to us and are surprised to find out that we act more like a neighbor than a business," states Bill Groce. By continuing to be both family-oriented and family-owned, the Groces anticipate that they will continue to provide funeral services for the citizens of Asheville into the twenty-first century. ▲

In addition to providing traditional funerals, Groce also handles national and international transfers, cremations, and prearrangements.

JROTC
RPEX

CHAPTER SIXTEEN

EDUCATION AND QUALITY OF LIFE

The Asheville area has a strong commitment to education, offering a high quality of life for its citizens. The area's educational institutions prepare students, challenge scholars, and prepare those seeking to enhance practical skills.

The University of North Carolina at Asheville

UNCA, a four-year public liberal arts university located one mile from downtown Asheville, has earned a national reputation for its programs in the humanities, undergraduate research, and environmental studies. UNCA was named one of the nation's top 10 public liberal arts institutions in a recent edition of the *Fiske Guide to Colleges.*

Quality education lies at the core of a community's strength, fostering its young, readying its workforce, and inspiring its citizenry. Asheville is fortunate to be home to one of the nation's premier public liberal arts universities, the University of North Carolina at Asheville (UNCA). Across its 265-acre campus, students of all ages study a curriculum that ranges from economics to computer science, history to foreign languages.

The value of a liberal arts education grows increasingly important in our modern, specialized society. Liberal arts help develop the big-picture view that leads to creative responses and workable solutions. Liberal arts students acquire the knowledge and skills that enable them to become leaders in business, professional, and civic life.

As a public university, UNCA makes quality education available at a remarkably low cost. Part of the University of North Carolina system, UNCA is the only one among the system's 16 campuses whose mission is undergraduate liberal arts education. With its focus on undergraduate teaching and learning, UNCA offers students the opportunity to study under senior professors, rather than graduate teaching assistants, in small classes averaging only 21 students. In fact, UNCA is earning a reputation as a trendsetter among the nation's colleges.

UNCA is a pioneer in promoting opportunities for undergraduates to pursue and present their own original research. UNCA created the National Conference on Undergraduate Research, which has become a nationwide forum where students present their research findings.

The university's humanities program is an important component of its liberal arts curriculum. When the program began in 1964, UNCA faculty showed unusual vision in initiating an integrated sequence of required humanities courses to form the cornerstone of UNCA's academic program. UNCA's program spans disciplines. From Moses to Marx, Darwin to Dickens, it introduces students to diverse ideas, world views, and cultures. The program has been recognized as a national model by the National Endowment for the Humanities and the Association of American Colleges and Universities (AAC &U).

UNCA's Undergraduate Research Program provides students the chance for in-depth exploration of any field from drama to physics. Students design and conduct their own research side-by-side with faculty mentors, an opportunity usually reserved for graduate students. UNCA is nationally recognized for its leadership role in multidisciplinary undergraduate research, which it pioneered in public higher education a decade ago.

UNCA also shares its expertise through the annual Asheville Institute on General Education. Produced in partnership with AAC &U, the institute brings together faculty from across the nation for an intensive, week-long campus workshop. UNCA is also a cofounder of the nation's first consortium for public liberal arts universities.

UNCA's leadership role is garnering national attention. It has been named a "best buy" by the prestigious *Fiske Guide to Colleges*. Noting that "UNCA has matured into one of the finest colleges in the South," the guide gave high marks to UNCA's small class size and its professors, "who aid and challenge students to succeed."

The university enriches the quality of life in the community through a wide variety of cultural and intellectual offerings such as concerts, plays, seminars, and lectures. UNCA's basketball teams have an avid following in the wider community, and Asheville area residents are often found on the university's track and tennis courts. UNCA's leadership programs help create a pool of informed and motivated citizens to lead community service activities. The faculty and staff contribute their expertise to the region by serving as volunteers and consultants to a wide range of community organizations, businesses, and schools.

The North Carolina Center for Creative Retirement serves the community through the development of innovative programs and services that enhance the quality of life in older adulthood and foster the growth of an intergenerational society. Through its programs, center participants learn and serve in activities ranging from the immensely successful, peer-led College for Seniors to the widely heralded Seniors-in-the-Schools, which extends tutoring and mentoring by seniors to public school children.

UNCA also hosts opportunities for graduate education. The Asheville Graduate Center, located on UNCA's campus, provides master's and doctorate level programs offered by several of the University of North Carolina campuses. Among them is UNCA's own master of liberal arts degree, a natural extension of its primary curriculum.

From its role as a model and mentor to its progressive academics, the University of North Carolina at Asheville is a vital component in Asheville's outstanding quality of life. ▲

UNCA faculty and staff contribute their expertise to the Western North Carolina region as volunteers and consultants to community organizations, businesses, and schools. Here, a UNCA student joins a faculty member from UNCA's Environmental Studies Program who is conducting research that will help reclaim a wetlands area in Graham County.

An undergraduate institution with 3,200 students, UNCA is noted for its small classes, superior teaching, accessible professors, and friendly atmosphere.

Western Carolina University

Western Carolina University (WCU), one of 16 branches of the University of North Carolina system, ranks among the nation's premier state universities, combining high academic standards, nationally accredited programs, and convenient access to the cultural, recreational, and natural resources of Western North Carolina.

In addition to courses at its 265-acre main campus in Cullowhee, Western Carolina also makes a broad range of advanced undergraduate and graduate level courses available to students through the university's off-campus resident center, located on the campus of the University of North Carolina at Asheville (UNCA), 52 miles to the east.

In addition to commencement exercises, WCU's 8,000-seat Liston B. Ramsey Regional Activity Center hosts athletic contests, concerts, conferences, and hundreds of other events annually. *Photo by Mark Haskett.*

It is not a new idea: Western Carolina has been offering courses in Asheville since 1937, and at UNCA since 1975. It is a cooperative effort between the two schools in which UNCA provides the facilities, and Western handles the administration and day-to-day operations.

Students in the WCU program in Asheville can expect to receive the same high-caliber instruction they would get at the main campus. Almost all of the courses are taught by regular WCU faculty—not by graduate students. Western's roughly 330 faculty members hold degrees from some of the finest universities in the United States and overseas, and many of these skilled teachers commute to Asheville from Cullowhee. In addition, small classes—62 percent have less than 20 students, and 78 percent have less than 30—help ensure that every student receives individual attention.

The program is designed to complement; rather than compete with, UNCA's own programs. WCU offers roughly 80 courses each semester. Eighty percent of them are graduate level; the remainder are undergraduate. About 750 students are enrolled in the programs, most of them part-time. WCU's programs in Asheville are fully accredited by the Southern Association of Colleges and Schools and by all appropriate professional accrediting agencies.

Nestled in a valley between the Great Smoky and Blue Ridge Mountains, Western Carolina University's campus setting rivals the most beautiful to be found anywhere. *Photo by Mark Haskett.*

While not all of Western Carolina's course offerings are available in Asheville, particular emphasis is given to the areas of education, business administration, human resource development, nursing and health sciences, public affairs, engineering technology, and criminal justice. These programs primarily serve the residents of Buncombe and surrounding counties from which many students commute.

Students can fulfill all of the course requirements for a master's degree in Asheville in the following areas: business administration, elementary education, English education, middle-grades education, health sciences, counseling, human resource development, mathematics education, general special education (with concentrations in behavioral disorders, learning disabilities, and mental retardation), public affairs, school administration, and school supervision. The university also offers the education specialist degree (Ed.S.) in educational administration and supervision in Asheville. Two-year college programs are available at both the master's and the Ed.S. levels.

In addition, some of the required courses leading to a master's degree in other fields are also available in Asheville. Among those fields are business education, English, history, home economics, technology, mathematics, music education, physical education, project management, psychology, and science education. Some of the course work for the doctor of education degree (Ed.D.) in educational leadership is offered, as well. All WCU programs in Asheville are affiliated with the Asheville Graduate Center.

A portion of the course requirements for bachelor of science degrees in both criminal justice and health services management and supervision are offered through

Western Carolina University's Alumni Tower, constructed during the university's centennial celebration in 1989, is a campus focal point. *Photo by Will & Deni McIntyre.*

the WCU programs in Asheville. An interinstitutional agreement between WCU and UNCA allows students based in Asheville to earn a bachelor of science in nursing degree from Western Carolina University, with the stipulation that the junior year of study must be completed on the Cullowhee campus.

Registered nurses who are graduates of an associate degree or diploma program can complete all remaining requirements for the bachelor's degree in Asheville. Also, through an interinstitutional partnership with Asheville-Buncombe Technical Community College, most of the course requirements for a bachelor of science degree in electronics engineering technology and manufacturing engineering technology are offered.

Western Carolina University administers its programs in Asheville through its resident center staff offices located in Room 120 of Karpen Hall on the UNCA campus.

Students in the Asheville programs enjoy the same quality facilities as their counterparts on the main campus. The classrooms for courses scheduled through the resident center are located in UNCA's Karpen Hall, a new, modern building. Technology classes meet in the engineering classrooms and laboratories in Elm Building on the Asheville-Buncombe Technical Community College campus. All major types of media equipment and computer support are available on-site to ensure a high quality educational experience.

Classes are normally scheduled evenings from six until nine P.M., with each course meeting one evening each week during a regular semester. This schedule seems to accommodate the needs of most working adults.

Western Carolina students in Asheville are encouraged to participate in many aspects of university life. Students enrolled in courses offered through the resident center have full access to student services such as library privileges, student health services, counseling services, and recreational facilities on the UNCA campus. Students also are admitted to WCU-sponsored athletic events on the Cullowhee campus.

Western Carolina University's tenth chancellor, Dr. John W. Bardo, arrived on the main campus in the summer of 1995. Almost immediately, Dr. Bardo identified regional outreach as one of his three top priorities for the school (the other two are academic excellence and the fine and performing arts). In addition to WCU's course offerings in Asheville, a number of other programs support the university's regional development efforts.

Many of these programs are housed in the recently established Mountain Resource Center. The Local Government Training Program links the region with the North Carolina Institute of Government in Chapel Hill, providing training in technical skills, networking opportunities, and updates on trends and developments affecting local government. The North Carolina Small Business and Technology Development Center provides direct assistance for the state's small businesses via 16 host sites, two service centers, and one satellite office. The Mountain Resource Center also houses the headquarters of Western North Carolina Tomorrow, a 17-county regional leadership organization.

Western's various academic disciplines, such as business, health, and education, also seek to incorporate regional outreach activities into their curricula. Together, all these programs are making Western Carolina University a leader in providing training and assistance for mountain residents, helping them address the region's key problems, needs, and challenges. ▲

The emphasis is on learning at WCU, and an exceptionally strong faculty of more than 350 professors is committed to providing excellence with a personal touch. *Photo by Will & Deni McIntyre.*

Montreat College

Founded in 1916, Montreat College has enjoyed phenomenal growth in recent years, and is now offering its first graduate level program.

Montreat College combines a rich heritage of quality education with innovative programs for the twenty-first century. Founded in 1916, this fully accredited school is affiliated with the Presbyterian Church (U.S.A.). Montreat College has enjoyed phenomenal growth in recent years, and is now offering its first graduate level program.

Nestled in Western North Carolina's beautiful Blue Ridge Mountains, the scenic main campus with stone buildings and dormitories is set in a tree-filled mountain valley, just 15 miles east of Asheville and its varied cultural attractions. Just down the road lies the historic town of Black Mountain, and the scenic Blue Ridge Parkway runs nearby. Several larger metropolitan areas, including Charlotte, Knoxville, and Atlanta, are within a few hours' drive.

Montreat is a relatively small college offering big possibilities. It serves more than 1,000 students, who can choose from a wide variety of majors and concentrations, including American studies, Bible and religion, business administration, English, environmental studies, history, human services, mathematics, music, and outdoor education. Montreat College is included in *U.S. News & World Report's* annual list of America's Best Colleges.

There's a lot more to the college than just conventional academics, however. This Christian liberal arts institution seeks to integrate faith and learning, helping students discover the call of God in every sphere of life.

"Montreat really provides a safe, accountable, Christ-centered environment," says human services major Leslie Dalton. "People really live their faith, but no one tries to impose their views on you; there's a balance present... an attitude of acceptance."

Experiential learning is also stressed. "The professors here believe experience is a major part of your education," notes recent graduate Rob Lewis. "They encourage you to take internships and other hands-on opportunities while you're in college."

A Christian liberal arts institution, Montreat College seeks to integrate faith and learning, helping students discover the call of God in every sphere of life.

Montreat students also roll up their sleeves and get involved in a wide variety of worthy local causes, including serving in area nursing homes, Habitat for Humanity, the Big Brother/Big Sister Programs at the Presbyterian Children's Home, and local shelters for the homeless.

It's not all work at Montreat, however. The 10 Montreat College Cavalier athletic teams compete in the Tennessee-Virginia Athletic Conference, NAIA. Many campus teams have enjoyed winning seasons and post-season play, and the baseball Cavaliers are recent conference champions.

Other college programs provide less conventional experiences. Discovery, a 20-day wilderness adventure, lets students explore backpacking, white-water canoeing, rock climbing, route finding, and more in the pristine mountain environments of Pisgah National Forest and Linville Gorge Wilderness Area, both within an hour's drive of the campus.

Available off-campus study programs offer invaluable internship opportunities. Locations include Los Angeles; Washington, D.C.; Costa Rica; Cairo; Moscow; Oxford; and others. These opportunities across the country and abroad are available through the Coalition for Christian Colleges and Universities.

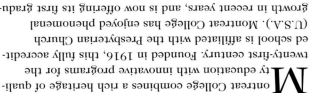

It all adds up to a multifaceted educational experience that helps each student fulfill his or her unique potential. Montreat graduates have gone on to achieve successful careers in every imaginable field. Samuel Fields, '71, is the pastor of a wilderness church in Alaska. Kristine Newman Bennet, '72, teaches at the American International School of Zagreb. Richard Shroyer, '76, is a management-information analyst at Martin Marietta Space Launch Systems at Cape Canaveral. Noted alumni of the college include Franklin Graham, the son of world-renowned evangelist Billy Graham (who lives in Montreat), and George Darden, associate conductor of the Metropolitan Opera Orchestra.

The college also serves adult students. Montreat's School of Professional and Adult Studies prepares career-minded adults for the workplace of tomorrow, offering accelerated business degree programs through a growing network of satellite campuses, including permanent extension facilities in Asheville and Charlotte. Intensive, weekly classes serve working adult students needing a nontraditional college schedule. Through study groups, students work together to learn problem-solving skills related to all areas of business operation and development.

Networking opportunities abound, and each student uses a notebook computer to supplement classwork, group, and individual study. The MBA program is available in Asheville and Charlotte. Core courses provide a broad, challenging program of study that ranges from applied management theory and marketing strategies to quantitative methods in business and international business.

Montreat College is a vital part of a unique community, with which it interacts in a variety of ways. McCALL, Montreat College's Center for Adult Lifelong Learning, offers noncredit educational experiences to community members, who use the college's facilities but run their own programs. They take (and sometimes teach) courses ranging from history and languages to travel, art, and literature. This successful program has grown to more than 200 members in the last few years, roughly half the full-time population of Montreat.

The fine arts also play a vital role in the life of the Montreat community. Each year, the college brings in many distinguished guests and special events, including the acclaimed North Carolina Shakespeare Festival; the internationally renowned Symphonic Choir and Orchestra of Kiev, Ukraine; arts festivals; the student acting troupe, The Greybeard Players; Christian performing artists; and the Staley Lecture Series.

McTEER, the college's volunteer program, enlists enthusiastic, gifted community members to serve as tutors, assist in many offices, including housing the families of students visiting the college. McTEER has grown enormously (and rapidly), from a mere 11 volunteers several years ago to about 165 today.

Thanks to innovative, nontraditional programs and significant investments in computer technology, Montreat students are being prepared well to meet the challenges of a new millennium. Montreat College is a historic institution with its sights set firmly on the future. ▲

Montreat College provides a multifaceted educational experience that helps each student fulfill his or her unique potential.

Montreat is a relatively small college offering big possibilities. It serves more than 1,000 students, who can choose from a wide variety of majors and concentrations.

Each year, some 30,000 conference attendees enjoy the beauty, tranquility, and rich cultural and educational offerings of the Montreat Conference Center, which today is one of three national conference centers for the Presbyterian Church (USA).

Montreat Conference Center

Cradled in the heart of the beautiful Blue Ridge Mountains, the Montreat Conference Center offers its guests a time-honored tradition of friendly, gracious hospitality. Founded a century ago as a place for spiritual renewal, continuing education, and physical refreshment, the center today strives to honor its rich heritage as it evolves to meet the needs of a more diverse community of visitors. Each year, some 30,000 conference attendees pass through the gate and enjoy the beauty, tranquility, and rich cultural and educational offerings of the Montreat Conference Center, which today is one of three national conference centers for the Presbyterian Church (USA). Generations of Presbyterians and other Christians have found inspiration here. Guided by a strong ecumenical vision, however, the conference center is reaching out to other denominations, as well as nonreligious groups, to share with them the wonders of Montreat. The center's 4,000-acre campus provides a stunning setting. Much of that acreage is carefully preserved as wilderness, with a network of well-maintained hiking trails. Physically active guests can also enjoy boating and canoeing on Lake Susan, fishing in nearby streams, swimming in the Olympic-sized pool, or perhaps a game of tennis on one of Montreat's seven all-weather courts. And there's golf just down the road in Black Mountain.

Montreat is also home to a unique residential community. When the Presbyterian Church purchased Montreat in 1905, it raised the needed funds by selling stock. Those original shareholders received residential lots as well, and the 578 cottages they built have attracted a diverse group of talented, enthusiastic residents.

Visitors to Montreat can choose from a range of accommodations, all of them convenient to conference activities. The landmark Assembly Inn, built on the site of the original Montreat Hotel, offers lodging, dining, and meeting facilities for larger groups. For more intimate accommodations, the Guest Lodges offer country ambiance and irresistible, breezy front porches. And, for lovers of the outdoors, there's also a family campground, with a bath house, a quiet stream, and lovely native rhododendron. Each campsite is equipped with a picnic table and grill.

The heart of the Montreat experience, however, is the conference center's wide variety of educational programming and learning experiences, offering information and inspiration to a diverse and growing audience. Arts Alive, a highly successful series of musical and dramatic performances, provides a taste of the rich mountain heritage

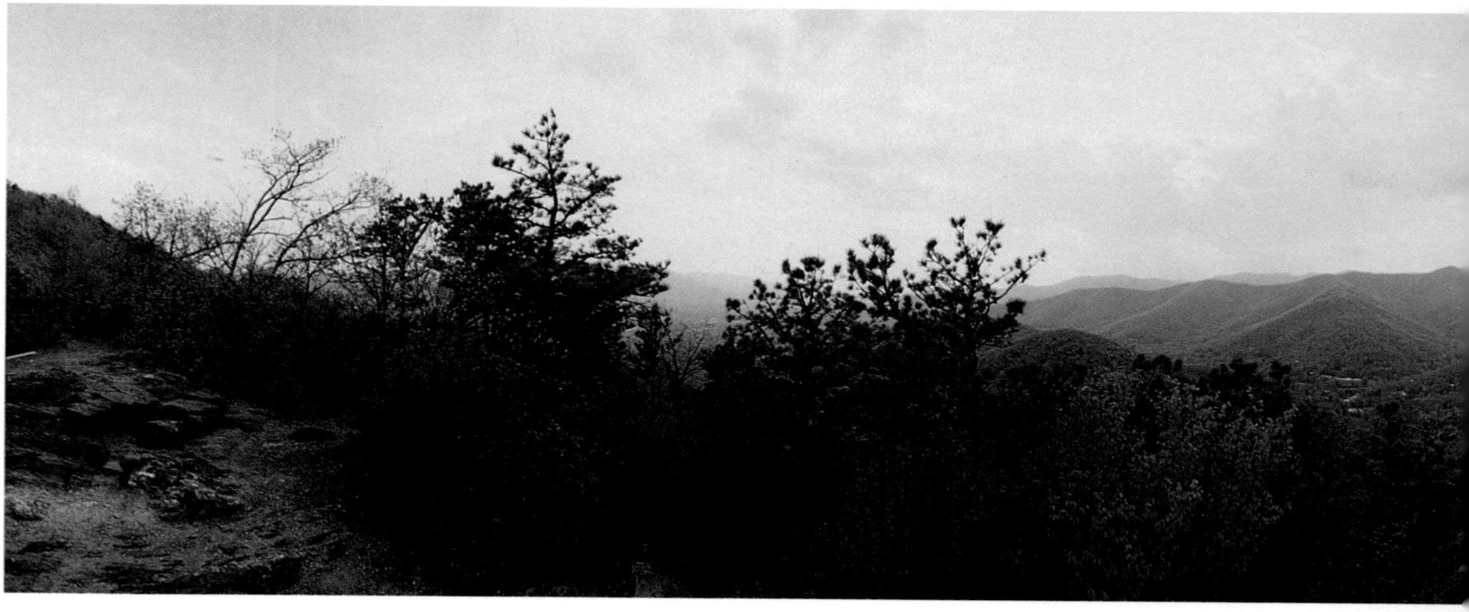

and a chance to sample the talents of visiting artists. This joyous celebration of the performing arts is making the center a cultural mecca, helping new constituencies discover what Montreat is all about. Anderson Auditorium—a warm, inviting facility that comfortably seats 2,500 people—provides the perfect setting for these enriching evenings, as well as hosting the traditional Sunday morning summer worship.

Montreat today is a proactive place that strives to discover and respond to what its visitors want. The center's in-house programming department develops conferences to meet the stated preferences and needs of an increasingly diverse clientele. Timely programming, closely tied to current issues, seeks to enhance participants' understanding of the world they live in. One exciting new direction involves carefully planned, off-site learning opportunities, both across the United States and overseas. The international travel component, still in development, will combine unique experiences abroad with time at the center for orientation and reflection. In the coming years, the conference center plans to substantially increase its capacity to span geographic areas. And, of course, a continuing highlight of the program year is the center's annual Youth Conference Series, which brings some 6,000 high-school students to Montreat to enjoy creative, productive, life-enriching experiences at a pivotal time in their young lives.

A variety of rental facilities can accommodate groups from 15 to 2,000 people, and they are regularly rented out for retreats, concerts, meetings, workshops, and even child care programs. A wide range of audiovisual equipment is available, and the catering and food service departments keep everyone well fed. The retail sales operation includes several specialty shops, all housed in the Moore Center. Ten Thousand Villages features handcrafted items from around the world. In addition to helping support the center and enhancing visitors' experience, the bazaar is also an economic development tool for artisans from developing nations, who receive a significant portion of the income from sales. To help reduce overhead, the shop is staffed by volunteers. The Presbyterian bookstore and gift shop, on the second level, offers cards and books, as well as authentic Appalachian crafts, including ceramics, weaving, and some jewelry made by local artisans. The general store, on the first level, is a convenient, year-round place to purchase Montreat T-shirts, hats, and sweats, as well as groceries. And the Huckleberry Snack Bar can satisfy that sudden craving for a quick sandwich or sweet. The newest addition to this growing family of services is the retail sales catalog, which makes the wonderful items sold in the shops available to a broader audience.

Montreat Conference Center's annual Youth Conference Series brings some 6,000 high-school students to the center to enjoy creative, productive, and life-enriching experiences at a pivotal time in their young lives.

From the time of the Cherokee right on through to today, Montreat has been a special place—a spiritual place. For many years, this was the single spot from which Presbyterian missionaries left the United States, on their way to all corners of the world. This unique mountain retreat tends to leave an indelible mark on its visitors, who often return, either for conferences or even to live here. And now, more than ever, new people are meeting each other, exchanging ideas and life experiences, here on these historic front porches. "Heritage is important," observes Executive Director William Dunifon, "but only as a context for our attempt to embrace the future. We aren't looking at life in the rearview mirror." ▲

Cradled in the heart of the beautiful Blue Ridge Mountains, the Montreat Conference Center offers its guests a time-honored tradition of friendly, gracious hospitality. *Photo by John Warner.*

Warren Wilson College

Warren Wilson College, located in the picturesque Swannanoa Valley, is a community of students, faculty, and staff who have come together from 45 states and 25 foreign countries to learn in a fresh and challenging way. *Photo by David Dietrich.*

First-time visitors to Warren Wilson College might mistake the campus for a small community nestled in the picturesque Swannanoa Valley. And they would be right. Community is at the heart of the college's mission and the distinctive place it holds in American higher education, having received several national recognitions in higher education surveys.

Warren Wilson College is a community of students, faculty, and staff who have come together from 45 states and 25 foreign countries to learn in a fresh and challenging way. They come not just to learn a given set of methods, values, and ideas but to truly understand and appreciate them.

Since its beginnings more than 100 years ago as the Asheville Farm School, the idea of work and serving community has been strong. Today, a Dean of Work oversees a program which requires 15 hours weekly on one of 80 work crews across the 1,100-acre campus. Students learn about responsibility to a community, time management, and work ethics, the very qualities that make employers eager to hire them.

Community service programs require a 100-hour minimum of off-campus work before graduation, and collectively students give 15,000 hours to the community each year. Locally, they work at projects such as tutoring in the schools, counseling at drug education centers, and winterizing homes for the disadvantaged. International outreach includes projects such as building a health center in Haiti or a water catchment system in Kenya.

Warren Wilson College offers an academic major in outdoor leadership. *Photo by David Dietrich.*

There is much written about the importance of independent liberal arts colleges having a distinctive mission, and Warren Wilson College's triad approach—strong liberal arts curriculum, required work program, and required community service program—sets a new standard. In addition to its liberal arts curriculum, there are also professional program areas in education, social work, and business. And in its ongoing search for ways to expand offerings, the college has formed a partnership with North Carolina Outward Bound, which now has its administrative headquarters on campus and offers a new academic major in outdoor leadership.

Summer is a time when many campuses slow down. Not here. With a strong commitment to continuing education, Warren Wilson College provides a wealth of summer programs that celebrate the arts and humanities. Started in 1992, the Swannanoa Gathering offers four weeks of courses in traditional music, dance, and storytelling, attracting primarily adult students from all over the world. Celtic Week, Dulcimer Week, Dance Week, Old-Time Music and Dance Week, and Guitar Week are just some of its programs. In addition to the dig-related activities at a significant Native American archeological site by the Swannanoa River on campus, background studies in Cherokee music, history, culture are planned to complement the project. Other popular summer programs include the nationally renowned residency of the Masters of Fine Arts in Creative Writing program, which attracts writers from all over the country; the five-week residency of the Swannanoa Chamber Music Festival, which celebrates chamber music through teaching and performing; and the North Carolina Shakespeare Festival's summer residency.

Warren Wilson College is so much more than a campus. It is a strong community nurturing skills vital to building better communities around the world. ▲

Carolina Day School

It is morning at Carolina Day School: A fifth-grade class in the Lower School writes and designs its own newspaper on computers. A Middle School student constructs a three-dimensional landscape from what she's learned about the movement of the earth's crust. And in the Upper School, seniors chat with their teacher—in French. These are all scenes from a school which balances a demand for academic excellence with the support and encouragement students need to achieve it.

Carolina Day's Upper School science curriculum includes nine courses, with electives ranging from analytic chemistry to freshwater ecology to genetics.

Carolina Day, a coeducational, college preparatory school, was founded in 1987 through the merger of Asheville Country Day School and St. Genevieve/Gibbons Hall. This new partnership created a school that was at once old and young: old in the traditions of its parent institutions—founded respectively in 1936 and 1908—and young in its rejuvenated aim to instill in students a love of learning and a thirst for personal growth. Located on 23 acres of land adjacent to the Blue Ridge Parkway in south Asheville, the school currently has an enrollment of 450 students in pre-kindergarten through grade 12.

The academic program at Carolina Day is designed to impart the skills that students will need to become lifelong learners and independent thinkers. As a result, good study habits and self-discipline are promoted alongside skills in communication, critical and creative thinking, and computer literacy. A student-faculty ratio of 10 to 1 ensures that classes remain challenging yet flexible, and that children are able to receive personal attention as they need it. The success of the school's program can easily be measured by a student's senior year. Carolina Day students consistently score 200 points above the national average on the SAT, and virtually 100 percent of its graduates go on to college, with 82 percent accepted at their first choice.

The small size of the school also allows students to participate and take leadership roles in many extracurricular activities. After-school activities include intramural and varsity sports, drama, Odyssey of the Mind, and community service opportunities through such groups as Habitat for Humanity and SADD.

Underlying all levels of Carolina Day's curriculum is a core belief that it is equally important to develop the character of students as well as their minds. Both in the classroom and out on the playing field, students of all ages are encouraged to strive for personal excellence and to demonstrate the qualities of respect, responsibility, integrity, and compassion. Through outreach activities such as cleanup of local highways and serving as buddies to Special Olympics athletes, students learn to take their place as citizens in the larger community.

Carolina Day's faculty, parents, and administration have worked in close partnership to create a caring, tightly-knit atmosphere, where all students are asked to achieve the simplest and hardest of goals: their full potential. Recently the school began to raise funds for an ambitious plan to expand and improve its facilities, a project which will give Carolina Day School more room in which to educate the minds and hearts of Asheville's children. ▲

Young writers work together to record observations and ideas about their world.

The Asheville School

Near downtown Asheville, a road flanked by towering oaks and maples winds past stately homes and buildings that speak of days gone by. At the crest of the hill, a commanding vista of the region's magnificent Blue Ridge Mountains presents itself, a glorious backdrop for the 300-acre campus of The Asheville School, the leading coeducational boarding school in the Southeast. Through the combination of challenging curriculum and embracing community, the school prepares its students not only for success at the most competitive colleges and universities but also for a life based on strong personal values.

Founded in 1900 by Newton M. Anderson and Charles A. Mitchell, founders of the renowned University School in Cleveland, Ohio, The Asheville School strove to educate the "whole young man" in the classics, manual arts, and physical and spiritual growth. Glance at a list of its illustrious alumni—names like Studebaker, Kimberly of Kimberly-Clark, Ball of Ball Bros. Jar Company, Johnson of Johnson & Sons Wax Company, and prestigious Asheville natives—and it becomes apparent how well the school has succeeded. The Asheville School became coeducational almost 25 years ago, and has subsequently added many women to its list of prominent graduates. An average of 200 students attend each year, representing more than 20 states and 14 foreign countries.

As a traditional boarding and day preparatory school, The Asheville School believes strongly in the individual worth of each student and stresses sound scholarship, self-reliance, a sense of responsibility, and the development of strong character and leadership abilities. The unique and challenging academic curriculum is taught by a dedicated, caring faculty in small classrooms averaging only 12 students. With 44 full-time and 4 part-time faculty, the overall student-faculty ratio is a low 5 to 1. As a result of the close personal attention and outstanding academics, the school averages two National Merit Semi-Finalists per class and a median SAT score more than 150 points above the national average.

But teaching extends beyond books and classrooms. Valuable lessons are learned on the playing field, in throwing a pot or painting a canvas, and through the fellowship that is so much part of The Asheville School experience. The spacious new dining hall, for example, is designed to foster a family atmosphere where important social skills are learned. At the other end of the spectrum, the Mountaineering Program—outdoor activities conducted as an integral part of the educational program—builds teamwork and group communication skills in the great outdoors. A new Alpine tower and ropes course on campus enables students to learn the fundamentals of climbing and rappelling before taking weekend camping trips in the nearby mountains.

Students at The Asheville School compete in 12 different interscholastic sports.

The Asheville School also shares its resources with the surrounding community. Lectures, performances, and art exhibitions at the Walker Arts Center are all open to the public. Community, after all, is what distinguishes The Asheville School. It is through a strong community of learning and fellowship that The Asheville School is able to accomplish its mission of nurturing character and fostering the development of mind, body, and spirit. ▲

Mitchell Hall, the administration and classroom building, is typical of The Asheville School's Tudor architecture.

Mars Hill College

At Mars Hill College the grandeur and sweep of the Blue Ridge Mountains form a majestic backdrop to the school's mission of providing students with the individual support and direction needed to guide them to future success. A college that is committed to the education of the total person, Mars Hill emphasizes the importance of reaching for individual goals, fulfilling spiritual needs, and serving the community—values as fixed and unwavering as the mountains in which they're taught.

Founded by the Baptists in 1856, Mars Hill is the oldest college on its original site in Western North Carolina. Each fall just over 1,000 students from 28 states and 10 foreign countries arrive on the campus, located 18 miles north of Asheville. There, through relationships with each other, and faculty and staff, they become part of a caring and tightly knit community. The college offers the security of a small-town atmosphere and the diversity of cultural and recreational activities that characterize the region.

With a student-faculty ratio of 13 to 1 and a computer-student ratio of 6 to 1, Mars Hill students are assured of personal attention in their classes. To prepare students for the challenges posed by a rapidly changing world, the college offers a curriculum of liberal arts courses designed to help the formation of basic learning skills, critical abilities, moral and ethical judgment, and theoretical understanding.

Each fall just over 1,000 students from 28 states and 10 foreign countries arrive on the campus of Mars Hill College, located 18 miles north of Asheville.

At Mars Hill College the grandeur and sweep of the Blue Ridge Mountains form a majestic backdrop to the school's mission of providing students with the individual support and direction needed to guide them to future success.

Faculty at Mars Hill are dedicated to teaching and advising, and their credentials reflect their academic preparation. Of the college's 80 full-time faculty members, 75 percent have earned terminal degrees in their disciplines. Many have also been recognized through grants, publications, and appointments to national panels as having made outstanding contributions to their professional fields.

The college also recognizes that opportunities for learning are not confined to the classroom and encourages students to take advantage of internships and involvement in campus activities, as well as student exchange and travel experiences both in the United States and abroad. Through service programs that include visiting with residents at a nearby nursing home, volunteering at a shelter for the homeless, and tutoring area school children, students are also taught to assume their role as stewards of the community.

Mars Hill College is proud of its heritage in southern Appalachia and is involved in keeping alive the craft and musical traditions of the region. The college's Bailey Mountain Cloggers are five-time national champions and recently performed at the Kennedy Center. The college also sponsors a yearly schedule of events that showcase the achievements of other cultures, such as a concert by the Vienna Choir Boys or a performance by the Ballet Gran Folklorico de Mexico. And sometimes Mars Hill puts on concerts that are just for fun, as demonstrated by recent appearances on campus by Hootie and the Blowfish and the Indigo Girls.

Since 1856 the educational philosophy of the college has been to give the opportunities, guidance, and learning experiences necessary to graduate students who are developed as total people. At Mars Hill College, students receive not only an academic education, but also four years of growth linking mind and spirit, spirit and community. ▲

Christ School

Christ School defines its curriculum as everything a boy experiences from the time he enters the school until the time he leaves. This broad-based curriculum extends well beyond the classrooms, across the pastoral, 500-acre campus onto the playing fields and into the residence halls, dining hall, chapel, and workplaces.

Arts and technology are prominent on campus. The campus is being hardwired in all buildings—offices, dorms, classrooms, library—connecting them to one another and to the Internet.

Founded in 1900, Christ School is a boys college preparatory school affiliated with the Episcopal Church. The school is strongly committed to its mission to produce educated men of good character, prepared for both scholastic achievement in college and productive citizenship in adult society. The mission is a four-fold process. First and most important, faculty challenge and encourage each student, in the nurturing environment of a close-knit campus, to develop academically to his maximum potential. Second, through competitive sports, student self-government, and a variety of extracurricular activities, students develop their physical fitness and leadership skills, as well as a respect for others regardless of their origins, cultures, or beliefs. Third, by involvement in the care of the campus home, civic duty is learned, along with a sense of the dignity of honest labor. Finally, through religious instruction and regular participation in chapel activities, each student learns the sustaining value of faith and spiritual growth throughout his life.

Christ School's academic curriculum prepares the students for acceptance and successful work at a wide range of colleges and universities (ranging from Ivy League to state universities to liberal arts colleges) by providing an integrated, thorough, and rigorous study of the basics of history, mathematics, foreign language, science, English, and the new basics of character and moral development. Arts and technology are prominent on campus as well. An artist-in-residence program, for example, complements a curriculum that already features music, drama, creative writing, art, and photography. And the campus is being hardwired in all buildings—offices, dorms, classrooms, library—connecting them to one another and to the Internet.

The faculty consists of 34 full-time members, the majority of whom have advanced degrees and reside on campus to contribute to the family-like atmosphere. The average class size is only 10 students, with a student-faculty ratio of 6 to 1 that ensures the best possible learning environment for the boys in grades 8 through 12. (SAT scores are high, averaging 1135, and students receive regional and national recognition for their scholastic achievements.) The student body of 165 represents 15 states and 10 foreign countries with 20 day students from Asheville. Christ School plans to expand to 200 students by the turn of the century.

Christ School aims is to build character, community, and civility as a means of preparing students for living the ideal of servant leadership. Rather than climbing a ladder to success, servant leadership is about holding the ladder for others, serving as they go. With this kind of dedication, vision, and leadership, there is little doubt Christ School will meet its goal to become the best boarding school for boys in America by the year 2000. ▲

Christ School, a boys college preparatory school affiliated with the Episcopal Church, is strongly committed to its mission to produce educated men of good character, prepared for both scholastic achievement in college and productive citizenship in adult society.

CHAPTER SEVENTEEN

THE MARKETPLACE AND ATTRACTIONS

The area's hospitality industry vitalizes the economic life of the Asheville area.

Great Smokies Holiday Inn SunSpree Resort

The Great Smokies Holiday Inn SunSpree Resort offers its guests the best of both worlds. Established in the early 1970s, when spacious, rolling grounds close to downtown were still feasible, the resort is an oasis of natural beauty overlooking the beautiful Asheville skyline. At the same time, guests enjoy the modern renovations that are the trademark of SunSpree Resorts. An on-going $4-million renovation plan is evident everywhere, starting with the attractively landscaped grounds and impressive stone and white beam entranceway. The new look extends into the spacious lobby, where guests are encouraged to have their afternoon tea or an evening cocktail in the comfortable seating surrounding the 30-foot native stone fireplace. The fresh decor continues into the elegantly appointed restaurants and attractively decorated guest rooms. Throughout, the resort is a charming blend of the warmth of a mountain lodge and the hospitality of a Southern plantation.

Families are a focus at SunSpree Resorts. More and more, business travel includes spouses and children, and SunSpree caters to their needs. "We have a children's area known as the KidSpree Activity Center," states General Manager Steven Laney, "with a dedicated staff from 8:30 A.M. to 8:30 P.M. They plan activities and take the kids on nature hikes around the golf course, to tennis training activities, or for a fun romp in the pool. We also serve them lunch or dinner. Parents are not required to stay with their children, but they must be readily available, so we provide a beeper that gives them the freedom to play golf or relax by the pool, while we take care of the kids. This is a great way for families to travel together—it means business and family life do not have to be separated."

Doing business on the road is easier at SunSpree, too. The hotel now features upgraded amenities such as 37 business rooms with fax, copy machine, voice mail, and E-mail hookups. "I am a technology buff," Laney adds. "People need these services when they are traveling, so we have completed a lot of infrastructure work that makes this a very modern hotel."

All 280 newly remodeled guest rooms include refrigerators, coffee makers, hair dryers, remote control color TVs, and in-room movies. Renovations also include new beds, chairs, case goods, and telephone systems. Televisions are hooked into property management systems, allowing guests to review their bills before checking out.

The hotel's 10,000 square feet of convention space is undergoing complete renovation, as well. Facilities can accommodate all types of events from small receptions, to important business conferences, to major conventions.

The Great Smokies Holiday Inn SunSpree Resort offers its guests the best of both worlds. The resort is an oasis of natural beauty overlooking Asheville. *Photo by Tim Barnwell.*

In 1996 the hotel committed more than $450,000 to golf course renovations, including new manicuring equipment, new golf carts, new pathways, and other improvements to make it one of the premiere facilities in the area. *Photo by Tim Barnwell.*

An on-going $4-million renovation plan extends into the spacious lobby, where guests are encouraged to have their afternoon tea or an evening cocktail in the comfortable seating surrounding the 30-foot native stone fireplace. *Photo by Tim Barnwell.*

Current space includes four boardrooms, four meeting rooms, and a grand ballroom. In the spring of 1997, an additional 7,000-square-foot ballroom is planned which will overlook the golf course and downtown Asheville. In addition to convention activities, the new ballroom with its picturesque setting will be a popular setting for wedding receptions, parties, and events of all kinds.

The Pro's Table, the hotel's upscale yet moderately priced restaurant, shares the spectacular view overlooking the 18th green. Rave reviews of its Sunday brunch tout the menu of crab legs, shrimp, and oysters on the half shell, complemented by waffles, French toast, and eggs Benedict. There are also stations for freshly carved roast turkey and roast beef, pasta, vegetables, and luscious desserts. And the menu is just as exciting throughout the week. "We are introducing a new menu concept," Laney states. "Traditionally, hotels try to offer a lengthy menu in an effort to attract all potential tastes. Instead, we have selected 12 well-researched items that are absolutely the finest value. They are offered at one price for the complete meal—appetizer to dessert. In addition to the entree selections, a chef prepares appetizer and salad selections table-side every evening."

For casual dining, guests head to The Marketessen—a New York-style deli and convenience market featuring salads, sandwiches, fresh fruit, and bakery items, plus a wide range of beverages including espresso and cappuccino. Selections are available to take back to the room or enjoy on the run.

Another new offering popular with local residents and guests alike is the Equinox, an English-style pub just off the main lobby. With rich, dark woodwork, its own fireplace, and clusters of wingback chairs and camelback sofas, the pub creates a comfortable and cozy atmosphere where friends can unwind and share the events of the day.

The 6,800-yard golf course has received an extensive facelift, as well. In 1996 alone, the hotel has committed more than $450,000 to the golf course renovations, including new manicuring equipment, new golf carts, new pathways, and other improvements to make it one of the premiere facilities in the area. Local residents agree and can often be found playing the par 70 course. "Our course is very well known around here. We host a lot of local players," Laney adds.

To take the course to an even higher level of excellence, the hotel hired a talented, enthusiastic superintendent, Jeremy Boone, who comes with the right mix of college degrees and good common sense to do the job right. According to Laney, Boone is working with the Sierra Club to make sure the golf course is in tune with the environment. "We are creating natural areas where wildlife can live and come onto the golf course. This is not an overly urbanized golf course. The wildlife is part of the attraction."

The tennis center, although very nice, is slated for renovations in the not-too-distant future. With four indoor courts and four outdoor clay courts, it is one of the best in the region. The 35,000-square-foot center is slated to serve as an additional convention and private event site once renovations are complete. The hotel also features two outdoor swimming pools, a pro shop, exercise room, and gift shop.

Boasting one of the best views in town, excellent cuisine, and a full array of modern amenities and services, the Great Smokies Holiday Inn SunSpree Resort is set for an even longer history as one of Asheville's most popular destinations. ▲

Biltmore Estate

The curving road is so quietly beautiful that the impact at its destination—the majestic Biltmore House—is a powerful surprise. *Photo courtesy of The Biltmore Company.*

Only two miles south of Asheville's historic Pack Square, a graceful road winds through lush stands of colorful rhododendron and heavy-boughed hemlocks. The curving road is so quietly beautiful that the impact at its destination—the majestic Biltmore House—is a powerful surprise. The 250-room French Renaissance chateau—nestled in the Blue Ridge Mountains on 8,000 acres—is the largest private home in America.

On Christmas Eve in 1895, George Vanderbilt, grandson of industrialist Commodore Cornelius Vanderbilt, formally opened the doors for the first time to friends and family. In the late twentieth century, Biltmore House remains much as it was when Vanderbilt occupied it 100 years ago. His original collection of furnishings, art, and antiques are part of the collection of 70,000 objects still in Biltmore House today: artworks by Renoir, Sargent, Whistler, and Pellegrini; furniture by Sheraton and Chippendale; a chess set and gaming table which belonged to Napoleon; sixteenth-century Flemish tapestries; and Persian and Oriental rugs adorn Biltmore's four acres of floor space.

Step outside the House to the estate's glorious Gardens and grounds, designed by the father of landscape architecture in America, Frederick Law Olmsted. A dazzling array of color and the sights and sounds of abundant wildlife greet you. Formal gardens include a four-acre English Walled Garden, a sixteenth-century Italian Garden with three reflecting pools, and a dramatic Rampe Douce and esplanade lined by an avenue of 100-year-old trees. A master of naturalistic landscaping, Olmsted used a variety of indigenous flora and added the rare and exotic, in true Victorian fashion, to create this unique setting.

Beyond the formal gardens there are acres of trees and shrubs, wildflowers, and ferns. Tall, ancient trees that knew the land long before George Vanderbilt walked here, come in more shades of green than even Monet could imagine. Countless species of birds sing in every octave, geese honk their syncopated cacophony, and an expanded network of woodland trails encircle the Bass Pond and meander through the Azalea Garden and meadow.

Each season brings forth something new to admire. Biltmore's unique horticultural environment creates a blooming season that begins in early spring and continues until the first frost. In the Gardens, 50,000 Dutch tulips and acres of azaleas brighten spring. Summer annuals, autumn chrysanthemums, and hundreds of other varieties add to the year-round splendor. Even during the winter months, the glass-roofed conservatory is full of colorful tropical plants such as poinsettias, orchids, lilies, cacti, and bougainvillea.

The family's long tradition of enterprise continues to this day, preserving George Vanderbilt's vision of a self-sufficient American estate. Modern innovations and

The 250-room French Renaissance chateau—nestled in the Blue Ridge Mountains on 8,000 acres—is the largest private home in America. *Photo courtesy of The Biltmore Company.*

The estate's glorious gardens and grounds were designed by the father of landscape architecture in America, Frederick Law Olmsted. *Photo courtesy of The Biltmore Company.*

improvements maintain the style and taste of the original plans, while providing an enhanced guest experience. For instance, the Winery, America's most visited, opened in 1985 as a state-of-the-art facility where guests can learn about viticulture and sample Biltmore's award-winning wines. The estate currently bottles approximately 75,000 cases of wine annually.

Creative cuisine presented in ambient country elegance is the trademark of the estate's three restaurants. Deerpark Restaurant, set in a restored farm building, features elegant and leisurely luncheons in an outdoor atmosphere. The Stable Cafe, a beautiful renovated space with seating in former horse stalls and hay loft, serves the freshest rotisserie roasted meats and poultry, accompanied by crisp salads and tantilizing desserts. The estate's newest restaurant, The Bistro, is located at the Winery and offers a unique setting for late lunch or early dinner, featuring wood-fired pizzas, homemade pastas, and creative Bistro specials. All menu items are homemade and prepared with the freshest seasonal ingredients, many grown and harvested on Biltmore Estate.

While memories of a visit to the estate last a lifetime, unusual shops offer an assortment of remembrances. Five shops in the renovated stable area feature Victorian-style gifts, regional crafts, toys, confections, and decorative accessories. The Gate House Gift Shop, located just outside the main entrance, showcases the Biltmore Estate Collection of reproductions and decorative accessories. The Winery Gift Shop includes distinctive wines, gourmet foods, and kitchen and dining accessories. A Gardener's Place, located behind the Conservatory, features estate-grown plants, books, tools, and gifts for the gardener.

Special events punctuate an already exciting schedule. From mid-April to mid-May, Festival of Flowers adds live music and evening events each weekend to the already bedazzling blossoms. On selected warm-weather weekends, the sounds of live jazz resonate in the Winery courtyard. And Christmas at Biltmore, the grand holiday tradition George Vanderbilt began in 1895, continues annually with more than 35 magnificent trees, hundreds of wreaths and poinsettias, and 10,000 feet of evergreen roping decorating the house. Candlelight Christmas Evenings add crackling fires, glittering trees, and hundreds of candles, casting a warm glow through the richly decorated rooms.

Groups of 20 or more are warmly welcomed on the estate. Whether seniors from Iowa or business executives from New York, group tour guests are treated to discounts and special opportunities to call the estate their own. Deerpark, for example, is available for private events, featuring chef-selected or custom-tailored menus. A professional staff assists with arrangements such as flowers, decorations, photography, music, and entertainment.

With so much to explore, it only makes sense to come back to the estate again and again. And it's easy to do just that with a Twelve-Month Pass, which includes unlimited daytime visits for a year, discounted tickets to special events, invitations to seminars and event previews, and the *Ambassador* newsletter.

For all the fun and fantasy of the estate, the economic impact of the Biltmore Companies on the region is considerable. Its direct impact in sales, payroll, and taxes alone is almost $120 million annually. Calculate the indirect effects, such as lodging, fuel, and meals, and the figure soars to $215 million each year. Biltmore Estate is a microcosm of what is so special about Asheville—an extraordinary combination of unparalleled beauty thriving amidst an environment of economic development. ▲

Creative cuisine presented in ambient country elegance is the trademark of the estate's restaurants. *Photo courtesy of The Biltmore Company.*

The Grove Park Inn Resort

Forged from massive gray granite boulders, with a roof of red tile folding softly like a cloak over its eaves, The Grove Park Inn Resort rises with a grandeur to rival the surrounding mountains.

Forged from massive gray granite boulders, with a roof of red tile folding softly like a cloak over its eaves, The Grove Park Inn Resort rises with a grandeur to rival the surrounding mountains. The inn's old-fashioned charm serves as a counterpoint to the modern luxuries of its accommodations, a careful blending that yields a seamless tribute to the best of the past and present.

It was the dream of E. W. Grove, a Saint Louis pharmacist who first came to Asheville in 1900 in search of a respite from the Midwestern summer heat and a case of the hiccups so chronic that even the elixir that made his fortune—Grove's Tasteless Chill Tonic—could not cure him. At the time, Asheville was a small town of less than 20,000 people in the midst of a real estate boom. Grove, at heart an entrepreneur, made sure that when deals were made, he was on one end of the handshake; he soon snapped up hundreds of acres in and around the town. Choice among these holdings was a site on the western slope of Sunset Mountain, to the north of Asheville. It was here that Grove decided in 1912 to build a resort hotel that would overlook the panorama of the Blue Ridge Mountains.

After an exhaustive search for an architect, Grove turned to a sketch by his own charismatic son-in-law, Fred Seely. Like Grove, Seely was a jack-of-all-trades who had tried his hand at a number of different lines of work, each time with success. On Grove's urging and with no previous experience, he now set about building a world-class hotel—in 12 months' time.

Scores of men were recruited to the job and slept at night in a tent that had been pitched on site. Teams of mules dragged in granite boulders and rocks from nearby mountains, which were then hoisted into place by pulleys. Meanwhile a group of artisans in East Aurora, New York, was turning out over 700 hand-hammered copper chandeliers, lanterns, and lamps. Called the Roycrofters, the group is now celebrated for their role in the Arts and Crafts movement. Its furniture shop also fashioned banquet chairs for the inn as well as writing desks and sideboards. When it became evident that the small shop would be unable to finish the rest of the pieces needed in time, the White Furniture Company of Melane, North Carolina, stepped in to make the oak beds and dressers designed by Seely and the Roycrofters for the guest rooms.

The determined push to complete construction paid off when the Grove Park Inn opened in 1913 to wide and instant acclaim. The guest register in the ensuing decades included the names of many American luminaries. In the mid-1930s, new arrivals alighting in the tile entrance court were scanned from a window above by F. Scott Fitzgerald, who was never too paralyzed by writer's block to give up girl-watching. Calvin Coolidge mulled over his presidency from one of the rows of rocking chairs on the same front porch that Franklin Roosevelt would pass through many years later with a wink and a wag of his cigarette holder. Thomas Edison thought inventive thoughts as he strolled through the Grove Park's hallways, as Will Rogers talked his trademark talk in the inn's Great Hall. And although it's not documented, Harry Houdini must have delighted in the magic of the elevators housed in the two massive fireplaces that flank the Great Hall.

But a clash between personalities that were perhaps too alike for comfort ended the Grove Park's golden era: Seely and Grove fought in court, and the inn was sold by

The inn's old-fashioned charm serves as a counterpoint to the modern luxuries of its accommodations, a careful blending that yields a seamless tribute to the best of the past and present.

Indoor and outdoor tennis courts and swimming pools, a sports center, and a century-old, Donald Ross-designed golf course round out the resort atmosphere at the Grove Park Inn.

Fine restaurants and theme weekends make the four-star hotel a favorite getaway spot.

Grove's estate in 1928. The Great Depression and a world war also took their toll, and the glitter of its former days had almost faded into local memory when the Grove Park Inn was purchased by Dallas businessman Charles Sammons and his wife, Elaine, in 1955.

Grove's vision for the inn had been "a big home where every modern convenience could be had, but with all the old-fashioned qualities of genuineness with no sham." The simple, straight lines of the handcrafted Roycroft furniture blended with the unfinished boulders of the inn's construction. Even the copper chandeliers bore hammer marks. All seemed in harmony with the Grove Park Inn's craggy mountain background. Under the Sammons' direction, this integrity was painstakingly restored and the inn placed on the National Historic Register.

Today, The Grove Park Inn Resort is a living museum, home to the world's largest public display of Arts and Crafts antiques, a design style that's again popular because of its simplicity, quality, and timelessness. The inn hosts a three-day Arts and Crafts conference each February to celebrate that world-renowned heritage. Most recently, the restoration of its Palm Court, one of the country's first indoor atriums, received an award from the Preservation Society of Asheville and Buncombe County; and the inn was featured in *Architectural Digest*.

Vice President and General Manager Jim France makes sure that for every step the Grove Park Inn takes to perpetuate its past, another is taken to solidify its future. Fine restaurants and theme weekends make the four-star hotel a favorite getaway spot (not to mention the children's programs that keep kids and their parents happy.) With the addition of two wings in the 1980s, it now boasts 510 rooms and full convention facilities. Indoor and outdoor tennis courts and swimming pools, a sports center, and a century-old, Donald Ross-designed golf course round out the resort atmosphere, and its recycling, food redistribution, and energy conservation programs have won regional and national acclaim. In its ninth decade, The Grove Park Inn Resort continues to demonstrate that the best of traditions can be maintained and built upon. ▲

Radisson Hotel Asheville

The Radisson Hotel Asheville is not only in the heart of downtown Asheville, but it is also the heart of downtown for many visitors to the city. For everyone from the casual overnight guest to an international troupe of performing artists, the 281-room hotel becomes their home away from home and is only blocks from the center of town.

But the Radisson never takes its convenient location for granted. "We are partners in the development of downtown Asheville," states General Manager Eileen Connolly. "We work closely with the downtown businesses and retailers because we are part of a growing tourist attraction—Asheville's downtown with its 40 restaurants, 150 shops, and attractions like Pack Place. It is an exciting place to be."

The hotel's prominence in downtown, of course, is based on far more than its address. Award-winning services and first-class amenities figure strongly in the hotel's reputation for excellence. For the past two years the hotel has earned Radisson's prestigious President's Award based on guest satisfaction and other important criteria. What that means to guests—whether tourists, business persons, or convention delegates—is that the Radisson consistently provides them the highest quality experience possible. The 18-year-old hotel has been owned by New York City-based Golodetz from the beginning and became a Radisson Hotel in 1989.

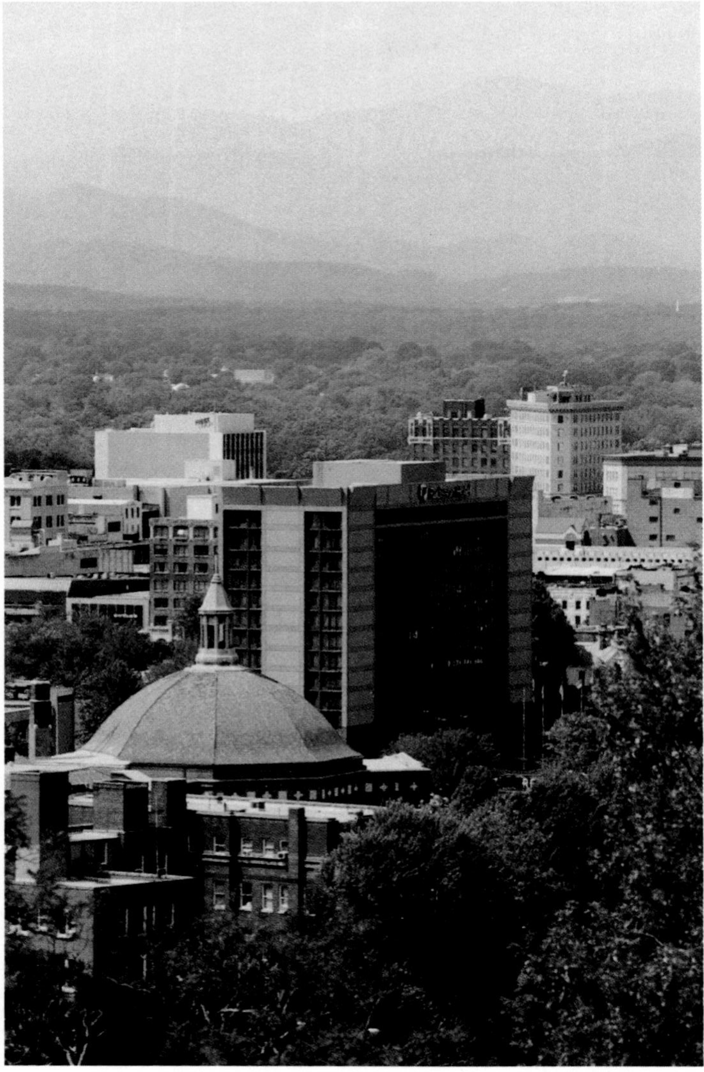

Nestled in quaint downtown Asheville, the Radisson Hotel Asheville is within walking distance of 40 restaurants and 150 unique retail shops.

Hotel management recognizes the need for professional training and meaningful incentives to continually deliver this high level of service. Matching the right employee to the right position, coupled with effective orientation programs, gets things off to the right start. Once an employee is properly placed and trained, good communication is encouraged between personnel and department heads to keep teams working together. An ongoing training program entitled "Yes I Can" is Radisson's trademarked, nationwide program to encourage adaptability and flexibility when dealing with guests. "Yes I Can" also symbolizes an attitude that runs throughout the hotel. All 150 employees attend annual training seminars addressing ways to ensure superior guest service. Workshops include discussions of new procedures, old-fashioned courtesy, and role playing designed to help employees find effective solutions to difficult situations.

Employee incentives also contribute to Radisson's success equation. "We do a lot of incentives for our staff to keep them motivated," states Michael Kryzanek, director of sales and marketing and assistant general manager. "Our Quality Management Task Force, for example, is a problem-solving employee group that meets monthly. Representatives from each department get together to brainstorm problems they are facing. We need their input—oftentimes they find the best solutions because they are so familiar with the procedures. We host a monthly employee luncheon and award employees with a "Yes I Can" attitude cash incentives and prizes. We also feature an Employee of the Month who wins a cash award, a prime parking space, dinner for two at our rooftop restaurant, Top of the Plaza, and their picture displayed at the desk."

The Radisson's community outreach extends beyond its active promotion of the region. The hotel serves as an important meeting site and entertainment facility for businesses and individuals in the greater Asheville area. Management also works with numerous arts and nonprofit organizations to assist with rooms and other amenities. "We work with Pack Place, Downtown Development, Bele Chere, to name a few," Kryzanek adds. "We want to help with festivals and other events when we can be of assistance."

The Radisson's three distinctly different restaurants attract local and out-of-town guests alike. Atop the hotel's 12th floor overlooking the surrounding mountains, Top of the Plaza is one of those special restaurants that offers elegance without pretention. Casual attire is welcomed among the linen tablecloths and fresh flowers, and guests can order carefully prepared entrees of fresh pasta, prime rib, or seafood at a very reasonable price. Newly redecorated, the restaurant's decor of teal, peach, and ivory complements the lovely rich wood paneling in the dining room and bar. For sheer dramatic effect, though, nothing compares to the 100 feet of windowed wall with a view across the city and the mountains beyond. "Top of the Plaza has become a tradition for a regular clientele who always have their holiday meal or Sunday brunch with us," Kryzanek adds. "We typically

With 281 mountain-view guest rooms, the Radisson Hotel Asheville is one of the region's largest hotels.

offer special buffets for Thanksgiving, Christmas, Easter, and Sunday brunch."

Just off the main lobby, Izzy's Sports Bar is a popular spot to unwind. Large screen TVs fed by satellite carry sports events not available on cable or major TV networks. And Izzy's is well stocked with interactive video games such as QB1 and Trivia, pool, darts, and other sporting games. For a change in pace, guests enjoy the menu of steaks, pizza, and lighter fare while watching a sporting event or playing a game in the relaxed, comfortable atmosphere.

Overlooking the Thomas Wolfe Memorial, Burt and Harry's New York Deli serves up classic overstuffed deli sandwiches, large salads, and daily specials to satisfy any craving.

The Radisson is one of only three hotels in the region that can accommodate sizeable conventions. Facilities include 10 different meeting rooms for a total of 15,000 square feet of meeting space and a grand ballroom that can serve 650 for dinner or seat 1,000 people theater style. According to Kryzanek, the hotel hosts more than 400 different groups every year in meetings ranging from 10 to 700 people. They run the gamut from professional associations, family groups, garden clubs, card collectors clubs, and exhibitions to SMERFS—social, military, educational, religious, and fraternal groups. We do a lot with those groups, as well as corporate groups from Atlanta, Charlotte, and local businesses."

Each day the staff at the Radisson Hotel Asheville works hard to create an environment that will make visitors feel good about their visit to the hotel and the entire region. "We take our role in Asheville very seriously," states Connolly. "We are a strong part of the community, and we strive to maintain—and enhance—its reputation as a wonderful destination." ▲

Richmond Hill

Richmond Hill is a special place for special people—the kind who like their travel to be leisurely and soul-restoring. It's an island of serenity, surrounded by streams and stunning mountain views. Indeed, with its easy pace and exquisite cuisine, Richmond Hill is virtually a way of life, a gracious remnant of a bygone era. No surprise, then, that guests settle in so readily and often find it difficult to leave.

Built in 1889 as the home of Congressman and Diplomat Richmond Pearson, Richmond Hill is Asheville's finest remaining example of Queen Anne-style architecture. The grand mansion was also a showcase for Pearson's substantial collections of art and furnishings, acquired during his extensive travels. The great home's common rooms—the magnificent Oak Hall, the elegant front parlor, the drawing room, and the library (which once housed 3,000 books)—help bring the past alive. The inn's 12 guest rooms are individually decorated with draped canopy beds and Victorian furniture. Some feature fireplaces with elegant mantles, oriental rugs, and even the original, claw-footed bathtubs.

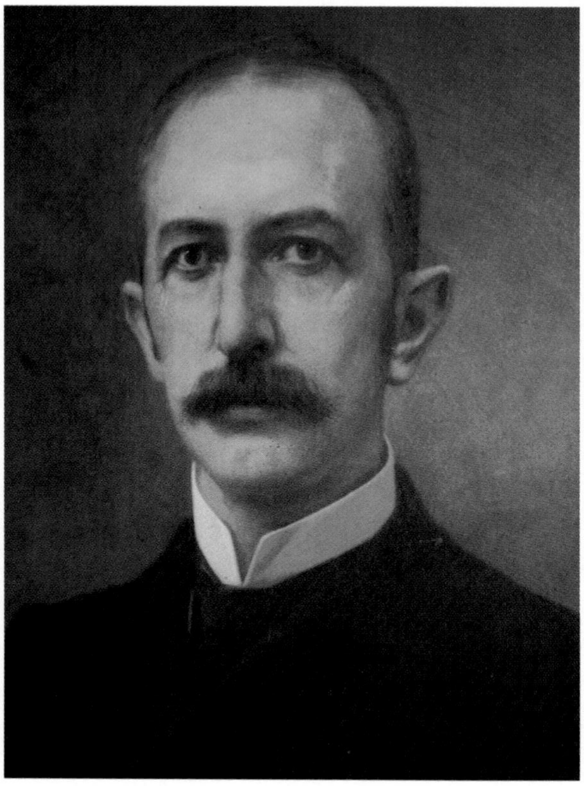

Richmond Pearson, lawyer, assemblyman, congressman, and diplomat, traveled the world, but always returned to his home in Asheville, North Carolina–Richmond Hill.

Visitors seeking greater seclusion may prefer the Croquet Cottages, opened in 1991. Each of the nine cottages, named for indigenous tree species, boasts its own front porch—complete with a breathtaking view of the mountains—as well as fireplaces, pencil-post beds, and all modern amenities. The traditional-style cottages are grouped around a flawlessly manicured croquet court. Guests who succeed in escaping from their porch rocker's gentle embrace can play a game themselves—or just lean back and enjoy the free show.

The latest addition to this unique inn is the Garden Pavilion, 15 rooms nestled in a secluded setting and overlooking a waterfall and bubbling stream. In the Garden Pavilion, the new Arbor Grille features more casual fare. Here each guest has a splendid view of the waterfall and parterre garden.

In its heyday, Richmond Hill was the scene of many lavish parties, hosted by Pearson's gracious wife, Gabrielle, the beautiful daughter of a wealthy Virginia tobacco planter. Today, that same tradition of fine food and warm hospitality is carried on in Gabrielle's, the inn's acclaimed restaurant, which serves creative and varied cuisine designed to please the most discriminating palate. A full breakfast is included in the price of each night's lodging. Gabrielle's also offers dinner nightly, plus an elegant Sunday brunch. Guests may savor the Victorian ambiance of the mansion's formal dining room, with its rich cherry paneling and triple-tiered brass chandelier, or they may opt for the more informal atmosphere of the glass-enclosed sun porch, with its comfortable wicker furniture and mountain views.

A tradition of hospitality timeless as the sun, illuminates Richmond Hill Inn. Attention to detail and uncompromising standards have earned this Victorian mansion a coveted four-diamond rating.

Today, the inn offers visitors a full range of gracious amenities and services, a tradition that would please Richmond Pearson, whose estate in its heyday was almost entirely self-supporting. Pearson, the scion of an illustrious North Carolina family, was a statesman, orator, and diplomat who served in both the North Carolina General Assembly and in Congress. His diplomatic career included service as United States Consul in Belgium and Italy, Minister to Persia, and Envoy Extraordinary and Minister Plenipotentiary to Greece and Montenegro. Pearson's father, Richmond Mumford Pearson, was Chief Justice of the North Carolina Supreme Court for 20 years, and also ran his own law school in Yadkin County.

Throughout its rich history, Richmond Hill has been a testament to those who loved it. Pearson, himself, lived in his grand mansion whenever his career permitted, and he died there in 1923. Gabrielle died a year later, shortly after returning from a trip to Persia. The surviving children, Marjorie and Thomas Pearson, left the estate in a caretaker's hands for many years as they traveled abroad. But decades later, in 1951, they returned to their beloved home, which they opened to the public as a museum. When Marjorie died in 1972, the house passed to a cousin, General Hayne Davis Boyden, triggering a series of events which seemed to spell almost certain doom for the historic property. Boyden sold the estate to the Western North Carolina Baptist Homes Corporation in 1974. The terms of the sale, however, stipulated that the house be preserved for at least 10 years.

The Preservation Society of Asheville and Buncombe County began negotiations in regard to the possibility of restoring Richmond Hill in such a way that it could be used as a retirement home. In 1977, the Baptist group decided that restoration would not be possible and built a retirement home on the property next to Richmond Hill. In 1981, the Preservation Society bought 7.5 acres of land that adjoined Richmond Hill. Following that purchase of property, the Baptist group offered to sell the house to the Society for $1. Over the next three years, the Preservation Society struggled to raise the $100,000 needed to move the 750-ton mansion 600 feet to the east. The prodigious task was finally completed in 1984; the threat of destruction had been staved off, but the house was still in desperate need of restoration.

The final link in this century-long chain of love was forged in January of 1987, when The Education Center, Inc., a Greensboro firm that produces educational materials, bought Richmond Hill and owners Dr. Albert J. and Margaret Michel began the massive task of restoration. Every effort was made to preserve as much as possible. The original slate roof was removed, boxed, stored and eventually replaced. Amazingly, the home's 100-year-old plaster survived the move in such good condition that only minor repairs were needed. Doors and windows were removed, restored, and replaced. Four fluted chimneys were rebuilt, and the original brick fireplace tiles reglazed.

Inevitably, though, changes were required to convert the former private residence into a grand country inn. Several rooms were reconfigured, and new ones were added, along with new plumbing, wiring, insulation, and heating and air conditioning systems. The result is spectacular. And more than a century after Richmond Pearson first realized his dream of gracious living, Richmond Hill still surrounds its visitors with unsurpassed romance, history, and elegance. ▲

The Oak Hall is one of the common rooms of the inn. Raised panel walls form a backdrop for the portrait of Gabrielle Pearson. Exposed beams traverse a 12-foot ceiling. An oak staircase rises to the second floor where stained glass windows softly color the first landing.

The Chestnut Room, in one of The Croquet Cottages on the grounds of Richmond Hill Inn, is favored by expansive views of the Blue Ridge Mountains. Just outside, a croquet court beckons.

Ramada Limited

Location, location, location. Had this business adage not already been coined, it surely would be after a look at the Ramada Limited. First, of course, is its location in Asheville. Every day a growing number of business clients and travelers discover the seemingly unlimited appeal of this region. Then consider that this newly renovated 120-room hotel is only moments away from many of Asheville's landmarks: the Blue Ridge Parkway, Biltmore Estate and Winery, Folk Art Center, and downtown Asheville's wealth of concert halls, museums, and galleries. Business travelers will find the Asheville Convention Center only a short five-minute drive away.

Located at 180 Tunnel Road directly off I-240, Ramada Limited is in the heart of a booming retail district. Forty restaurants, the ever-expanding Asheville Mall, specialty shopping outlets, several movie theaters, and bowling are all within walking distance. More than one guest has been seen leaving the hotel empty-handed only to return carrying everything from toys for the kids back home to hiking gear for tomorrow's excursion.

But most importantly, it is the service and accommodations the Ramada Limited offers that make the difference. The staff invite their guests to make this hotel their "home away from home." Third-generation hotel owners stand behind a commitment of quality, and the list of repeat customers backs it up. The rooms are overflowing with amenities to make guests comfortable: complimentary coffee makers; remote control television with complimentary HBO, ESPN, and cable; alarm clock radios; full-length dressing mirrors; and double vanity bathrooms. Rooms with the woman traveler in mind include hair dryers and makeup mirrors. Two Jacuzzi suites are available, and all guest rooms have electronic door locks. In addition to the heated outdoor swimming pool and Jacuzzi, there is also an indoor health club complete with exercise equipment, Jacuzzi, and sauna.

Recent renovations to the rooms, a handsome new front entrance, and the complete remodeling of the adjacent restaurant are part of Ramada Limited's continuing commitment to an attractive and comfortable facility.

The complimentary executive continental breakfast is even better than back home with its selection of English muffins, toast, Danish, cold cereals, fresh fruit, coffee, tea, hot chocolate, milk, and a selection of three juices. The expanded menu grew out of consideration for guests' needs ranging from senior citizens on tour to business executives and families on the run. To welcome the business traveler, the manager hosts a complimentary cocktail party every Wednesday evening where corporate guests make new contacts and repeat customers renew friendships.

In addition to the heated outdoor swimming pool and Jacuzzi, there is also an indoor health club complete with exercise equipment, Jacuzzi, and sauna.

Recent renovations to the rooms, a handsome new front entrance, and the complete remodeling of the adjacent restaurant, Arthur's, All Your Grilled Favorites, are part of their continuing commitment to an attractive and comfortable facility. Open for only a year, Arthur's has already earned a reputation with out-of-town and local customers alike for its grilled barbecue ribs, prime rib, and Norwegian salmon. Arthur's also features a full bar, two glowing rock fireplaces, and a meeting space for 50 with its own banquet menu to fit every budget.

Visitors always find it hard to leave Asheville, but at least they know they are always welcome back at Ramada Limited, their home away from home. ▲

Hampton Inns

Step inside either of Asheville's two Hampton Inns, and you will immediately sense the difference. An attractively appointed lobby with its crackling rock fireplace teams up with the soft music to create a cozy atmosphere. Then there's the hearty welcome from the staff. Their attention, while plenty prompt and efficient, seems more natural than studied. And that is no accident—outstanding service is standard here, with third-generation hotel owners standing behind it one hundred percent.

Good feelings continue as you settle into the spacious and comfortable rooms. Hampton Inns, after all, offer the best of both worlds—an outstanding assortment of amenities found only in luxury hotels but at very competitive prices. Consider the king study rooms which feature a sofa sleeper and private whirlpool. All rooms offer remote control television, HBO, clock radios, free local phone calls, and electronic guest room door locks. Seventy-five percent of the rooms are nonsmoking, and handicap accessible rooms are available. There are meeting rooms that can accommodate as many as 20.

The next morning something special starts at 6:00 A.M. Actually it starts well before that—it takes time to prepare a continental breakfast as nice as this one. Fresh fruits, bagels, biscuits, English muffins, fruited breads, oatmeal, grits, five cold cereals, three juices, coffee, teas, hot chocolate, milk, and even waffles are presented in the spacious dining area. Upholstered chairs and plenty of tables make guests feel at home. On chilly winter nights the staff serves hot cider and fresh baked cookies, their way of saying, "sweet dreams."

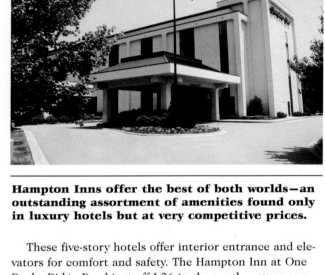

Hampton Inns offer the best of both worlds—an outstanding assortment of amenities found only in luxury hotels but at very competitive prices.

These five-story hotels offer interior entrance and elevators for comfort and safety. The Hampton Inn at One Rocky Ridge Road just off I-26 in the southwestern section of the city is just across from the 75-store Biltmore Square Mall and nearby is the Western North Carolina Farmers Market. The 204 Tunnel Road property, opened in April of 1995, is a stone's throw from I-40 and the Asheville Mall featuring 100 shops and boutiques. Both properties are within minutes of the Biltmore Estate, North Carolina Arboretum, Folk Art Center, and Blue Ridge Parkway.

Many amenities distinguish these inns, but maybe none more than the indoor pool and spa. Within the glass walls surrounding the clear green water, you half expect to see a tanned waiter serving beverages in pineapples. While the mountain views say no, this can't be, the warm, penetrating sun, the tables with umbrellas, and the lush green plants (one blooming bright red) shout yes. After a swim, grab a towel and head for the fitness center, sauna, or whirlpool spa to tone and tighten or just relax.

From the fireplace to the pool, continental breakfast to the evening snack, everything is fully guaranteed, 100 percent satisfaction or you don't pay. Isn't it funny how the companies that offer such guarantees don't need to? That's because at these Hampton Inns they are too busy making things right, right from the start. ▲

Step inside either of Asheville's two Hampton Inns, and you will immediately sense the difference. An attractively appointed lobby with its crackling rock fireplace teams up with the soft music to create a cozy atmosphere.

Young Transportation

When the people of Woodfin wished to visit the Chicago World's Fair in 1933, T. Ralph Young Sr. was happy to oblige. He rigged the back of his truck with wooden benches, and on these makeshift perches, three loads of travelers were taken to see the wonders of the fair. While that improvised bus has long since been replaced by a fleet of sleek motor coaches, Young Transportation remains a company on which people can depend to take them wherever they wish to go.

In the years following the Chicago venture, Young Sr. ran scheduled buses to Asheville from outlying areas such as Leicester and Elk Mountain. But the post-World War II boom that put a car in every driveway also slowed Young's business to a trickle. When Young Sr. passed away in 1960, there were only two buses left in operation from the once flourishing line. It seemed as though the company would be forced to fold, but under the guidance of T. Ralph Young Jr., Young Transportation shifted into the charter and tour business and was once again on the road to success.

Company President Ralph Young Jr. (center) is joined by Young Transportation's next generation, daughter Sarah Garbee and nephew Tom Crouch. ***Photo by Steve Dixon, courtesy of*** **Citizen Times.**

Attention to detail is a key component of all the company's services. The charter department provides transportation to meet the needs of each group. Whether it is a large group going to a popular destination such as an amusement park, or a handful of people going to an unusual location such as a business site, the customer need only to name the time and place, and Young Transportation will work with them. If a group needs more than just transportation, the tour department can plan every stage of the journey—from travel and lodging to meals and show tickets. These tours are no longer limited to motor coach travel: for example, on Young's Alaskan trip, travelers take a plane to Seattle, board a cruise ship, and then tour the state by train and motorcoach. The tour department also offers receptive tour planning services to groups coming into the area, whether by plane or with their own transportation.

The company also shows people the wonders and sights found right here at home in Western North Carolina. Young's Convention Services, with an office in The Grove Park Inn, provides both meeting planning and entertainment for organizations that are destined for Asheville. Here the company combines its attention to detail with creative and flexible schemes for recreational time. Activities range from whitewater rafting and steak dinners grilled outdoors to craft tours and mystery theater.

Safety is a top concern for Young Transportation. "We realize the responsibility of having an entire group in one of our vehicles," states Ralph Young Jr. The company's attention to safety has brought it recognition from the National Safety Council as well as a first-place rating—rare in the industry—with the Military Traffic Division of the Department of Defense.

With a new 5.5-acre facility on Riverside Drive in Woodfin, Young Transportation is ready to travel wherever future roads may wind.

Since the day when Ralph Young Sr. first tacked benches to the floor of his truck, Young Transportation has adapted to the changing needs of its customers. This tradition is now in its third generation, as Young Jr.'s nephew and daughter have joined the company: Tom Crouch is now a partner and vice president of the firm, and Sarah Garbee is tour manager. And with a new 5.5-acre facility on Riverside Drive in Woodfin, Young Transportation will be ready to travel wherever future roads may wind. ▲

Bibliography

Cabins and Castles. Asheville, North Carolina: Historic Resources Commission of Asheville and Buncombe County, 1981.

Crutchfield, James A. *The North Carolina Almanac and Book of Facts.* Nashville, Tennessee: Rutledge Hill Press, 1988.

Harshaw, Lou. *Asheville: Places of Discovery.* Lakemont, Georgia: Copple House Books, 1980.

Pacher, Sara and Linda Davis March. *The Insider's Guide to North Carolina's Mountains.* Charlotte, North Carolina: Knight Publishing Co., 1995.

Parris, John. *Roaming The Mountains.* Asheville, North Carolina: Citizen Times Publishing Co., 1955.

A Pictorial History of Buncombe County. Asheville, North Carolina: Asheville Citizen Times, 1993.

Sondley, Foster A. *A History of Buncombe County North Carolina.* Spartanburg, South Carolina: Reprint Company, 1977.

Terrell, Bob. *Grandpa's Town.* Nashville, Tennessee: Harris Press, 1978.

Tessier, Mitzi Schaden. *Asheville: A Pictorial History.* Virginia Beach, Virginia: Donning Company, 1982.

Acknowledgements

Special thanks to my wonderful family and to the many individuals who provided information, materials, and the encouragement to create this publication.

The following were especially helpful in the research stages of *Asheville: A View from the Top:* Angie Chandler and the very knowledgeable staff of the Asheville Area Chamber of Commerce and Asheville Convention and Visitors Bureau; Bob Terrell, historian; Mimi Cecil and Elizabeth Sims, Biltmore Estate; Chuck Reiley, BellSouth; David Tomsky, Grove Park Inn; Bob Burgin and Janet Moore, Mission + St. Joseph's Health System; Karen Cragnolin, RiverLink; Mary Nell Webb, WNC Film Commission; Terry Clevenger and Mary Fierle, Downtown Development Association; Linda Wilkerson, Arts Alliance; Becky Anderson, HandMade in America; Laura Rotegard, Ina Parr, and Phil Knoblet, Blue Ridge Parkway; Kevin McKee, Asheville Community Theatre; Tom Byers and Merianne Epstein, UNCA; Mary Ritter, Chimney Rock Park; Rick Webb and Pat McCabe, Advantage West; Charlie Price, Price McNabb, and Stuart Canter, Mountain Folk Festival; Bob Shepard, Land of Sky Regional Council; and Mona Cornwell, A-B Tech.

Lisa Bell
Author

Enterprises Index

Index

This book was set in Trajan, Veljovic, Caslon 224, Bodoni, and Garamond at Community Communications in Montgomery, Alabama.